Charles Dudley Warner

A Roundabout Journey

(Edition 4)

Charles Dudley Warner

A Roundabout Journey
(Edition 4)

ISBN/EAN: 9783744752978

Printed in Europe, USA, Canada, Australia, Japan

Cover: Foto ©Andreas Hilbeck / pixelio.de

More available books at **www.hansebooks.com**

A ROUNDABOUT JOURNEY

BY

CHARLES DUDLEY WARNER

FOURTH EDITION

BOSTON
HOUGHTON, MIFFLIN AND COMPANY
New York: 11 East Seventeenth Street
The Riverside Press, Cambridge
1884

CONTENTS.

CHAPTER I.
OUT OF THE FOG INTO THE SUN 1

CHAPTER II.
THE FOUNTAIN OF VAUCLUSE 7

CHAPTER III.
AVIGNON TO NÎMES 17

CHAPTER IV.
MONTPELLIER 29

CHAPTER V.
CETTE 39

CHAPTER VI.
AIGUES-MORTES 46

CHAPTER VII.
LA BELLE MAGUELONNE 59

CHAPTER VIII.
MUNICH TO ORVIETO 68

CHAPTER IX.
PALERMO 78

CHAPTER X.
GIRGENTI AND CATANIA 91

CONTENTS.

CHAPTER XI.
Taormina 104

CHAPTER XII.
Syracuse 118

CHAPTER XIII.
Malta 132

CHAPTER XIV.
Gibraltar and Tangier 144

CHAPTER XV.
Across Africa 162

CHAPTER XVI.
Along the Spanish Coast 191

CHAPTER XVII.
A Ride in Spain 199

CHAPTER XVIII.
The Alhambra 235

CHAPTER XIX.
The Bull-Fight 255

CHAPTER XX.
Monserrat 283

CHAPTER XXI.
Random Spanish Notes 304

CHAPTER XXII.
Wagner's Parsifal 333

NOTES OF A ROUNDABOUT JOURNEY.

CHAPTER I.

OUT OF THE FOG INTO THE SUN.

WE left Paris on the morning of November 8, 1881, in a dense fog. The difference between the fog of Paris and the fog of London is that one is yellow and the other is black; both are raw and piercing, and when I am in Paris I am not prepared to say that I prefer the latter. The Paris sky is gray, like its houses. I do not know why it is that all the large capitals of the civilized world have such unpleasant climates, — London, Paris, St. Petersburg, Berlin, — New York, even with its extremes, is better than either.

We did not escape from the fog until we had run through the forest of Fontainebleau, when the sun came out in all its splendor, and we were whirled along through a cloudless day, and over a smiling land, every inch of which is cultivated. The effect is that of a prairie, so extensive is the view; but there are low hills, now and then, and water-courses, with miles on miles of sentinel poplars, and now and then, on an elevation, a ruined tower marking some old feudal domination. The fields, without fences, are cultivated in long narrow strips, in colors of green, brown, and gray. Gautier says the country looks like the cloth patterns pasted on cards which his tailor sends him. Gray houses dot the landscape everywhere; gray villages with curious old spires and towers are frequent; the long strips of gray roads are dazzling white in the sunshine. Gray is the prevailing color, for France seems to be all limestone and chalk, and houses, fields, and people take this color of decadence. At this season there are no vivid greens to make a contrast. The foliage, however, has warmth, the forests showing rich brown and the mulberries golden yellow.

We travel express, none but first-class carriages being on the train. The fare also is first class. The distance from Paris to Avignon is about four hundred and sixty miles, and the fare is over ninety-one francs — over eighteen dollars. This includes only a little baggage, so that there is a large extra charge for that. However, there are some compensations. We travel fast and we reach places at the time named on the schedule. This surprises Americans, who are accustomed to regard time tables on long routes as arranged for the amusement of directors and not for the information of the public. We made the distance, four hundred and sixty miles, from Paris to Avignon, in twelve hours and forty minutes, and arrived on time. This includes stops of a half hour for breakfast at twelve, and a half hour for dinner at six. There are, besides, five other stops of five minutes each, so that the running time is actually only a little over eleven hours, or (if I have figured correctly) over forty-one miles an hour.

Another good thing about the journey was the absence of "hot boxes." The only thing that could bear that name was the hot-water cans that were given us for foot-warmers. Now, a real American is not comfortable without a "hot box" occasionally in the course of a long journey. It seems to him that something hasn't happened.

The cars also were exceedingly easy. This was due to comfortable seats and good springs partly, but mainly to the excellence of the road-bed and the perfection of the steel rails. We glided along on our very rapid course without a jar. And another discovery we soon made was that the road was so perfectly ballasted with stone that we had no dust. We were neither jerked about nor banged up and down. This splendid steel highway from Paris to Marseilles is run over as smoothly as if one were in a gondola, a dustless journey, on time.

And we were little visited by conductors, ticket-men, or other inquisitive persons, and not once by boys who desired to improve our minds and destroy our stomachs by their merchandise. Having once put us into a car for Avignon and been satisfied that we had paid, the officials let us alone. We might have got out anywhere, and forfeited our tickets and left our baggage.

Not till we reached Dijon at night did a ticket-taker open the door. But then four simple words that he said — "*Billets s'il vous plaît*" — so deluged the apartment with garlic that we had to open all the windows. If he had added another solid word, I think we should have been compelled to jump out of the car. Such a mighty power is the breath of a single man in this great nation.

I am sorry to say that the climate of Paris extends far south. The isothermal line takes a dip almost down to the Mediterranean. By the middle of the afternoon we were in a cold, dense fog again, as thick as we have on the banks of Newfoundland, and it was not until we were well away from Lyons and the sun had ceased to draw the moisture from the ground that we saw the stars. But by nine o'clock we had changed our climate totally, and when we saw in the moonlight the towers of the ancient Palace of the Popes at Avignon, we knew that the sort of winter to which we are accustomed was left behind us, and we had not to look forward with apprehension to Thanksgiving day.

The ancient hotel received us in its ancient courtyard, where the big sycamore-tree grows and the galleries run round, and where there are benches for loiterers to sit in the sun. The next morning was cloudless, delicious. The soldiers and the children were sunning themselves in the Place de la Ville, at the head of the Rue de la République, where stands the statue of Crillon, friend of Henry of Navarre, and the pretty theatre with the figures of Racine and Corneille seated in front. We were come to a land where statues can sit out doors with comfort in winter. I returned to the hotel with my hands full of the open air roses of Provence, which are blooming everywhere.

It is only truth to say, however, that the "mistral," an odious, cold, cutting northeast wind, blows here in the winter and gives Avignon a bad name. It is not so very far from the spurs of the Alps, and one of the finest sights from the Dome of Rocks, above the old palace, is Mt. Ventoux, eighteen miles away and 6,421 feet high, a lovely purple mountain, said by Petrarch, who ascended it, to be covered with eternal snow. The snow may be eternal or internal, but we could not see it.

Avignon, crumbling, old, crooked in its ways and indecent in some of its smells, is, after all, a most romantic, delightful old town, interesting in its architectures, its superb old palaces, its historical associations of the Popes and the Two Lovers, and has, altogether, a most fascinating atmosphere for the traveler.

But it is afflicted, as all France is, with soldiers, barracks full of them, streets full of them. They sleep in the Palace of the Popes; you see one of their unintelligent heads at every little window of the fortress-palace, and squads of conscripts, the rawest of raw recruits, are always in sight. And they seem poor material for soldiers, short in stature, ill-made, inferior in every way, light weights in head as well as in body.

This is the general character of the conscripts and troops we have seen everywhere south on our journey, and it is very poor stuff to oppose to the stalwart, intelligent German soldiers — if they are to be opposed to them.

CHAPTER II.

THE FOUNTAIN OF VAUCLUSE.

THE lover has almost as good a chance of immortality as the warrior. A romantic attachment to a charming woman, especially if it is hopeless or ought to be hopeless, put into literature, does very nearly as well for a man's reputation as if he murdered a great many of his fellows. Not quite; for killing is still the most popular thing a man can do in this world. Witness, the prominent industry of France at this moment is the training of the most awkward of conscripts into the most unsoldierly-like-looking soldiers, for the purpose of killing Germans and other outside barbarians.

The quaint old walled city of Avignon, however, owes more to Petrarch than it does to any or all of the Popes who once made it the centre of the shows and pilgrimages of the Christian world; more even than to that fighting Pope Benoit XIII., who was n't a very good Holy Father, as holy fathers go in this world, although he stood a siege in his palace-fortress in Avignon that lasted a year longer than the siege of Troy. All Avignon is saturated with the story of Petrarch and Laura, and it is a pity that the name of the handsomest street in the city and the only straight one, which was *Rue Pétrarque*, has, in the access of Republicanism — for Avignon is fiercely Republican — been changed into Rue de la République.

I know very well that it is the fashion now not to believe very much in Petrarch's love-affair, and to say that the sweet but cold Laura de Sade, dying at the age of forty, a faithful wife and the mother of eleven children, was only a literary flame of the sentimental Italian. But I like, while I am here, to believe the old romance in all its details. And if the poetically amorous poet mingled his taste for letters and his love of renown with a convenient and idealized passion for a beautiful woman, and made every event of his despairing love the theme of a sonnet, I like to believe that the name of Laura, which was always on his lips or at the end of his pen, was something more than a name.

It was, says the simple narrative, on the Monday of Holy Week, at six o'clock in the morning, that Petrarch saw at Avignon, in the church of the nuns of Sainte Claire, a young woman whose robe of green was sown with violets. Her beauty struck him: it was Laura. Daughter of Audibert des Noves, chevalier, she had recently married Hugues de Sade, of an old patrician house of Avignon. Her features — so Petrarch describes her — were fine and regular, her eyes were brilliant, her glance was tender, her physiognomy sweet, her behavior modest, her gait noble, her voice vibrant with feeling; her waist was slender, her eyebrows were black, her hair was blonde; her complexion was of dazzling whiteness, animated with the most lively colors; in short, she had a charm more seducing than beauty.

To see this lovely person was to love her. To be absent from her was a torture. It was necessary to Petrarch to be near her always. He sought her everywhere. She had the air of inviting him. If he approached her, she fled; but she fled slowly; she fled to be pursued. Petrarch was timid. Laura was a woman of sense, and yet, like all women, *au fond*, a coquette. It was a coquetry which nature inspired, which modesty confessed. Laura was flattered by his devotion, not insensible to the renown which his sonnets brought her; distinguished strangers from afar wished to see the divinity who inspired the famous poet. They could not always recognize in her the raving beauty whom Petrarch saw.

Did Laura love him? The love of Petrarch flattered her pride. But she had the air of ignoring the passion of the young poet; she treated him with kindness; but a sweet severity came to the aid of her virtue. She attracted him and repelled him. He seemed always to pursue an enticing shadow which always just evaded his grasp, and yet invited him with a sweet smile into some heavenly place.

In the despair of a lover whose love was in the air, in disgust of a sycophantic court whose favor was only got by fawning, in hatred of a city whose morals were decayed, and in order to have uninterrupted leisure for the cultivation of the muse, Petrarch sought a retreat in the solitude of Vaucluse. Even there the image of

Laura pursued him; he heard her voice in the garden at evening, and in the murmuring stream that ran before his door his thought swiftly traveled to Avignon, where she lived. He wrote there many sonnets upon her. Upon her beautiful eyes he composed three poems full of grace, delicacy, *esprit*. Drawn back to Avignon by his passion for her, or drawn from Vaucluse by missions political or poetic, Petrarch returned to it again and again. But it was never more than a retreat of convenience, a summer residence.

What is this Vaucluse, whose fountain is such a perennial spring of poetic longing? Vaucluse is to-day a little town of some five or six hundred inhabitants, in the foot-hills of the French Alps, about eighteen miles east of Avignon. I went there by the railway to Cavaillon, which was the home, you may remember, of Pierre de Provence, whose romantic love for La Belle Maguelonne is the theme of one of the most charming stories of the twelfth century. The road was through a level gray limestone region, planted everywhere with the vine and the olive. Here and there are little hills, and on one of these, to the north, is the Château Neuf du Pape, whence comes a very good red wine of that name, which even the temperance traveler in this land of the grape and the madder may drink if he gets an absolution from the Pope. Before us, however, all the way, rose one of the loveliest of mountains — the last southern effort of the Alps to sustain their majesty — a barren height, lifted up in a purple light under this blue sky of Provence; a mountain which has a special fame from the fact that Petrarch once ascended it, and describes it as in perpetual snow. Things are not now so perpetual as they were in mediæval times, or this season has been unfavorable for snow. We could see none. It is the Mt. Ventoux. It has an air of repose in lonely grandeur, and gets the full benefit of its altitude, for this plain descends with only a gentle slope to the Mediterranean.

The day was lovely — it was the 12th of November — like our choicest and most inspiring October days. Olive orchards gave a silver shimmer to the air, and flowers bloomed in the open without fear of frosts. At every little station upon low trellises were trained rose vines, and sweet-scented red roses, the red rose that used to be a shy confession of love in June in New England, made brilliant banks of color.

We left the train at L'Isle du Sorgue, a sleepy, gray, and dusty little village on the river Sorgue, and took an omnibus for Vaucluse, three or four miles distant. The stone houses are gray, the roads are gray, the landscape is grizzly. The road, however, is broad, and hard, and smooth. As we go on, by vineyards and olive orchards, with a Virgin and Child at odd angles and corners by the portals in the walls, the country becomes rougher and less arable. We are approaching the mountains, or rather the gray limestone cliffs which are their outposts.

The road descends to the narrow valley of the Sorgue, and follows its tortuous course into the very bosom of the mountain. Soon we pass under the arches of a fine modern viaduct, and find ourselves in a ravine, with the rapid little river and high cliffs on both sides. There is a house with a garden now and then, but there is no room for many houses. We pursue this way until we come to a veritable *cul de sac*. In this *cul de sac* is Vaucluse. It is a sorry little town, rather Italian than French in its appearance, with its few houses on the edge of the stream, and perched on the hill-sides. In one place the rock has been tunneled, and the tunnel leads to other stone houses jammed under the ledges. There is a little square with a high commemorative column (erected in 1804), and a big sycamore-tree. This is where the omnibus stops, and the horses are unhitched, and where old women, not so pretty as old women might be, offer to sell you dried grasses colored, and sprigs of lavender, and photographs of the fountain and the town. There is, of course, a café on this square, the *Pétrarque et Laure*, and a bridge across the stream leads to a modern paper-mill.

Taking the right bank of the river we ascend by a stony path, always attended by the woman with the lavender and the photographs and babies, until we reach the end of the horse-shoe inclosure. In the last few hundred yards the river has disappeared. We mount by the side of a dry cascade. The bed of the stream is strewn with big moss-covered bowlders, and over these the torrent pours when the fountain, in the spring, is high enough to overflow. Its outlet now is under this stony bed. These bowlders in the dry stream (for it is here dry the greater part of the year) are thickly painted with the names of distinguished Frenchmen. I know they are distinguished or they would not be here. Every square foot of the vast cliffs about us, as far as moderate ladders can reach, also bears in white paint the same noble names. The Frenchman always paints or carves his name on every object that is available whenever he ventures into the savage and unknown world outside of Paris. His appreciation of himself is of the same sort as the modesty of the ancient Pharaohs.

Mounting above this dry cascade, we were faced and hemmed in by a perpendicular limestone precipice eleven hundred feet in height. Before us in the cliff is a cavern, perhaps a hundred feet long by thirty deep. At a descent into it of thirty or forty feet from the brink where we stood was a pool of water, perhaps thirty feet across, and probably, at this time, about thirty feet deep. But it is impossible to say how deep it is, for the water is absolutely pellucid. I have never seen any mountain stream clearer. And yet its color is a sort of blue black. Petrarch describes it as "a mirror of blue-black water, so pure, so still, that where it laps the pebbles you can scarcely say where air begins and water ends." I found this literally true, for stooping on the shingly edge to dip the water in my hand I only perceived by the touch where the water began.

This is the sole source of the river Sorgue, which issuing from this ravine parts itself into many canals;

it refreshes the prairies of Vaucluse, it waters Lille and the beautiful plain of Contat, and at last throws itself into the Rhone near Avignon. " O Vaucluse ! " exclaims the poet in his absence, " who will transport me to thy fresh banks! O fountain marvelous! would that I were seated near thy source ! "

Returning to the square, we crossed the bridge to the rock-hewn street behind the mill and passed through a rock tunnel in search of the site of Petrarch's house. On the height above us, perched upon the rugged rocks, are the ruins of the castle of Cardinal Cabasole. The Cardinal was Petrarch's friend, the seignior of this district, and part of the time Petrarch's companion here. At the foot of the precipice, under this castle in the air, was Petrarch's modest house. This site is tolerably well defined. The house has long ago gone, but another, which is said to be exactly like his, stands in its place. It is a two-story stone house, jammed under the precipice of which it seems to be a ragged part, with small windows, and looks very much like a poor stable and hen-house. In front of it is a little garden fenced in. This was a part of the larger garden of Petrarch, which extended to the river. In Petrarch's day this may have been a charming retreat. In the stream he drew his nets for fish. Melodious birds chanted in his ear, and farther off he heard in the meadows the lowing of herds and the bleating of sheep. The birds sang on one side; on the other, the waves murmured. Figs, grapes, almonds he had — these were his delicacies. His habit was that of a shepherd. At mid-day he was in a vaulted grotto impenetrable to the rays of the sun. At evening he wandered in the meadows, where he had a second garden.

It is a little difficult to imagine all this now, in the midst of these surroundings so grim and commonplace. But the stream is there, and the everlasting gray cliffs are there; and the ruins of his friend's castle still look down upon this marvelous gorge in the mountain. I plucked some pink roses of Provence and a leaf of magnolia from this dusty and blooming little garden, as romantic aids to imagination and faith.

In this solitude I can believe that the image of Laura pursued Petrarch as it had followed him in the forest of Ardennes. He believed that he saw her. He saw her start from the trunk of a tree, from the basin of the fountain, from the crevice of a rock, even from the edge of a cloud. "Three times," says he, "in the midst of the horrors of the night, all the doors fast shut, I have seen her appear at the foot of the bed, with an air assumed, with a countenance haughty. It was her very self." She rebuked her slave; she reclaimed him. What did Laura wish? "Perhaps," says the *naïf* chronicler, "to be the first and perhaps the only woman who was ever loved with an angelic love."

On the front of the café of *Pétrarque et Laure*, in the little square, is an inscription saying that on the site of this building Petrarch had his study, and that on this very spot he composed his one hundred and twenty-ninth sonnet, beginning (written here in French and in Italian) : —

> "O sweet country !
> O pure river !
> Which bathes the beautiful visage
> And the dear eyes of my Laura !"

CHAPTER III.

AVIGNON TO NÎMES.

PUT a man in red trousers and blue jacket and make his red legs move in unison with a lot of other red legs, and the man is perhaps relieved a little of his original insignificance. We have been witnessing the manufacture of soldiers, out of poor material, all the way across France. We have seen the forlorn squads of conscripts on their way to the stations; we have seen the first attempts on the drill ground to make four of them stand in a right line; we have seen their awkward efforts to make the musket anything but a murderous instrument for themselves, and we have finally seen them march off in columns — this thousand red-legged machine of war — with slanting bayonets and the intent to kill.

I did not intend to say anything more about the soldiers. But as I opened my window to the south to let in the sweet morning air, I heard the toot-toot of the everlasting trumpet-call, and while I sit down to begin this page a red-legged regiment is crossing the esplanade. I wish I could say anything good of them. Individually they are insignificant; but their red legs do go very well together. At any rate they are the prominent fact in all these towns and cities. The air is full of soldiering. The trumpet-call is the first thing one hears in the morning and the last in the evening, and all day the tan-ta-ra tan-ta-ra is liable to break out and a squad of uniforms appear round the corner. In the streets everywhere are soldiers and officers, the most familiar figures; but nothing seems able to give any of them the soldierly bearing that the Germans have.

I don't know, however, that it is any of my business, if the republic chooses to use up its energies in this way. But I wish they would put some good-sized men into the army, just for appearances. There are Frenchmen of fair proportions; you see occasionally a large man on the street, and they make a brave show — especially the commercial travelers — at the *tables d'hôte*. A row of Frenchmen at the table of a first-class hotel is likely to be a row of exceedingly good heads and highly intelligent faces, and men of more than ordinary size. To be sure, their table manners are apt to be barbarous, but then one would not go to a hotel in America to learn manners. It seems to me on the whole, taking the conscripts and the crowds in the streets, that the French in the south are under-sized. Perhaps it is a significant and decisive fact that the bedsteads at the hotels are all a trifle short for a man of good honest proportions to stretch himself at ease. We have plenty of men in Hartford to whom these bedsteads would be the mere mockery of repose.

They have in this region a new use for men. They

make "chambermaids" of them. Nearly all our chambermaids since we left Paris have been of the awkward sex. It seems to outrage the nature of things to see one of these unhandy creatures making up a bed, and trying to give that touch to it which is instinctive in a woman. The fact that men are employed to do this domestic service in hotels speaks volumes. But what is in the volumes I don't know.

From Avignon to Nîmes is a very pleasant ride of some twenty-five or thirty miles by rail of a sunny morning. The view is very extended, though the land is not flat; there are charming slopes and great sweeps of well-tilled land. The prominent feature — everywhere in this region, indeed — is the vast olive orchards. Together with the grape vines they cover the land.

In coming only this short distance we have changed, however, the *milieu*. There are not so many roses and other flowers in the open air as at Avignon. That old town, although it has, as I said, a bad name for the *mistral*, is nevertheless very good to the flowers all the year round, and is a bower of roses. In the garden above the Palace of the Popes they were setting out new beds of mignonette, as if they expected it to bloom through the winter. The cemetery was odorous with sweet flowers. About the sarcophagus where lie, in a nook sheltered by hedges of pines, John Stuart Mill and his well-beloved wife, are banks of roses, red and pink and yellow, rejoicing in the sun and robbing the grave of half its lonesomeness.

We left behind, too, at Avignon, the strawberries. Strawberries, they say, they have there every month in the year. To be sure they are the small, seedy, Swiss variety, of which it takes a great many to make a mouthful. But a strawberry is a strawberry in literature as well as on the table, and to come in of a winter morning from a walk in the abounding sun with a hand full of roses, and see on the breakfast-table even the humblest strawberry, is more pleasing than a stalled ox and snow in New England.

This Nîmes is a large city — 63,000 inhabitants the guide-book says — and it has the reputation of being one of the most cheerful and pleasant cities in southern France. It is open and sunny, and wide-spaced, but somehow, after one has seen the Roman ruins and the public garden, where there are also lovely Roman remains, there is not much to interest the traveler. It is too modern and lacks altogether the picturesqueness of Avignon, with its crooked, ill-savored streets and its decayed grandeur.

The Hôtel Luxembourg, where we stay, has a lovely sunny front south and west on the esplanade, a great esplanade of gravel in the middle of which is a lovely fountain with statues by Pradier, and about which are the public buildings and the vast and imposing Roman Amphitheatre. It is a good place also from our balcony to see the sun set and to hear day and night the toot-toot of the trumpeting soldiers, and the tooting horns of the omnibus and street-car conductors. If there is any one thing the French like more than another it is noise.

This old hotel has a sort of imposing appearance interiorly, with its large court and open staircase and galleries. It is a curious place, however. We were met on entering by two old women, in mob caps, black fronts, and short black dresses, who regarded us with the curiosity of magpies — nice, friendly old magpies — tottering about and solicitous to know our wants and to turn the last penny on them. It seems to be quite in the way here for old ladies to keep hotels. The Europa at Avignon was kept for sixty years by two lively, comfortable old ladies — they were not always so old — who had just departed this life the year we were at Avignon before (in 1875). In the little waiting room hangs a portrait of their gracious old mother, who, I suppose, kept the same house ages before. They have certainly transmitted their sweet and hospitable spirit to their successors, the present agreeable landlord and his lovely wife, who make the old house seem like home to the wayfarer.

The fussy old magpies at Nîmes transferred us to a queer old waiter, older even than themselves, who hobbled up-stairs before us. There was an assuring air of decrepitude about the whole ménage. The *bonne* who sat in the bureau was lame, and all the servitors were more or less venerable. Indeed, we got the notion as soon as we went into the streets that inferior and crippled and ugly people were very common in Nîmes, and the whole population — as we saw it — seemed to have suffered somehow a blight. This may be very unjust, but with all its Roman grandeur and spacious lay-out, Nîmes seems to be ill-favored in respect to population. Pretty women, or passable looking women, are even scarcer than at Avignon, and the men are inferior.

You do not expect me to instruct you on the Roman remains of Nîmes, indeed you do not wish information about them. You already know that twelve miles from here the Pont du Gard, the ancient aqueduct over the river Gard, is one of the most imposing Roman remains in existence, much more striking than anything about Rome itself. You know that the vast amphitheatre here, where 17,000 spectators could see, under awnings and at ease, gladiators pound each other and wild beasts eat persons professing the Christian faith, is the most perfect large amphitheatre left to us from Roman times. I saw the other day the Roman theatre at Orange. It is unique. The semi-circle seats for the spectators are hewn out of the rocky hill, like the theatre of Dionysius at Athens, and it is separated from the town by a wall thirteen feet thick, a hundred and twenty-one feet high and three hundred and thirty-four feet long. This high wall made the background for the stage; and built on it next the stage were the spacious green-rooms for the actors. This amphitheatre at Nîmes was not for plays at all, but for spectacles, combats, and the circus performances of the arena. The amphitheatre is elliptical in form, four hundred and thirty-seven feet in the greater axis and three hundred and thirty-three in the less. It is altogether one of the noblest ruins in the world, and is in such repair that it is still used for circus sports, and, I believe, for mild combats of the bull.

Another charming specimen of the grace and architectural refinement of the Augustan age is the Maison Carrée, a beautiful little Corinthian temple, still in good preservation, and used as a museum of local curiosities.

Perhaps the most pleasing feature of the city is the public garden, an artificial pleasure-place, very attractive. It is in front of a high rocky hill, on top of which is a noble Roman ruin called Tourmagne. From the summit of this tower there is a most extensive prospect of the city and variegated country. Below this is a pine forest with lovely walks. The side of the hill is terraced and adorned with circular balustrades in marble. At the foot is a basin of water, a living fountain, limpid and larger than the famous fountain of Vaucluse. It supplies the water for the canals and baths of the garden. This garden is a skilful adaptation of the old to the new. Adjoining it is the ruin of the Temple of Diana, built in the year B. C. 24, and in the garden are the Roman baths, about twelve feet below the level of the promenade, the vaulting being supported on slender columns over which rise open stone balustrades. The garden is adorned with vases and statues, gay with flower-beds, enlivened with the sparkling waters from the spring at the foot of the hill, shaded with elms and palm-trees, protected from the wind, and loved of the sun. Altogether it is a pleasant place for a northerner to saunter in a November day, and make the acquaintance of the children and babies and the old women who knit in the sun.

Nîmes is full of idlers, idle young men and idle old men. I have never seen a city where loafing is so much an occupation. It is a contrast to industrious Avignon. Perhaps this is the loafing time of the year.

Before you leave Nîmes, if you ever do leave it, you ought to make yourself acquainted with the works of M. Boucoiran. When this genius describes the cities of Provence and Languedoc in his native language, it is not difficult to comprehend him. But in an evil hour it occurred to him that he was capable of instructing the English travelers through this region in their own tongue. He has had a great success, and produced a book more amusing than he has any idea it is.

We cannot always understand M. Boucoiran's descriptions, but his reflections are always valuable, as when, standing on the top of the wall of the amphitheatre, he views the city on one side, while "from the other side your sight plunges into an immense and destroyed crater, the picturesque accounts of which induce the mind to reflect upon the most lasting works of men. We are inquiring, before so much devastation and solitude, if the monuments are not formed as the sports of going over civilizations, which conserved or mutilated them according to their necessities, or the employments to which they may be appropriated." Which seems altogether probable.

But the author is at his best in dwelling upon his sensations in search of such a marvel of architecture as the Pont du Gard: — "If you may have the least artistic mind, you will scarcely resist certain sensation of curiosity in seeing for the first time this aqueduct bridge. . . . The most you approach and the most it increases and astonishes, as all those conjunctive shafts that the man exercised to leap over the rivers and the valleys; it seems therefore that the solitude may be more hard, so as to *Roque-favour*."

This is true. And the author justly adds: "There are many people who at the sight of a handsome site give way to their impressions, and take a peculiar pleasure to the infinite sensations that inspire a bright sunrise after a storm-day, in the midst of the young nature — and near the dampish rocks. The early beams that play through that lofty wall as an open work, prepare the mind to sweet sensations, and the hours go rapidly over in that solitary spot that you will see again with a new delight."

The city of Arles is famous, you know, not more for its many and splendid Roman remains than for its beautiful women. I heard an Englishman at Avignon raving about them. They also are survivals of the Roman times, preserving in their regular and handsome features, their noble bearing, their alluring manners, the traits of the girls of old Rome. This is a topic that evokes the full powers of M. Boucoiran: —

"The modern city of Arles saved the prestige of its olden times. What seduces the more the foreigner, what charms him, is surely the sight of handsome women. The successive dominations crossing the country, each brought there its tribute for the performance of such beauties. They like flowers, fondle various perfumes, and are not indifferent to all sorts of poetry. The noise or motion transport them in joy; they take great pleasure in walking, desire the dances, the concerts, the holidays. Every spectacle attracts them, less for itself than for the incidents whereof they raise up.

"The women of Arles are in some way the Athenians of the Provenza; they are specially cited for the superiority of their manner of speaking and dressing, so that the attire is the most important work of their youthfulness. Preserved amidst the Arlesian girls of the middle classes, in spite of the universal invasion of Paris fashions, their dress contributes very much to their attractions and they exhibit, in its improving, the most exquisite art, and the most dexterous inquiries."

These women, we are assured, have the forms and the features of the antique statues. Perhaps they have a dash of Moorish blood also, for some Andalusian customs obtain in this region. One of these is the yearly gathering of the bulls in a great plain, for the purpose of marking the half-wild animals with the names of the owners. The custom is described by a writer in the sixteenth century. Our author dilates upon it:—

"An amusing pleasure, which has so many attractions for the Arlesians as for the Andalous, is the bull runnings. It is not, we must say that, the sole relation that may be found between those two types, separated nevertheless by great distances. But it is then proved that the handsomest childs of the Prophet found sometimes sympathetical affinities, yet evident at Arles as on other places of Spain.

" You may observe on the spirit, either on the skin as in the veins of the Arlesian girls, of that same blood which reveals itself among the Malaguenes, by the brilliancy, as alike ingenuity of conversing, or by that adorable forsaking which makes of them any dangerous spoiled children whereof you will love till the imperfections.

" That similitude of kindness, that irresistible propensity for the dressing art, have not been drawn up at the same spring? Those are not primitive sins reckoning from a little far!

" The marking of young bulls, which is called *Ferrade*, keeps yere so numerous adepts as at the foot of the Alpujarras mountains, among the girls than among the young men."

After this, if we do not go to Arles, it will be because we are entirely wanting in the classical spirit and the love of beauty.

I have neglected to speak of an institution at Nîmes more entertaining and lively than its Roman remains. It is the public *blanchisserie*, or wash-house. The great spring or fountain which waters the public garden flows away in walled canals. It also supplies the washing place. Sunken in one of the wide streets, several feet below the surface, and surrounded by a high wall in the form of a parallelogram, perhaps two hundred and fifty feet long and fifty feet broad, is the washing place. Through this slowly flows the stream, let in and out by small gates. In the middle is a stone platform, and on each side of this is a canal of water, about eighteen inches deep. All along the edges is also a stone platform.

As I approached this sunken place I heard a tremendous spatting and pounding, and chattering and laughing. Looking down into the long pit over the wall, I saw four rows of women· and girls, old and ugly, and roguish and indifferent, all ages and degrees of feminity, some two hundred and fifty women in all, standing in the canals and beating clothes with little mallets on the stone benches. Each woman stood in the canal, but each one stood in her own wash-tub, with her skirts tucked up, so that her feet were kept as dry as if she had been on land. I have been accustomed to see the clothes put into the wash-tub and the women standing outside, but here the women stood in the tubs, and from time to time dipped the clothes into the canal, which was a mass of soap-suds, and then dragged them out for another pounding on the stones. Splash, splash, thump, thump, chatter, chatter, chaff, laughter, thump, whack — blackbirds could not talk faster, mermaids could not splash more. Each woman in her own tub, each tub standing on its own bottom — *voilà!* independence, and convenience. All in the open air, and the sight of the world.

CHAPTER IV.

MONTPELLIER.

You need n't desire a pleasanter autumn ride of an hour than that from Nîmes to Montpellier. In the spring this region must be a sort of paradise. The slope is towards the south, towards the Mediterranean, which we all the time approach. On the north prolongs itself the purple range of the Cévennes. The olive orchards spread themselves out to the sun. Their silver sheen is already toned by the fruit, which is ripening to a dead black.

Long before we reach the city our sight is fascinated by two mountain cliffs, rising up from the plain like a gateway, with perpendicular faces of gray limestone, shapely, handsome peaks — the last of the Cévennes. Rarely do you see, even in a mountain region, such striking and beautiful hills. They lie exactly north of Montpellier, and give dignity and romantic beauty to all the landscape.

Although Montpellier is only five miles from the Mediterranean, it occupies high ground — 300 to 400 feet above the sea — and is, in fact, perched on the very irregular foot-hills of the mountain range. Its position is thus picturesque, and the views from its highest places are charming. The city itself is old, but it has the advantage of being full of active, modern life and trade — one of the busiest and most lively of all the old towns in the south of France. It has about the same population as Hartford — something under 50,000. It does not, however, enjoy such a climate as that of Hartford.

Considering that it is a very gay and cheerful city, with many handsome modern buildings and open sunny streets, it is exceedingly interesting, for it preserves for the most part its ancient character of tortuous, narrow streets, which wind about most unexpectedly up and down the hills, and you are constantly entertained withun expected architectural effects.

In fact, as my friend Boucoiran says, " almost the whole town partakes of that boldness of irregular directions, that they are desirous to redress the utmost in our utilitary ages." And he adds, with as much poetry as perspicuity, " the name of Montpellier reminds always in the foreign countries the remembrance of Hyeres or Nice, and smiling thoughts as the emblem of the spring. The renown of the medical school, as well as the clearness of meridianal sky, attracts every year numerous foreigners, because for the northern nations, Montpellier is a sort of hot-house, suitable for the weak constitutions; it is besides the fortunate land of the troubadours to sweet language." There is no doubt about the genial climate. The first four days of our stay here the weather was perfection, a clear sky with an invigorating but still soft breeze from the Cévennes. And now for three or four days it has been cloudy, with occasional bursts of sunshine, and now and then a warm shower — the thermometer standing somewhere from 58° to 65° Fahrenheit. In the sun it is always pleasant, and people here make a business of sitting in the sun. The windows of our apartment in the Hôtel Nevet look south over a little garden, and although all vegetation is in its decay, the grass is yet green and the magnolia trees rejoice in full leaf and vivid color.

Near the hotel is the esplanade, a vast tree-planted promenade, and parade-ground for the soldiers, who are quartered in the citadel beyond the sunken railway. The trumpet is always tooting, and the red legs are always trotting around there. The conscripts are getting so that they can trot together very well. I see that drafts of them are being trotted off to Tunis every few days, after only a drill of three months, which is hardly enough to get the slouch out of their bumpkin gait.

This esplanade has been occupied now some time by a temporary fair, the cheap booths of which in long streets always attract a crowd. There is another street of cheap side-shows, peep-galleries, shooting galleries, fortune-tellers, games and little lotteries and go-rounds, paste-board theatres, a traveling menagerie, and a circus. In front of the booths men in fancy costumes and women in fancy paint stand and beat drums or turn hurdy-gurdies, and call the passers-by to enter their show. It is a cheap Vanity Fair, and at night when the lamps are lighted and everything is in full blast, rather an entertaining one. There are traders and sorcerers here from Algiers, swarthy women and men in fezes. The ground is a study of petty games and feats of legerdemain. I made friends with a lively and lying little Oriental from Algiers, who sold me inedible *nugat* from Zanzibar, and a queer confection from Algiers, which I believed from his toothsome and lively recommendation of it was a sort of ambrosia. America? Oh, yes, he had been in that America in the Philadelphia in 1876 — and he liked it not at all, and shrugged his shoulders in recollection of the *mauvais temps* in that country there.

Montpellier has many attractions. Being of a literary turn, you would probably come here because Petrarch in his youth sojourned here for some time, pretending to read law, but cultivating the muse instead, in the law school which was already in his day very famous. Not more so, however, than the medical school, which owed its existence to the learning of Arab scholars. Their knowledge of medicine was one of the many benefits that the Saracens brought into benighted Europe. Not only was the school of medicine famous here, but here was the first Botanical Garden instituted in France. It is still one of the most interesting, and I do not know where the botanist and the arborist could go to be better pleased. There are nine acres in the grounds. I recognize in the arboretum a great many trees indigenous in America. The grounds are divided into charming walks by allées of trees, by hedges, by paths festooned with ivy. In the Botanical Garden are the busts of the botanical professors, whose names are famous all over Europe, from the middle of the sixteenth century down.

Montpellier has always been the home of culture and of schools. It sustains its reputation to-day by a number of excellent schools for girls and for boys, and by a conservatoire of music and a gallery of the fine arts.

The Museum, with its picture gallery — largely the gift of one man, M. Fabre — passes above provincial pretensions. It is indeed a charming gallery, with works of old and new masters, the lovely heads of Greuze and busts of Canova being prominent.

But the glory of Montpellier, after all, is the Promenade Peyrou. This is on a great eminence at the west side of the town. It is an elevated esplanade, planted with trees — many of them large — and flowers, and adorned with statues. I do not know such another airy, light, and cheerful place. The view from it is one of the finest in Europe. Beneath you is the sunny, irregular city, with its outlying villas and villages, its orchards of olives and groves of pines. To the north are the lovely cliffs of the Cévennes, already spoken of. On the south lie the blue waters of the Mediterranean, not more, in a right line, than five miles distant. On a clear day, at sunrise or sunset, you can see in the west the Canigou, the last outpost of the Pyrenees, and in the east Mt. Ventoux, the first sentinel of the Alps. With the Cévennes, the Alps, the Pyrenees, and the Mediterranean in sight, one ought to be satisfied.

But the charm of this promenade seems to be quite as much in itself as in its commanding prospect. It is so lifted up and cheerful, and elegant in itself and in its surroundings. This great rectangular terrace, built up on rocky foundations, is inclosed by low walls and balustrades, and here and there steps descend to other tree-planted terraces and allées below. In the centre of the terrace is an equestrian statue, in bronze, of Louis XIV. The original one was sent down here from Paris a year or two after the death of this great conqueror of heresy, as a sort of witness that he had upheld the true faith in his province of Languedoc. Religious feeling still ran high, and the statue was first set up out of the city on ground used for winnowing corn. In 1792 it was destroyed. The present one is by Deboy and was erected in 1838. Opposite the entrance of the Promenade Peyrou is a magnificent triumphal arch which was raised in honor of the victories of Louis XIV., in his life-time. Near it is the Palace de Justice, a fine building with two wings, thrown in advance, and a beautiful Corinthian portico with figures sculptured in high relief in the pediment. This and other edifices are in keeping with the noble situation.

In one of the little divisions of the promenade, amid flowers and half hidden by trees, is one of the most charming groups of modern statuary I have seen. I could not learn the name of its creator. A noble male figure, seated, is holding upon one knee the figure of a woman. He supports her with his right arm. Her left arm is clinging about his neck, and her face is upturned to his, which regards her with all tenderness and pity. His left hand clasps her right hand. At their feet and crouching beneath them are two lovely children, one apparently nodding in weariness, and the other leaning upon his comrade's shoulder as if weeping. It is the little Cain and Abel! On the base of the statue are the words: —

PARADIS PERDU.

The figures are exquisitely modeled; it seems impossible for marble to appear so yielding and flexible, and to express more tenderness, grace, and sentiment.

On this promenade also is a fountain with a basin of pellucid water, in which a couple of white swans are enjoying the sun and the pure air which comes gently down from the Cévennes. In the terraces below are other fountains and basins, with swans, white and black.

Above this basin and at the west end of the plateau is a beautiful hexagonal Corinthian building. It is the Château d'Eau. Into it pours the water from the aqueduct, which, on high double rows of arches, stretches across the country and is an exceedingly picturesque addition to the landscape.

You comprehend now that this lovely terrace, tree-planted and flower-adorned and statue-set is a reservoir. You never would suspect it. The water comes in a long covered way, partly on arches, from springs in the Cévennes, eight or ten miles distant. It is excellent, and clear as crystal. It keeps sweet in its covered way and in this reservoir, which is also, as I said, completely covered, but has openings in the side to admit the air. When shall we in America attain such civilization as to utilize for beauty a reservoir as this is utilized?

On Sunday we heard mass in the little Church of St. Denis, where the music was very good indeed. The people of Montpellier pride themselves upon their music, though I doubt if they have as much critical knowledge of it as the people of Avignon. It was a simple little church, full of devout worshipers. Rich and poor mingled together. Whatever else the churches are they are democratic. And there is something, I know not what, of the familiar in these services that is pleasing. Even the dogs come in and wander about at their will, seeking their masters or mistresses, and no one remarks or repulses them. I have seen a good-sized dog, even a little one, almost break up a Protestant worship in five minutes.

In the afternoon of Sunday at three o'clock the regimental band plays upon the Promenade de Peyrou. All the world goes there, all there is of fashion and *ton* in Montpellier is on view. The music was not very good, mostly light, trashy stuff — the French military bands are simply not to be compared with the German — but the whole town was out. There must have been nearly three thousand people on the terrace — a gay and animated concourse, a little provincial, but not the less interesting. One noticed that the people were in family groups for the most part. No young girls unattended, no young men promenading with young ladies.

At noon there was a street parade of the traveling circus, a motley procession with brass band and brazen faces; pseudo knights in soiled mediæval costume upon caparisoned steeds; painted women on horseback, with copper helmets and a faded, dissolute air, led performing horses, clowns of both sexes, and the usual vulgar show of such an affair. In the evening the fair on the esplanade, next to our hotel, was in more than full blast, and crowded with people.

We seldom have so animated a Sunday in Hartford. As we go away from Paris, and out of the through routes to Cannes and Nice, we see less and less English and Americans; only French, largely commercial travelers, wine and olive merchants, at the *tables d'hôte*. It is rare to hear a word of English from one day to another. At the Avignon hotel, which is a thoroughfare of the English, little else is heard besides their tongue, and the sensitive American who attempts to speak it is apt to be encouraged by his British cousin, who lets him know that he detects his accent, but likes Americans himself — has, in short, been so fortunate as to meet a good many pleasant people from America. If the American expresses surprise at this the Englishman pleasantly insists, and even goes so far as to name names. The American sometimes gets weary of this incessant flattery, and seeks to evade it by assuming at the outset his proper position. It was at the table in Avignon that I heard one of my countrymen reply to an Educator of the Globe and Standard of Manners, who followed his soup with the usual question — *Parler-vous Anglais, Monseer?* — "No, sir, I speak American, but I understand English, you can go on."

Here at Montpellier, the long table is filled day after day with men, prosperous, well-to-do looking merchants, all men of business apparently. Few women seem to be traveling. They are all French, and yet the types are somehow familiar, and we constantly see faces that remind us of well known people at home. There is one innocent old man who persists in remaining here who constantly reminds me of an old fool in Hartford, whose name I cannot recall. He is very annoying.

I should like before I close this wandering epistle to the gentiles to call the attention of the Hartford club, by way of eating, to a sort of small, soft-shell clam they have here, which comes from Cette or Palavas, and is called *clovise*. It is a very nice morsel, as a *hors d'ouvre* at breakfast. Worthy the attention of the club, also, is a tiny white fish — an inch long or so, also from the Mediterranean — which is a great delicacy when fried crisp. The club cannot do better, if it is out of white bait, than to direct its attention to this *bonne bouche*. It might also get from Montpellier — but it of course does not care for that — the best *vin ordinaire* I have ever tasted.

CHAPTER V.

CETTE.

ONE inducement to go to Cette was that the spelling of the word has some relation to its pronunciation, a novelty to attract the attention of the traveler in France. He sometimes feels like making suggestions on this point, but he is restrained by two reflections; one is the need of a spelling-reform in his own tongue, and the other is the unimportance of the suggestion in regard to the French language. The English and not the French is the conquering language of the world. The French was invented to enable people to talk interminably without saying anything. The language itself is full of little shrugs, ejaculations, refinements of trifling expirations of breath, which enable two people to keep up a friendly, exciting, inviting little noise incessantly without committing themselves to anything. It is called the language of love and of diplomacy. *Voilà tout!* Everybody knows what the words of lovers and of diplomats are worth. And when diplomats are also lovers we have the final use of the French tongue.

Cette was the ancient *Setion* of the Greeks. The name, until the end of the last century, was written Sette.

All this coast from Cette to Marseilles is a most interesting study of lagoons and sandbars. These marshes are intersected by the great Canal du Midi, which, coming from Toulouse, and thus by some river navigation connecting the Atlantic with the Mediterranean, follows the winding coast from Cette to Marseilles.

You approach Cette by rail on a long curved causeway over the lagoons, and sometimes close along the sea. You leave it, going southwest, by another long sand beach between the lagoon and the sea. Cette is in fact as good as an island. It is, however, a bold promontory, thrust out into the Mediterranean at the end of a sand spit. *Mons Setius* was its name before the Christian era. The bulk of the town is on a flat, cut by canals, the streets communicating by drawbridges. Its best street is a canal flanked by broad quays and high houses; so that the masts of small vessels appear amidst the houses of the town. It has also an artificial harbor, made by a stone pier and breakwater, an inclosed basin with a narrow entrance, and a light-house. The town has all the characteristics of an active seaport: quays crowded with drays, hogsheads piled up, noise, dirt, clamor, confusion, taverns, cafés, a floating southern population, sailors from all the Mediterranean ports, dark-eyed, bronze-cheeked women, able to give back as good as they get to the chaff of the sailors.

The population (as one sees it in the streets) is evidently mixed, dashed with the blood of Italian, Spanish, and Greek. The result is favorable. One sees many pretty, handsome faces of young girls. Until you get south the French woman is celebrated for anything but her beauty. In Paris a handsome woman is as rare as a good one in some places. And the race does not improve until you get to the Mediterranean coast. These southern towns are tolerably well supplied with attractive and piquant if not altogether handsome faces. I was in Cette only a few hours, and perhaps I did not see all the women in the city, but I probably saw most of them, for it is the habit to be out doors. The young women are on the street with babies; the old ones sit by the doors of their little shops or their houses and knit. There are groups in the squares. There are knots of them watching the soldiers drill on the parade. Soldiering is going on here as everywhere else. On the parade the raw conscipts, got into uniforms which do not fit, are being put through gymnastic exercises. Standing in rows each six feet from another, at the word, they all lift up the left leg together, put that down and lift up the right; bend forward till the head is as near the ground as possible, and then stay there for a while; squat down in unison and get up, squat down and get up, squat down and get up, — it is a most usful and beautiful sight in this age of the world.

The streets of the city are not all flat. Some of them climb up the round, steep hill. This conical hill, which in the upper half is all occupied by little villas and gardens, inclosed in high walls, is five hundred and ninety feet high. Try climbing up its stony way, half steps and half sharp stones, after a three franc breakfast (wine included) and see if you do not think it is half as high as Talcott mountain. On the very top is a telegraph signal station, and the queerest little church. The view from it of the sea dotted with sails, the lagoons traversed by causeways and canals, the mainland shore sprinkled with villages, Lake Thau and the Cevennes striding down from the north, is superb.

Half-way up the hill, on the top of a tower of a large church, stands a monstrous image of the Virgin in shining new bronze, perhaps the largest bronze figure of the Virgin in the world. It watches over the town, and must be an object of hope to the storm-tossed sailors.

We are most interested, however, in Cette as the place from whence come our wines. Cette has one of the largest wine manufactories in France. There are made here annually over one hundred thousand pipes of imitations of all the well known wines. M. Boucoiran says, " the fabrication of vessels and casks of every size procures a constant employment to numerous workers. But which makes the object of a considerable trade is the mingling of various wines, to imitate perfectly well those different soils and growths, such as Spanish, Greek, Sicilian, Portuguese, with their colors and natural perfumes." These wine factories partially explain why it is, in the bad years for wine even, all sorts of excellent wines are cheaper in New

York, after paying duties, than in Paris. You get, by the way, much better table wine — *vin ordinaire* — in these southern towns than in Paris. And the same may be said of coffee. I happen to know only one place in Paris where a cup of genuine coffee can be had. At the hotels and cafés generally you get little but chiccory. Whereas, in Avignon, Nîmes, Montpellier, and even in smaller places in the south, *café* is commonly made of coffee.

But if the wine in Cette is bogus, I can testify that the milk is genuine, unless the cows are party to a deception. In the middle of the afternoon I saw in a principal street what I supposed to be a couple of yoke of oxen. Drawing nearer, they still appeared by their size and the shape of their heads to be oxen. They were tied in couples, and their eyes blinded by fringed curtains. Behold, however, they were cows! About them stood groups of women, each with a little earthen pitcher that might hold two gills, waiting for her turn to have it filled. There was no deception here. The milk was milked straight into the little pitchers, under the inspection of the women, who carefully watched the process and took care that they did not get too much foam for their sous. How the cows like this "stripping," here and there, from street to street, and whether they will stand milking in driblets all day, I cannot say. This is, however, the only way, in this sinful, watery world, to get honest milk.

The weather in Montpellier, in the closing days of November, which has been a little cloudy, but calm and warm and free from the storms that have scourged the north of France, is again bright and sunny. As I write I have had to close the outside blinds to keep out the sun.

Montpellier is as lively and crowded as ever. Why so many strangers (all French) come here and fill the hotels day after day nobody seems to know. Perhaps it is trade, perhaps the schools, perhaps the courts which are in session. I looked into the court-rooms the other day. The lawyers and judges all wear black robes, cut with a gathered yoke on the shoulder, with white bands in front, and round fluted caps, larger at the top than at the bottom — a very becoming head-piece. Some of them have a black rosette on the shoulder, and a tab hanging from it tipped with ermine.

In the "court of the first instance," the inferior court, were three judges on the bench. Behind them on the wall hung a crucifix. On the same elevated platform, at the sides, were the clerks. The railed space in front was empty. In the benches before the bar sat the lawyers, among their clients and among the spectators. Whatever case was going on nearly every lawyer present seemed to take a hand in it, jumping up every few moments to make a remark or read a paper. On the bench of the court of appeals sat six judges. A lawyer was making an argument, chattering and jerking himself up and down with the utmost vivacity, and his colleague was so much interested in it that he occasionally gestured for his partner. The court was much like any other court. The fattest judge was fast asleep and nodding — he was probably the one who would write the opinion, being unprejudiced. The one next him was writing a letter. The two next were reading letters and conversing. Another was writing. And the last was regarding space vacantly. Nobody listened to the orator, who nevertheless kept on in the most persuasive and gentlemanly manner.

The criminal court was not in session. But the criminal business must be large, if one can judge by the newspapers, which are filled with accounts of most brutal crimes. The country, however, seems to be in a better state than Paris. Every day the Paris journals contain many accounts of crimes to the person, such as street assaults, stabbings, and murders. Paris is evidently not nearly so well in hand as it was under the empire, when, under the strict watch of the police, the stranger was safe to wander anywhere day or night. It is far from being so now.

CHAPTER VI.

AIGUES-MORTES.

"SEVERAL ways," says the most amusing guide-book for Provence and Languedoc, written by M. Boucoiran of Nîmes, who has discovered new incapacities in the English language, — "several ways are offered to the travelers to attain Aigues-Mortes; by earth or by waters, but the most practical is by railroad."

I found it so. The approach by rail is through the marshes and lagoons which lie on either side of the Rhone. This country, only a foot or two above the Mediterranean, and intersected by canals, is one vast vineyard. The wine produced is, I suppose, of an inferior quality, but the quantity ought to satisfy anybody.

"Before the arrival"—I cannot refrain from quoting the accomplished Boucoiran — "in sight of the Carboniere tower toward the left, upon a hillock, and between other modern rural constructions, an old arched wall that is yet up there. Upon that former house many centuries intrusted their architectural forms, and the tradition did maintain to that place the name of Psalmodi, because the Benedictine monks who were established there since the eighth century, sung unceasing psalms."

This old abbey was in one sense the mother of the later city, but Aigues-Mortes — the name signifies "stagnant water" — owes its importance to Louis IX., the saint. It required a saint to drop a full-walled city, a town completely inclosed with high ramparts and lofty fighting towers, in the midst of these swamps, and approached from the tideless Mediterranean only by shallow channels.

The view from the ramparts is largely of water and sandy ground saturated with salt, a narrow zone about the walls lending itself to cultivation. "The sight," says our instructor, "can only perceive a wide extent, in midst of which arise some pine forests that intersect ponds bordered by tamarisk trees and reeds. Upon these sandy shores and damp moors abound venomous reptiles; there whirl around swarms of winged insects, and feed on freely flocks of savage bulls or white horses. Among the numerous water fowls that fill these ponds the hunters often perceive, on the edge of waters, a company of long-legged ibis, and pursuing their career at the first alarm, they display in flock, at the sun their rosy wings."

From this inviting coast Saint Louis chose to embark for Palestine, and that is the explanation of the existence here of the most remarkable walled city in France, the most perfect and picturesque reminder of the Middle Ages. From afar off we see its high ramparts and heavy round towers, all in perfect condition; and it would occasion no surprise to see the crenlated walls manned with men in armor, and to behold a cavalcade of knights enter one of the narrow gates.

The city is so small and the walls are so solid that it seems as if it would be possible to pick up the whole affair and carry it away — that it would all hang together like a toy city which children play with. The embrasured wall is built in the exact form of a parallelogram, and it is only 596 yards long by 149 yards in breadth. The walls are thirty-six feet high, flanked by fifteen round towers. From the interior at regular intervals steps ascend to the top of the ramparts. The most remarkable, and the famous one, of these round towers is that of Constance, built out by salient walls from the northeast corner. This tower is ninety-six feet high and seventy-two feet in diameter, and contains a couple of vaulted chambers, the walls of which are, at the base, of enormous thickness. This tower is surmounted by a slender column, upon which a lantern used to be kept burning at night.

Within these narrow limits, Aigues-Mortes is a little city of straight, narrow streets. There are several entrance gates, and from one you look straight through the city out of another. It is said that in its prosperous days the city had a population crowded into it of 11,000. It is credited now with about 4,000, but it seemed to me there were scarcely 1.000 people in its silent streets. There are in it many vacant plots of ground and many deserted houses. Every other walled city I have ever seen has outgrown its bondage and spread into the surrounding country. Aigues-Mortes has shrunk within its stone shell, and rattles around in it like a dried nut.

It was in the summer of 1224 that Louis IX., being sick, and mindful of the necessity of propitiating Heaven, projected a crusade to Palestine. All the havens along the coast were in possession of his enemies or rivals. Montpellier, with its creeks, belonged to the King of Aragon, Maguelonne to a bishop, Narbonne to Count Aimery IV., and so on; while Marseilles was then not sufficient for the King of France, and he wished a less conspicuous place, where he could make preparations at his leisure, and assemble his eight hundred galleys and his forty thousand fighting men. Important works were undertaken, a sort of port was made, the channels were deepened, and on the 25th of August, 1248, Saint Louis with Queen Marguerite, having heard mass in the Church of Notre Dame des Sablons,— the ugly little edifice still stands in the principal square, and evidently has not been ventilated since 1248, for its smell dates back to the time when smells were first created, — embarked in great state and with much noise on his first crusade. He sailed again from Aigues-Mortes in July, 1270, on his second jaunt to Palestine, and he died that year in August amid the ruins of Carthage. These two crusades are known as the fifth and sixth. In the old square of the city there is a fine statue of the hero of these, by Pradier. King Louis, clad in a coat of mail and armor, has a beautiful face and figure.

Saint Louis, who so much loved Aigues-Mortes, did

not however, build its walls. They were erected by his son, Philippe the Hardy, after the plan, it is said, of the defenses of Damietta, the city at the east mouth of the Nile. The exact spot where Saint Louis embarked on his crusades has been in dispute. But our accomplished writer of English throws this light upon it: "It was discovered by chance, in 1835 a little vessel concealed under the sands, on the spot called *Les Tombes*, and where, it is supposed, Saint Louis had ordered to be built an hospital for pilgrims. That old carcass ascended until enough ancient ages, but difficult to precise exactly, and at least certified that, had existed at that place, before the thirteenth century, a passage for the ships going in the port of Aigues-Mortes."

But the city has other historic interests. In an old house one is shown a chamber — containing a famous carved mantel-piece, known as the *Cheminée de Saint Louis* — where was held in 1538 the interview between Francis I. and Charles V. of Spain, what time Hariadan Barbarousse, the Moslem corsair, was hovering along the coast to ravish the towns and carry away slaves.

Of still more interest to us are the religious persecutions of the sixteenth century, of which this city was one of the centres. The towns of Languedoc took eagerly to the reformation of 1560. It was impossible to repress the increase of proselytes to the new faith. Aigues-Mortes was the seat of a constant struggle between the Calvinists and the Papists, who held it turn and turn about. Louis XIV. visited this region with fire and fagot. After the repeal of the Edict of Nantes Protestant worship was forbidden in this region, houses of worship were pulled down, meetings for worship were forbidden, emigration was prohibited, and the faithful were immured in loathsome dungeons.

The tower of Constance was for many years the prison of unfortunate women whose sin was an humble profession of the Protestant faith. I saw the round chamber in the second story in which they were confined. It has several long, narrow slits in the thick walls to admit air, and one small, grated window. In this room, with never any egress, were heaped together the poor women, fed on the coarsest food, with little light and air, and deprived of the common accommodations of life. The wretched condition of these prisoners at length excited the sympathy of the Swiss, the Hollanders, and the Germans, who by their ministers protested to the court of Louis XIV., but without other result than to increase the rigors of the prisoners. Their confinement lasted during a good part of the reign of Louis XV. Finally, in 1767, a humane man, Prince de Beauvau, was made commandant of the province (Languedoc), and inspected the tower of Constance. I cannot, he says in his report, describe the horror of the first view of this appalling chamber, which had as little light as air. Fourteen women, the survivors of many, pined away in wretchedness and tears. Disgust at the sight of them was mingled with pity. At the unexpected visit the poor women fell together at his feet, seeking words and finding only sobbings. "Alas! their capital crime was to have been born and instructed in the same belief as Henry IV. The youngest of these martyrs exceeded fifty years, and she was only eight years old when she had been apprehended, going with her mother to hear a sermon, and her punishment yet continued." On the walls of this round chamber are scratched the names of these unfortunate women who for nearly half a century languished there.

So much for the historical interest of Aigues-Mortes, where, in a dirty little inn, ill-kept by friendly, simple people, I had a capital breakfast. But I confess that I was drawn to visit the city by an interest still more romantic. For it was at Aigues-Mortes that Pierre de Provence landed after his oriental captivity, and it was on an island near it that the fair Maguelonne founded her hospital for pilgrims and wayfarers.

Perhaps you do not remember the details of the charming story of "Pierre de Provence et de La Belle Maguelonne"? It was a favorite history in the twelfth century. This romance was turned into verse in 1178, by Barnard de Triviés, canon of Maguelonne, and it is said that it was one of the first books that Petrarch read when he came to Avignon, and that he attempted to perfect it.

The story is, in brief, this: Pierre was the son of Jean de Provence and his lovely wife, Isabelle, the daughter of Don Alvares, Count of Barcelona. He had considerable fortune, and the right to reign sovereign of the Comtal; but he preferred peace to glory, and did not dispute the title with his usurping brother, but lived with more content at Cavaillon, with his beautiful and virtuous wife, than if he had possessed the empire of the world. Pierre was their only child. He was most carefully educated, trained to all exercises in arms as well as letters; modest, virtuous, handsome. No one could excel him in the pastimes of chivalry; he could turn a neater verse than the professional troubadours, and he unhorsed and conquered all the knights that came from all Europe to his father's tournaments. Before he was of age he had the renown of an unconquerable knight. Attractive as he was in person, he was a stranger to the passion of love, and loved then, and all his life, virtue more than gallantry.

One day, at his father's table, some gallant knights whom he had overthrown in the lists spoke much of the court of the King of Naples and of the exquisite beauty of Maguelonne, the daughter of the king. Pierre was suddenly inflamed with the desire of seeing her, and playing a knight's part in the tourneys of such a court. With difficulty he obtained permission of his parents to go in search of adventures. When he departed, his inconsolable mother presented him with three precious rings. With a small following of servants, he reached Naples, where he took retired lodgings and remained unknown. At the first proclamation of the tournament he entered the lists as a nameless knight. Needless to say that he overturned everybody who opposed him. He saw La Belle Maguelonne, and was ravished with her beauty and her sweetness. She, on her part, was equally enamored of him. He was signally honored by the king, and invited to a banquet at the palace. There he exchanged words with the idol of his eyes, who was most gracious to the young knight. But he refused all solicitations to disclose his name and rank.

Tournament followed tournament. He was always victorious, and was advanced more and more in the favor of the king and queen. But the new-felt passion of love tormented him. It tormented also the fair Maguelonne, who had never felt it before. And with a fresh and sweet sincerity, which cannot be too much commended, she sent him word by her maid of her state of mind. The maid arranged an interview in her apartment in the palace. The two lovers, whose love was as pure as snow, vowed never to love nor to marry other man or woman. On her entreaty he disclosed his name. But there were political reasons why he could not ask her hand of her father. It is curious to note, in a story of that age, that she did not care for rank: birth, she said, was only an accident, and she wished she had been a simple peasant girl; only then she would have liked him to have lived on the next farm, so that they could have married without leave of anybody.

Obstacles to their union were many; she feared that some day her father would compel her to accept for husband a disagreeable knight whom she hated. The lovers took the bold resolve of escaping together.

Taking her personal jewels, they sallied forth at night on horseback, with a few faithful attendants. At dawn they stopped in a lonely wood by the sea-shore to repose. The tired girl, trusting always the honor of her pure lover, slept reclining in his arms. As she slept, a little wooden box, which contained the three rings of his mother that Pierre had given her, slipped from her pocket. A sea-bird, seeing it, swooped down and carried it off. Pierre, folding his cloak for Maguelonne to rest her head upon, gently laid her down and went in pursuit of the bird, who dropped the box into the sea. Pierre jumped into a leaky fishing-boat which had no oars, and pushed out to recover it. A wind blew the boat from the shore farther and farther. Pierre was in despair. The one accomplishment he lacked was swimming.

Result: The boat was blown out at sea. Pierre was picked up by some Moorish pirates, sold as a slave to the Sultan of Alexandria, became a great favorite with the Sultan, assisted him in council and in war. The Sultan would make him his son, and give him his daughter. Pierre said it was not the manner of his religion to have more than one wife, and that he was betrothed already. The Sultan thought the more wives the better. He attempted to convert his slave, but Pierre resisted all the arguments of the dervishes and all the blandishments of the seducing odalisques. At last, after eight years of captivity, the Sultan gave Pierre his liberty, embarked him on a vessel bound to Provence, and enriched him with loads of jewels and fine stuffs, which for security were placed in fourteen barrels covered with salt at each end.

The vessel stopped for water at a little island. Pierre wandered ashore and was left, while the vessel sailed on, and by chance came to Aigues-Mortes, and left the barrels of salt at a hospital on a little island near by, in charge of the Superior, who stored them away, having learned that they were the property of a passenger left behind. And in this passenger, for some reason, she took an uncommon interest. Pierre, after as many adventures as Ulysses, came at last himself to Aigues-Mortes, sick and forlorn, and sought the shelter of the hospital, over which presided a charming young Superior, who always wore her veil, whose name was concealed, and who was only known by her bountiful charity and her loving, tender spirit to all the unfortunate.

The story of Maguelonne, after her abandonment, is equally romantic. She dared not go back to Naples for fear of involving her attendants in dire punishment. Instead, she made a pilgrimage to Rome in company with an honest and lovely family, who were going there to get a dispensation from the Pope for the marriage of their daughter to her cousin. From Rome she sought Provence, the country of her lover. There she found that the story of her flight was known, and from what she heard of the anger of his parents against her she did not dare to present herself to them. She went to the little island near Aigues-Mortes, and founded a hospital for pilgrims. Her renown soon spread. Among those who came to see her were Count Jean and Isabelle his wife. They learned to love her for herself; and, finally, she disclosed to them her name, and all her faithful love and hope. She believed that Pierre had been captured by the Moslems, and that some day he would return.

One day a fisherman brought to the château at Cavaillon a fine turbot, and presented it to the Countess Isabelle. What was her surprise, on opening it, to find within a small wooden box, which contained the three rings she had given to Pierre. This was proof to the parents that Pierre was dead, and they had funeral services performed accordingly. But Maguelonne would not accept this as proof of his loss, and still waited for him.

In the hospital Pierre, who was very weak, was tenderly nursed by the veiled Superior, who, however, did not dare to disclose herself for fear of the effect of sudden joy in his exhausted condition. He told her his sad story. At length, when he was a little recovered, she told him that Maguelonne lived, that she knew her well; and one day she brought Pierre a letter written in Maguelonne's own hand, which he recognized. Then she feigned the necessity of three days' absence, and on her return she invited Pierre to supper in her apartments. What was his astonishment to see there his father and his mother, and Maguelonne herself, in all her radiant sweetness.

Does not all the world know that they were married immediately, and that they succeeded to the throne of Naples, probably the happiest king and queen who ever sat upon it, or on any throne, and that their only son united on his head the crown of Naples and that of the Comte of Provence? It is needless to say that the fourteen barrels of salt were not forgotten at the wedding.

When I stood outside the walls of Aigues-Mortes that night, toward the setting of the sun, the washerwomen of the city were gathering their clothes from the lines stretched on stakes driven into the sand. Children were playing around their mothers by the edge of the salt and tideless water. Under the high walls, in the full play of the generous sun, sat on the gravel a few old men, apparently contented in idleness and rags. Over the rosy water and the gray marsh, and under a sky blazing with broken clouds of orange and pink and green, I fancied I could see the happy island and hospital walls where the constant Pierre was nursed back to life by La Belle Maguelonne. Perhaps they were only in the sky.

CHAPTER VII.

LA BELLE MAGUELONNE.

I HAVE at last found Maguelonne: the lonesome little island which seems to float among the lagoons, and might any day drift out to sea, or pass away among the mountains of clouds of which it seems to be a part on a hazy day, or at sunset when its church tower and pines are lifted up and magnified in the rosy, transforming light.

This tiny island is the seat of the very ancient bishopric and church of Maguelonne, and I doubt not the romantic scene of the charming story which I have sketched of "Pierre de Provence et La Belle de Maguelonne." Whether grave history takes any account of the fair Maguelonne, I cannot learn, but local tradition preserves her name among the most cherished stories of mediæval times; and, for myself, I do not doubt that the heroine of the romance and of the desolate island are one and the same person.

All this coast from Cette to Marseilles is a series of lagoons and sand dunes, irregular in its lines, traversed by the great Canal du Midi and strewn with little fishing villages.

I went one day by rail, half an hour, from Montpellier to Palavas, across the lagoons and canals, the marshes haunted by the bird-hunters and set out in vineyards wherever there is any firm ground. Palavas was until recently a poor fishing village on each side of the little river Lez. Now it has become a resort for summer bathing for all this region of Hérault, and has many pretentious hotels and lodging-houses, which being closed at this season give the place a particularly deserted air. It smells, however, of fish and clams. The stream and the canals are full of small boats, nets are spread on the stone pavements, and the ruddy-cheeked girls, brown women with black eyes, and the loutish men proclaim the hardy nature of the occupation of its inhabitants.

On my way down I had marked, away to the right, across the lagoons, at a great distance as it seemed in the hazy autumn air, an island with an elevated mass of buildings amid trees. I thought that could not be my Maguelonne, but upon inquiry I ascertained that it was, and that it could only be reached by an hour's good walk along the curving shore.

This long sand dune might be compared to the Lido at Venice, but it is not so high or so attractive. Indeed, a more solitary promenade could not be desired by a misanthrope. The road stretched across the sand in a seemingly endless line, and was utterly uninhabited. On the right hand was the lagoon and the Canal du Midi, and beyond the lifted-up villages of the mainland, and the Cévennes behind them. On the left the Mediterranean was pounding the sand and the clam-shells, for the wind had been blowing some days from the south and a good surf was on. All along, however, the sandy ground was laid out in vineyards, which are slightly protected from the breath of the sea by high palisades of thickly-plaited straw. The vines seemed hardy and flourishing. I was surprised to find the grape growing on such a mere damp sand-spit, so near the sea.

With a fresh breeze and a sky of broken flying clouds and the dashing of the sea, the walk was an inspiring one and did not seem long, although enlivened by no company except some black-winged birds that were fishing in the lagoon. But somehow Maguelonne seemed little nearer when I was half way there than when I started on the level road. It was certainly a long three miles.

At length, however, the road bent to the right, and I crossed a narrow channel and was on the little island. Still no inhabitants, and no sign of life except the good road and the vine culture. I entered the island, which rises twenty or thirty feet above the surrounding morass, through a pretty avenue of pines, which changed as I came upon the plateau into a way bordered by low hedges of roses in abundant flower. Everywhere now were signs of culture and thrift. On the left were two stone magazines, or store-houses; and on the right, partially hidden by the pines and half overgrown with ivy, was the old church, still erect and imposing, although its towers had crumbled and many of its buttresses were tumbling down. I had passed at the entrance of the grounds a large crucifix among the pines. This symbol is never far away from business, or work, or pleasure, in this region. We come upon it unexpectedly in the fields and highways, and stepping into the court of appeals in Montpellier, the other day, it hung behind the bench of the judges. Upon the roof of the church is a small bell, which still calls to service every Sunday.

On the left of the church, toward the sea, are the remains of a chapel, said to be a part of the old hospital, and beyond it, close to the water's edge, a bit of ruin surmounted by an image of the Virgin, or some sea-saint.

Close to the church and partially in front of it I found the farm-house, a neat, cheap " château," where the proprietor, whose capital and energy have reclaimed from sandy desolation this island, lives with his family in the summer. A part of it is occupied by the farmer. Gardens about the house, and near, cultivated fields sloping down to the edge of the water. Flowers in beds, ivy climbing over the ruined church-tower, birds flitting about the vines and chattering in the sun, and the soft sea-air swaying the roses on their stalks. It was altogether charming. I was quite unprepared for so much beauty in a place of such sad and desolate aspect at a distance. Perhaps the romance of La Belle Maguelonne lent something attractive to the scene; and I could well believe that her sweet spirit yet dwells there.

Perhaps it is a question if she had a sweet spirit, or

if she existed there any more than Amy Robsart at Kenilworth. I confess that the grave histories of the old church do not mention her; they dwell fondly upon the bishops and archbishops and canons who thought they made the place famous by living there, but they are silent about the memory of this fair virgin, whose name gives a romantic sentiment to all this coast. The local tradition is, however, more considerate, and it is supported by the remains of her tomb in the old church — a tomb of white marble. La Belle Maguelonne was not a recluse. She was a woman of the world, who enjoyed the world and her own beauty, I doubt not. But she was pious, and good as well as pious, and delighted in charities and sweet ministrations to the sick and the unfortunate. Why should not beauty go with divine goodness and self-sacrifice, now and then? It is said that La Belle Maguelonne thought that she should never lose her beauty, and never grow old, and never die. I scarcely believe this, from what I know of this sensible woman. But perhaps she was a lovely "perfectionist." It is true, however, — at least they say so, — that when she perceived in herself some premonitions of weakness and of failing she had prepared for herself a white marble tomb, under which she might repose in sweet peace in the little island she loved. This is so much like the calm and undismayed spirit of La Belle Maguelonne, who, in the romance, after building the hospital here and nursing the pilgrims, at last married her faithful lover and went to assume her birthright as Queen of Naples, that I do not doubt that they were one and the same person, and that the poet of the eleventh or twelfth century, whoever he was, had her for his model when he wrote the romance of "Pierre de Provence et la Belle de Maguelonne."

How old this edifice is I do not know, but there has been a bishopric here and a church ever since the third century. It was in the old warlike times as much a fortress and place of refuge as a church. The devoted men who dwelt here were prepared to defend it against the roving bands of plunderers from the main-land and against the corsairs of the sea. Once the building had battlemented walls, and a great many buildings and houses were grouped about it. Twelve hundred years ago its warlike bishop resisted the assault of Wamba, the king of the Visigoths, but was finally compelled to capitulate. After that the Saracens, who ravaged all this coast, took the island and fortified it; and they in turn were expelled by Charles Martel. In the year 737 the see of the bishop was transferred to Substantion, for the bishop was tired of continual sieges and attacks. In 1037 the good Bishop Arnaldus set up the see again there, enlarged the church, repaired the causeway to the mainland, deepened the port, and recalled there his chapter and his vassals. In the beginning of the sixteenth century it was only a precarious monastic retreat, and the episcopacy, when Pius III. was pope, was transferred to Montpellier. After that it had few dwellers, who languished there with fever, although the spot was so loved that noble families continued to bear the bodies of their dead there from all the neighborhood, as to a holy ground, to inter them. Until its present proprietor reduced the island anew to cultivation, I suppose that for a long period it has been simply one scene of ruins, of desolation, swept by the storms of the sea, and only a sad historical monument. The thrifty owner has swept and garnished it, and made of it a most charming oasis in this waste of marsh and sand. The church has become again a sanctuary, and every Sunday mass is said here; though where the congregation comes from, unless the departed and buried of thirteen centuries are present at the ghostly service, I do not know.

Over the small portal is some good and quaint old carving in low relief. The interior is unexpectedly large and impressive. Denuded as are its walls, I am not sure but it is more impressive than if they were hung with the common daubs of pictures and the tinsel of a loving credulity. It has a nave without aisles, and a short transept. At the beginning of the transept a circle let into the pavement marks the place of the apse in the time of Charles Martel. The present apse was added by Bishop Arnaldus in 1037. In the pavement of the choir are entombed bishops and archbishops and other holy men, whose worn and broken effigies attest the long time they have lain there. In a glass case in the transept are preserved the skulls of dignitaries and men of note which were exhumed at some time when the pavement was repaired, and which belonged, said the farmer's wife who opened the church for me, to the sixth century. Some of them had preserved their teeth. I did not recognize in the case the skull of La Belle Maguelonne. I am sure I should have known her if she had been there.

The church has one architectural peculiarity in what is called a "tribune." A considerable portion of the nave from the entrance is covered by a roof — like an organ loft extending far out into the church. This roof is the floor of a large apartment. Ascending to it by a long and broad staircase, between the inner and outer walls, I found a spacious room, large enough for a chapel, and commanding a view of the choir and apse. This was the tribune.

Passing out of this room, my conductress led me to the roof of a part of the building now in ruins, a platform inclosed on three sides by high walls heavily draped with ivy, and vocal with the twittering of birds; and from thence by a steep, narrow stairway to the roof of the great building, from whence all the kingdoms of the sea and part of the land were spread out before me.

Nothing could be pleasanter than this great expanse of water, of low lands fringed with villages, and this green, peaceful little isle, bathed in a genial sun of November. It is, however, said my peasant guide, a pleasant black-eyed woman, in white cap and apron, — the universal costume of her class, — very cold in winter. It is bitter. Ice forms in the lagoons. Exactly how cold it was I couldn't make out, for the French zero, which is our thirty-two degrees above, is a frightful thing to them. I told the good woman that it was also cold sometimes in America. I tried to explain to her about Winnipeg, and Lancaster, N. H., and sixty degrees below our zero. But Winnipeg failed to impress her, and I think she had no conception of cold weather. The French thermometer is not constructed, as ours is, with the view of freezing people to death. As near as I could ascertain, winter in Maguelonne is like some of our most severe July weather in New England, when we have to cover up the flowers at night. Still, as people think about the weather, so is it with them.

When I came away I had permission to gather as many roses from the wayside as I pleased. I plucked literally an armful. Anything more fragrant, more splendid in color, than those roses I do not know. They were as large and fine as some of our best conservatory varieties, but, blowing about freely in the salt air, they had a touch of wildness and freedom in them that made them fascinating. In general color they were pink, pink of many shades; but the outer petals were dashed with a deep carmine, ensanguined, brilliant, as if stained with the blood of priests and warriors, Goths and Saracens, who had for centuries contended for the possession of this little isle of the sea.

"They are," said my guide, "*roses de l'Autome.*" But we named them *roses de La Belle Maguelonne.*

CHAPTER VIII.

MUNICH TO ORVIETO.

THIS Roundabout Journey, which was intended to be only round-about the Mediterranean, got a severe twist in December. It was not choice that rapt us from the sunshine and roses of the land of La Belle Maguelonne, through the tomb-like damps of Switzerland into the fogs of Munich, in the darkest month of the year. Nor was it curiosity to test the vaunted geniality of a Vevay winter. I could defend Munich, which is in the foggy season of December mild compared with Paris or New England, but the defense of Vevay must be left to those who like an atmosphere surcharged with moisture that chills through bone and marrow. It was Providence that gave us in those dark days the concerts at the Odeon and Clara Schumann instead of the palms of Palermo.

It must have been about the 10th of January that I left the city of the little monk, for it was after the festival of the Three Holy Kings. And very lucky it was that I waited, before setting out on my journey, for the blessing of Caspar, Melchior, and Balthasar. The day of the "Hl. 3. Könige" is January 6th, but for some days thereafter the priests go about with holy water and censer, to any house where their presence is desired, and purify and bless it for a year. We were sitting at dinner when two priests in full splendor of canonicals knocked and begged pardon for entering. One of them swung the censor until the room was that holy with frankincense that we could hardly breathe in it, and the other sprinkled it with holy water, and then with a piece of white chalk wrote over the door the date and the letters, "18 C. M. B. 82;" only he made a monogram of the letters and chalked above each one the cross. Every bedroom and apartment in the house was entered and fumigated in the same manner, and over every door was written the mysterious monogram. The priests were sent by the landlord of the house, at no expense to the tenants; and I am bound to say that they went through their task with perfect gravity. After they had departed, with a final swing of the censor my Catholic friends opened doors and windows, to get rid of the stifling fumes; but the chalk marks over the doors, they laughingly said, should remain, and that for a year we should be safe under the protection of Caspar, Melchior, and Balthasar.

Under the guidance of these three great travelers, — I need not mention that one ought to do very well with three kings, — I left the fog of Munich and came safely into the clear and scarcely colder air of Innsbruck. This picturesque and painted mediæval town is particularly attractive in winter, when the steep peaks that stand about it are dusted with snow, and peak and swift river sparkle and dance in the sunshine.

Everybody stops over a day in Innsbruck to see the wonderful tomb of Maximilian in the old church, and no monument is better known by photographs and descriptions. Indeed, there are fewer more impressive sights than the twenty-six heroic bronze figures of kings and queens, in the sumptuousness of armor and royal garments of state, standing motionless about this splendid tomb. Nor do I know anything in ivory carving superior to the panels of the tomb itself, each illustrating some scene in the fighting life of the hero, who provided for his remembrance better than any long-headed Pharaoh who hid his mummy in a decorated rock mausoleum. Nobody else has for sentinels about his resting place the proudest kings and queens of the world. The only fault the traveler finds with the situation is that the church is not large enough or fine enough for the jewel it contains. There is an incongruity in the spectacle and its inclosure. The tomb and the heroic attendants dwarf the edifice, and you feel that this is only a temporary store-house for a great work of art that should have a majestic setting.

I lodged at the Goldern Adler, an ancient inn, as famous in its way as the Tomb. I went there because Goethe and Heine stayed there when they were on their sentimental and satirical pilgrimages. I was shown into a large chamber, having two beds and a gigantic porcelain stove and only one window, but that one looked, between angular roofs and corners of narrow streets, upon the iron bridge over the river Inn. It was a comfort to know that Heine's room was next mine, and that Goethe's was opposite. The latter is large, and has three cheerful windows, looking down into the picturesque streets, which in this part of the city have not been changed since the resolute hotel-keeper, Andreas Hofer, here incited the sharp-shooters of the Tyrol to make head on the Austrian side against Napoleon. We do not commonly associate heroic courage — except in the matter of charges — with an innkeeper, but in the Tyrol the keeper of a Wirth-house, or inn where beer is more in demand than beds, is the most important person in the village. It requires resolution and courage as well as tact to manage the brutal peasants, who are quite ready, under the ennobling influence of beer, to whip out a knife, in the pause of the dance, to contest the possession of a comely and solid *sennerin*, or Alp-girl. These stalwart maidens, who pass the summer months alone on a high Alp, in a solitary hut, tending the feeding cows and doing the milking and butter-making and all the stable work with their own broad hands, are quite able to take a refractory bull by the horns and teach him manners. I have read that in a peasant dance — which would not be a holiday pastime for a "leader of the German," one of our gilded youths — a *sennerin* will catch her stout and heavy swain by the waistband, while he puts his hands on her shoulders, throw him aloft till his heels strike the ceiling, where they continue on the boards the lively rat-tat-too of the dance, the girl meantime continuing her round, with her lover in the air, and never missing a step dictated by the jig of the fiddle. Such a woman as this is evidently worth fighting for, and is only to be won by the strong hand and the craft of the champion chamois hunter. The control of a crowd of this description, on merriment and deviltry inclined, is no sinecure, and the inn-keeper, if he would not have his house come down about his head, must be a man of force and courage. Hofer had ample training in the mastery of men before he became a leader of them in the field.

I told my landlady that for some literary and sentimental reasons I should have preferred to lodge in the chamber of the great German poet. But she, having no doubt divined my republican predilections, said,— "But you have the chamber once occupied by the Emperor Joseph II. In this very room he slept on the nights of the 29th, 30th, and 31st of July, 1777, and here he gave audience to his officers."

That was enough, I humbly said, as I looked about the bare but transfigured apartments. What am I that I should not be content with an emperor's bed, if the sheets have been changed? We must all, one day,— for has not the poet Bryant, not to mention the psalmist, said it? — sleep with the kings and princes of this earth, and why not lie with an emperor now!

Yes, I said, the Emperor Joseph will do, since I cannot have Goethe, and I shall have a kindlier feeling for the Hapsburgs ever after. "Besides," said the landlady, with growing pride, "in the chamber above you lodged Andreas Hofer, and it was from the window above yours that he harangued the populace on the 15th of August, 1809."

That was just before Hofer set out for Italy, and just about a year before Napoleon, who always knew how to pick out the best men, had the patriot shot at Mantua.

I revolved these things in my mind as I lay in my imperial couch, — too short at both ends, — becoming gradually conscious of the heavy weight of dignity put upon me, and wondering whether the Great Joseph had the heroic patience *not* to do as I did: kick into the middle of the room the vast and fluffy featherbed under which I was sweltering, vast, and yet, as Mrs. Browning says, "too scant to cover doom."

It was, after all, a heroic place to sleep in, if only good sleep could make a hero or a poet. Heine on one side, Goethe on the other, Andreas Hofer overhead, and the ghost of the Kaiser in the room! What Andreas Hofer said to the excited crowd on that memorable 15th day of August, 1809, at 12 o'clock noon, out of the window above, was not running in my head, because it was said in an antique Tyrolean dialect that can run in no foreigner's head. But roughly translated, it was this: —

"God bless you, my dear Inspruckers [*Grüess enck Gott meine lieb'n S'brucker*], that you have chosen me for your general; and here accordingly I am. And there are many here who are not Inspruckers. All who are willing to be soldiers under me must fight for God, the Emperor, and their Fatherland, as brave, honest, and good Tyroleans, if they wish to be brethren in the fight; and those who will not do so may now return home. I counsel you and all who may accompany me that you will not forsake my banner; and I never will forsake you, so sure as my name is Andreas Hofer. Now I have said it, and you have seen for yourselves. God preserve you!"

I cannot ask the reader to stop with me at Meran, that sheltered nest in the Tyrol, a bright and architecturally most picturesque winter hot-bed of gossip and invalids, surrounded by snow mountains and sentineled by castles; nor in Florence, sparkling under the blue sky, warm in the sun and chill in the shade. I had many times desired to have a day in queer Orvieto; not on account of its golden wine, but to see the most brilliantly ornamented cathedral façade in Europe. And now the direct through line from Florence to Rome permits one to do so. Still, it is not a convenient stopping-place in winter. The station of Orvieto is not attractive, even with its composite restaurant, kitchen, and bric-a-brac shop, where you can buy sausage, wine, chunks of meat and bread, vases, jars and tear-bottles from the near Etruscan tombs, and yellow majolica, warranted just as good as the antique, in appearance. I was put into a shackling, decayed, antediluvian carriage with two horses, and dragged for over an hour up the steep hill by a winding road that seemed endless. Brown and desolate looked all the winter landscape, and more and more desolate as we rose, and the view widened over barren hills and colorless valleys. No city was in sight till we actually passed the gate and entered it, on the very crest of the hill. The wind sweeps it in tireless fury, and goes marauding through the narrow streets, searching out the weak points in the traveler's raiment.

I cannot say what this dead and mediæval town is like. It is full of architectural surprises. You may wander about, up hill and down, lose yourself in angles and corners and stony lanes, and get little idea of it. You seem to be nowhere, for the chief streets are little more than lanes with blank walls on either side, with here and there a dark hole or archway in the wall, which is a shop; and yet there is every now and then a bewitching architectural glimpse, and the decayed old town has an indescribable charm.

The best description I know of the cathedral is Mr. Charles Eliot Norton's study of the building of it. The edifice is vast, and inside and out in process of restoration. Within are, however, still many delicious ancient mosaics of scriptural scenes. The whole front blazes with biblical history. This edifice, like that of Siena, is built of black and white marble, and like that it has many a scriptural story and scene of judgment and retribution carved in stone. But what distinguishes it from all others, and makes it worth a long pilgrimage to see, are the pictures in brilliant mosaics which cover nearly the whole façade. If you want to know what they are, I can only say, "Go read your Bible through." But you can hardly imagine how they glow and sparkle in the southern sun.

There is also at Orvieto an interesting museum of Etruscan antiquities, and there are Etruscan tombs, attractive to the antiquary — but I will not take my reader underground.

I lodged in the hotel Belle Arte. It is a splendid old palace, and a cold old palace. I think the original inhabitants must have been frozen out of it. It would make a good ice-house in summer, and I do not suppose it was ever warm, since its thick walls shut out the sun. It has a noble dining-room, the ancient family hall, with some tolerable paintings on the walls, and its high vaulted ceilings frescoed so brilliantly that the room had a sort of glow of warmth. If there were only warmth in color we should have been comfortable.

There were only three of us at *table d'hôte*, mere specks at the long table in that vast apartment; the two others were a handsome German and his handsomer bride, who were kept from shivering, I presume, by the internal warmth there is in a honeymoon. There were only three of us, but the ceremony of *table d'hôte* went on with all the solemn and slow majesty that characterizes that great European ritual. It needed all the bottled sunshine in the golden Orvieto wine to keep it from being funereal. At the end of the hall a wood fire glimmered in an open stove. It had about as much effect on the temperature of the apartment as a lantern would have on the air of Bushnell Park on a windy, wintry night.

My chamber was not as large as the dining hall, but it was no less brilliant. It never was warmed, and there is no method of heating it. It is an instructive room, to a vacant mind; the vaulted roof is a picture gallery, but it is severely instructive. No Cupids and Venuses and little lovers and graces floating about in this chill and virtuous sky. But in the corners of the ceiling there are portraits of Plato and Herodotus and Homer, and another sage whose name I cannot recall; and in the medallions overhead you see Poetry and History and Philosophy and Religion. There is nothing warming in painted philosophy and religion, and I would gladly have exchanged the colored consolation of both for a warming-pan. I jumped into bed without much ceremony — and let no Early Christian rebuke my haste — where my teeth played a tune like the castanets of a dancing-girl.

CHAPTER IX.

PALERMO.

PALERMO is the best dressed city in Southern Italy. It is also the cleanest; as clean as the best parts of Paris, and, for that matter, cleaner than any in the United States. It is a cheerful, spick-and-span city, and the gilded youth dress up to it. I have nowhere else seen more attention to style and clothes, and nowhere else a more bright aspect of modern life. Even the narrow and by-streets are neat, and I was told that the municipality pays something for every pan of refuse collected by scavengers. Whether this is so or not, the result is agreeable. But then the streets are superbly paved with stone and capable of being easily cleaned.

Palermo is also lively and patriotic and republican. Garibaldi is the idol of the populace, and cheap liberal newspapers abound. One of the principal boulevards is the Strada Lincoln, and there is a café Lincoln, with a portrait of "Honest Abe" over the door. Our martyred President is popular in Sicily, and there is another long and important street named for him in Catania. This is to say that in the public apprehension he represents "liberty" for the mercurial Sicilians.

PALERMO.

As we arrive here in March, the town is already in active preparation for the celebration of the sixth centenary of the "Sicilian Vespers," and peculiar significance is given to it this time by a revival of the ancient hostility to the French, caused by the grasping occupation of Tunis. It is supposed that it needs but a spark to produce an outburst against the French residents, and many of them are leaving the city to be out of the way of the celebration, which begins on Friday, the 31st. A medal has been struck in remembrance of the event, books and illustrated papers are published telling the story, and pictures are exhibited in the shop windows. One of them represents the scene in the old public promenade outside the Porta Nuova, which was the immediate cause of the outbreak. You remember that on the evening of March 31, 1282, — Easter Eve, — the inhabitants of Palermo were amusing themselves dancing and playing games in the gardens, and mingled with them were a number of the French officers and soldiers, who were already odious to the people, from their insolent and libertine manners. The public mind had been inflamed by the petty tyranny and hostility of the French conqueror, and especially by the murder of Conradin. Among the promenaders enjoying the refreshing air was a beautiful and noble lady leaning on the arm of her husband. Under pretense of searching for concealed weapons, a French officer approached her, and seizing her offered the grossest insult. The husband of course interfered, and a young Sicilian, the lover, or at least the admirer, of the lady, drew his sword and ran the officer through. A terrible tumult at once ensued, and it did not cease till every Frenchman on the ground, two hundred in all, was slain. The flame thus kindled spread throughout the city, and the massacre continued until two thousand French were slain,— every man, woman, and child whose speech betrayed French nationality. The whole island was involved until the French were all slain or hunted out of it. The lady who was first insulted was, with others, on her way to vespers, and the massacre took its name from this fact. But a single libertine incident would not have caused the fierce outbreak, if the people had not already been exasperated beyond endurance by the unbridled license of the French tyrants and by deeper political reasons. It is easy to see that such memories of French insolence and rapacity are heated anew by the present unprovoked raid upon Tunis, which the Sicilians have always regarded with friendly eyes.

Palermo is too modern and clean to be of absorbing interest to the searcher after the picturesque, but for all that it has some mediaeval and Saracenic remains, and enough to keep the sight-seers busy for three or four days. The harbor, which opens to the north and has an artificial breakwater, is very pretty. On one side rises the rocky height of Monte Pellegrino, and on the other a bold, rocky cape curves round with a sheltering arm. The town lies on the plain, which extends far back of it, and is exceedingly fertile. It is encircled by lofty bare limestone hills. The town, as I have intimated, is altogether modern, with the exception of a few buildings, and it has more bad statuary in it than Boston. I am not going to trouble the reader with details of the " sights," for it is quite impossible to bring them before the reader by any description, and he would probably skip any descriptions I wrote.

The most imposing building is the cathedral, a vast edifice of a mixed construction, parts of it dating from 1169. It has many charming details, especially what may be called Moorish or Sicilian Gothic, and in the interesting interior are four superb sarcophagi in porphyry, of Sicilian kings, Roger, his daughter Constance, Henry VI., and Frederick II., all before 1250. I have a great respect for an old king, buried.

But the treasure of the cathedral (called the church Ste. Rosalia) is the petrified body of Ste. Rosalia, the patron saint of Palermo. I did not see her, but from what I have heard she was a beautiful girl; and indeed if the marble effigy of her in the grotto on Monte Pellegrino is her image, she was a fascinating woman. But unlike most of the beauties of antiquity she was devout while she was young and beautiful. It is too often the case that devotion only sets in with the decay of personal beauty and charm. The story is that this lovely daughter of William II. (the Good, who died in 1189) retired in all the bloom of her maidenly charms to Monte Pellegrino, and immured herself in a cavern on those sterile and lonesome heights, from pure motives of piety. Sweet and lovely as she was, her charms seem to have been forgotten for nearly four centuries, when a hunter accidentally discovered her petrified body in a recess of the rocks. The plague was at that time (1664) prevailing in Palermo, as it was about the same date in London. But the body of the fair saint, brought to the city, stayed the pestilence by its gracious presence, and she became the patron saint of the town.

Needless to say that we made a pilgrimage to the grotto on the mountain where she lived and died. A magnificent road of solid masonry, broad and of easy grade, has been constructed to it, zigzagging up the mountain, and once a year all Palermo goes with banners and music and holy procession up this highway to the chapel over the grotto of the pretty and lamented virgin. It is a very damp and dripping grotto, but the shrine is enriched with precious marbles and pious gifts of value. In front of the decorated cavern, where the holy maiden prayed for the sinful world, is a recumbent statue of her, in gorgeous gilded robes. It is a gracious and lovely work, and so life-like and engaging is the face that it seems sleep rather than death that has been counterfeited by the Florentine artist. The chapel overlooks a bleak little hollow in the mountains, a basin of stones, and is the most desolate place that ever early piety throve in, or ever the seed of the church ripened in.

From the rocks above it you have a magnificent view of the bay and the city, and you look down upon the flat plain which cuts off Monte Pellegrino from the range of mountains, upon the Conca d'Oro, a golden valley strewn with handsome villas and gardens. On this ever desolate mountain of rock, where it must be a persevering goat who can live, forests once grew, and here Hamilcar settled with his family and troops, and raised grain, in his war with the Romans, a couple of centuries before our era. But the Carthaginian has vanished and left no mark, while a weak Christian maiden, by the simple act of dying in discomfort and devotion, has consecrated the whole mountain to her memory.

The gem of the city of Palermo, however, and a gem worth a long journey to see, is the Cappella Palatina, in the old royal palace, a building of Saracen origin. This rich chapel, which is, I suppose, of Norman-Saracenic style, is full of Oriental and Moorish feeling. This appears not only in the Saracenic ceilings and capitals, but in the mosaics which ornament pillars and panels. Nothing richer or more exquisite can the traveler see. The whole interior is a mass of subdued but rich color, and excites a feeling of most tranquil pleasure. Its harmony is that of a perfect sonata. The details are no less satisfactory than the general effect. The entire walls and space between the Arabian pointed arches are covered with gorgeous mosaics on a gold ground, quaint scenes from the Old and the New Testaments, many of them ludicrous, but all pervaded with sincere feeling, and positively dazzling in Oriental splendor. I spent nearly half a day in the little chapel, and the magic of its beauty and harmony so won upon me that I thought that it was the most beautiful chapel in the world. Except at Ravenna I know no Byzantine mosaics, or mosaics of any sort, comparable in interest with these and their companion works and perhaps originals at Monreale.

The cathedral of Monreale, in the village of that name on the mountain side, is less than five miles from the city of Palermo. It and the road up to it are in plain view from the city gate, and yet until recently it was the most dangerous road on account of brigands. Troops are now stationed along the road all the way up. A couple of weeks ago, the stage going above Monreale to S. Martino was stopped and robbed by so-called brigands, and the driver was killed. The "brigands" were inhabitants of clean Palermo. A few days ago, also, a gentleman and lady going up Monte Pellegrino, in sight of the city, were stripped of all their valuables by a couple of foot-pads. The robbers were, however, arrested, and the jewelry and money were recovered. These are exceptional cases. Brigandage is really about at an end in Sicily. The organization of the brigands is broken up, and they are discouraged. My own explanation of the change, however, is that the brigands have gone to keeping the hotels in Sicily, and take it out of the travelers in a legal but more thorough manner. I might as well say here, from considerable experience in Sicilian hotels, that they are on their way to be first-class. Their prices are already first-rate. They have only to raise the accommodation, the food, and attendance up to the prices, and they will be all right. The landlords have simply begun at the wrong end. The four robbers of the stage coach I saw afterwards at Girgenti. They had been arrested by the *gendarmes*, and were led along handcuffed; and four meeker, more stupid-looking highwaymen I never saw — off the stage.

The cathedral of Monreale, which originated in the twelfth century, is a Latin cross, three hundred and thirty-three feet long, a hundred and thirty-one feet wide, has three apses, and is flanked by two imposing square towers. The whole interior walls of this vast building are covered with magnificent mosaics — the guide-book says there are 70,400 square feet of them. The mosaics run round the walls in three classes: the stories of the Old Testament, beginning with the creation; the life of Christ; and scenes in the lives of saints. The splendor of this interior is unrivaled, and the details of the mosaics, in quaint simplicity, surpass all flights of the modern imagination. Adjoining the church are cloisters, which are very large and also of remarkable beauty. There are two hundred and sixteen columns in pairs, slender columns, in varied graceful Saracenic designs; all the capitals are different, and the mosaics remaining in the arches are exquisite. Wherever the Saracens have made an impress in Europe, it has been one of beauty, a charm that lingers to fill us with regret. The bewitching grace of Moorish architecture — for to the Saracenic teaching I think the Norman remains in Sicily owe their fascination — is one of the chief delights of this battleground of the classic and the mediæval world.

There is one curiosity of Palermo about which I hesitate to disturb the reader. If he were to see it, and let his mind dwell on it, he probably would not sleep for a week afterward. Of all the fantastic, ghastly, and sportive dealings with poor mortality that I have seen in my short pilgrimage, the convent of the Cappuccini furnishes the most astonishing. In seeing it I had a new revelation of the capacities of human nature for indulgence in the horrible and the grotesque. From the convent we descended into the subterranean corridors, where are exposed, not buried, the dried remains of wealthy inhabitants of Palermo. These corridors, of which there are several, are arched, broad, well lighted, and I should think each a couple of hundred feet long. The air in them is dry and apparently salubrious, and one might walk through these wide aisles of death in comfort if he were blind. On each side of these passages are long boxes, piled one upon the other; not coffins, but boxes, sometimes with brass nails, and looking not unlike old-fashioned hair trunks. You might imagine yourself in an emigrant's baggage-room on a steamer, but for some other things in the corridors. Each of these boxes contains a dead person. The occupants of part of them, which have glass fronts, are visible. There they lie grinning in arrested decay, with just enough dried skin and flesh on the bones to preserve the semblance of humanity.

The poor desiccated bodies have been forced into clothes, sometimes into finery, and many in this awful dress parade of death wear white kid gloves and fine shoes. But this is not the worst. Above these rows of boxes hang, in all the limpness of irresponsibility for appearance which characterizes the dead, ranks of mummies, hung by the neck, or attached in some way to the walls of the vault. They are pretty uniformly clad in sombre monkish robes of cotton, and but for the horrible faces staring at you might pass for scarecrows. The drying process has drawn the faces into all ghastly contortions, in which one might fancy that the real character of the departed is revealed. Some scowl, some grin with malevolence, some smile (that is worst of all), and some actually assume a comical look that forces your unwilling laughter. Sometimes groups of three or four incline their dreadful heads to ·each other, as if enjoying some post-mortem humorous story. His conceit must be infinite who can walk through these ranks of the dried and distorted dead, and not feel humiliated by such an exhibition of his kind. Is it possible that we shall all look like that? Must all beauty and manliness and bravery come to that?

There are many little children, some not a span long, lying in their little boxes, decked in all the finery of fond affection, the lace and ribbons adding I know not what of mockery to the weazened baby faces. One entire corridor is reserved for the women, and this is more pathetic and profoundly disgusting than the others. Those who died virgin have crowns on their heads, and palms or lilies in their hands. They were great beauties, I doubt not, before they came here, for the dark-eyed women of Palermo are comely; but maid, or bride, or wife, they are not beautiful now, although they repose in silk dresses, kid gloves, and satin slippers. These be dresses for a ball, and what a ball and dance of death is this! Is it any pleasure for my lady to have her partner or her lover come and see her in this guise?

I learned that at death the bodies are interred in a sealed pit in this cemetery for a year. There is supposed to be something peculiar in the soil which dries the body without destroying it. At the end of a year it is taken out, dressed, and either put into its box, or hung up in the corridor. Every year, at least on All Souls' Day, the friends of the departed come to look upon the frightful remains. What satisfaction they can have in the spectacle I do not know, nor do I understand how any man or woman of presentable appearance who has visited these corridors in life can consent to occupy them after death. Interment here was prohibited about a year ago. I do not know how long the wealthy people of Palermo have been exposed here, but we were told, as we walked along, that 8,000 bodies were in sight. Does such a mode of sepulchre, adopted by a gay and intelligent people, argue a want of sensibility, — sensibility to the ridiculous and to the horrible, — or is it an evidence of Christian willingness to mortify the flesh?

The museum of Palermo is extensive, and has many remains of classic times, of the Saracenic occupation, and of the Norman period. I shall only mention two things: a magnificent bronze ram, which was found at ancient Syracuse, and ancient Greek sculptures found at Selinunto (Selinus) and Segesta. The most remarkable of these are the Metopes of Selinus, from the temples of that city. They are archaic, the oldest made in the second half of the seventh century B. C., and they are the most ancient specimens of Greek sculpture known with the exception of the lions of Mycenæ. Some of the later Metopes are coeval with those from Ægina, now at Munich. The material is coarse sandstone; the subjects are mythological (Perseus slaying the Medusa, a combat in a quadriga between Peleus and another hero, Heracles and Hippolita, etc.). The work is vigorous and rude, and the ablest betrays the Oriental, let us say Egyptian, influence. A curious piece of refinement is that the nude portions of the female figures, like the hands and feet, are inlaid in white marble. Sicily is very rich in Phœnician and Greek remains, and the fragments in the museum are a good preparation for those who intend to pay any attention to the study of ancient art.

I have not yet spoken of what will be the first to arrest the new-comer's attention when he lands at Palermo — the two-wheeled, painted carts, common all over the island, but most highly decorated here. The accompanying harness for donkeys and horses is as gay as embroidery and colored worsted can make it; but the carts are almost a contribution to the fine arts. Every part and piece of wood in the cart is decorated with ornamental painting, either figures or agreeable designs; but each of the two panels at the sides, and the two end boards, have elaborate pictures. These are invariably in the Byzantine school of art, drawn with great *naïveté*, but pleasing for all that, and brilliant in color. The subjects are always poetic and romantic. The classic writers are drawn on for themes as well as the favorite romancers, like Ariosto. I saw on one cart depicted the story of Helen of Troy and the wrath of Achilles, and on many combats between knights and Saracens, in which the rescue of a lovely maiden was usually the point of interest. My patriotism was stirred by seeing on one cart the picture of Columbus in his famous act of discovering our native land. These are the ordinary carts of dirty traffic, for the carriage of lime, soil, and stones, as well as goods, and are owned and driven by men who do not appear to be poets. What then shall we say of a common people who have so much romance or poetry in them that it is lavished on objects of such meanness as the cart? My own opinion is that the present cartmen inherited the habit of decorating the carts, without inheriting the taste of their ancestors.

CHAPTER X.

GIRGENTI AND CATANIA.

WE left the city of Saint Rosalia at six o'clock in the morning. I was sorry not to see the patroness of the town. This lovely woman dates, as I have said, from the twelfth century, but was wholly restored in 1664; and now reposes in the cathedral, having gained rather than lost in interest, as the church has done, by restoration. Her sweet spirit seems to preside over this region, and I naturally had her much on my mind as we steamed away in the fresh morning through the endless lemon plantations which occupy the plain and skirt the beautiful bay.

It is a peculiarity of the railway trains of Sicily not to be in a hurry, and we had leisure to enjoy the perfume of the air and the hedges of geranium and roses along the way. All the stations have a pretty taste in flowers. I know nothing much lovelier than the sweep around the bay of Palermo in the morning, the curve of the shore, as we draw away from the city and Monte Pellegrino and pass among the picturesque rocks and lofty headlands that line all this coast.

For a long distance we had the sea in sight, with lofty hills inland, and now and then villages, and even cities of several thousand inhabitants, perched upon rocky eminences, cities with steep streets, flat-roofed, oriental houses, church towers, and flanking ruins of mediæval castles. It is rather humiliating to one's geographical pride to come across cities of 20,000 to 30,000 inhabitants of which he never heard before.

As soon as we turned southward we began to ascend among the hills. I do not know what altitude we attained crossing the water-shed between the Tyrrhenian and African seas, but it must have been as much as 1,500 feet, and we had peaks in view over 5,000 feet in height. The road frequently pierces the hills, and we spent a good deal of our time in tunnels. Sometimes we appeared to attain a speed of nearly five miles an hour, but later in the day we went at a breakneck rate of over fifteen miles, for the distance of eighty-four miles to Girgenti had to be got over somehow in seven hours. Sicily is a treeless island, but fertile in the valleys and on the uplands, and we passed some fine grazing land; but the main yield of these hills is sulphur and yellow marble. The scenery kept us on the *qui vive* all day, and was very pretty when we went down the valley of the Platani and came into the rich basin of Castronuovo. We ran out of the Platani into a side valley, and passed close by Comitini, and among the most valuable sulphur mines of the island. The owner is called the sulphur-king — Pluto would be a better name — of Sicily, a rank and dignity only attained in our country by the princes of petroleum and the kings of silver. Heaps of the yellow mineral lay at the mouths of the pits and at all the stations platform cars were filled with the yellow blocks of it. I never expected to see so much sulphur, for I did not know there was so much of it in *this* world. After passing Caldare, where the line branches off for Catania, we had a view over the hills of the blue sea. A magnificent sweep of mountain country was in sight, and three or four cities perched upon commanding heights.

One of these is Girgenti, the object of our pilgrimage. This you know was the ancient Agrigentum, or Acragas, " the most beautiful city of mortals," in the opinion of Pindar. It is as much as 600 feet above the sea, and we were nearly an hour in dragging up to its walls, and entering one of its gates. The modern city was probably the acropolis of the classic city, which lay on a sort of irregular table-land below it, but was itself some 300 feet above the seashore. This acropolis had a temple to Zeus — some embedded pillars of which you can see now under an old church, by the aid of a small boy and a candle. To the east of the city rises the rock of Athene, over a thousand feet above the sea, and the Doric founders of the town, who came here almost 600 years before our era, may have worshiped Athene there. The depression in the ridge between the town and the rock is said to have been scooped out by Empedocles to let in the north wind and dispel the malaria, which, in his day as now, scourged the plateau of the city and the low ground through which a slow winding stream finds its way down to the ancient port.

The view from the city, which has about 20,000 people more or less in rags and idleness, and stretches along the ridge, over the edge of which it hangs, is extensive and magnificent, and almost unsurpassed in classic interest. Immediately beneath is the great plateau where the old city stood; the walls of it ran along the edge of a cliff, and protected the town, and the splendid temples, whose ruins are now the most striking objects in the green and smiling scene. Beyond is the sea-plain and the old port, and to the right the new Porto Empedocle to which the railway descends. And along the curving coast sparkles the blue African sea.

Many travelers go to Girgenti, but the advent of our carriage in the long main street seemed to be an event to the inhabitants. The ordinary business of loafing was suspended to watch us, and our progress was attended by a running, shouting rabble of men and boys, who gave us the benefit of their company to the door of the Hôtel Belvedere. With inconceivable noise and clamor, and good-nature, a dozen of these seized upon the various pieces of our luggage, and ran in with them, using the most commendable agility in distributing them in various parts of the rambling hotel. The excitement of the landlord and his minions, male and female, equaled that of the townspeople. It was impossible to get intelligent speech of any persons in the house. They all rushed about, up and down stairs, banging doors, and yelling to each other. We could not have been received in a more promiscuous manner if we had come into a lunatic asylum kept by lunatics. At last wearied out with chasing about waiters, landlord, and chambermaids, and attempting to follow our baggage distributed all over the house, I fixed upon a room to suit myself, and collected my personal property, after a struggle, from various people who had a two-soldi lien on every piece — the most helpful folk in the world, but alas, not unselfish. The room, with a stone floor, was not much to look at nor did it offer a great deal in the way of comfort, but what a view it commanded! It had a balcony on the very edge of the cliff, and below was all the glory of land and sea, and the poetry left over from the old Greek world. I can scarcely imagine what it was when a great city spread out there, but nothing could well be lovelier then this array of Doric temples and ruins of temples, clusters of columns, and single columns, on a plateau rich with spring verdure, full of color from blossoming plants, olive-trees, and round-domed pines, sprawling cactus, and vines trailing over the gray stones. The cactus is here very abundant and rampant. This huge misshapen vegetable always seems to me out of place in this age; it is a survival of the old geologic eras, when all the animals were gigantic and badly put together. It is neither tree nor shrub, but a succession of fat leaves, the one growing out of the other in the most fantastic manner. The only modern thing it reminds me of is the German language. That grows, one word springing out of another in endless uncouth progression, in much the same manner. And the parallel holds good farther. For on the edge of these fat leaves in time appear scarlet blossoms, and the fruit which merits its name of prickly pear, just as the barbarous German flowers now and then into the sweetest poetic bloom.

But I am wandering from this hotel, which I wish to commend. It hasn't its like in the world, I think, out of Sicily, and here is only matched by those in Syracuse. How it is kept running I cannot imagine, since the keepers of it feel no interest in their guests until the time comes for making out the bill. They give all their energies to that. It is a hotel where you can call for anything you want. You have this privilege; but of course you do not get anything. It is not true to say that it contains nothing that you can eat, and nobody to serve it, for we did live after a fashion. But it is an exciting place, a place where you struggle for existence, and the landlord looks on in an amused manner.

When we went into the dining room a surprise awaited us. We found something that I had never seen before, and did not expect so far from the centres of civilization. This was an electric bell on the table, a cord, passing over the chandelier, terminated in a knob which rested on a glass dish convenient to the hand. We at first supposed that this was intended to administer an electric shock to the boarders exhausted with waiting. But we ascertained that by pressing a button in the knob, we could ring with great violence a distant bell. I never saw anything so convenient.

Without rising from the table, we could ring this as much as we liked. It is a great improvement, and I wonder the invention is not introduced elsewhere. There is no harm in it, for no one in the house paid the least attention to it. The people were superior to their own invention. Occasionally the waiter made his appearance, but never in response to this bell. The landlord is on the eve of a great discovery. When he discovers that the object of ringing an electric bell is to have it answered, that it should summon a waiter, and that the waiter in request ought to bring something to eat, he will have taken a great step in the art of keeping a hotel. As it is, I can think of only one thing that is needed to complete his dining room, and that is a placard with the legend, "*The Lord will provide.*"

Whenever we walked in the street of Girgenti, (there is one street where you can walk, in the others you must climb), we were attended and followed and beset by crowds of most importunate young beggars, impudent and imperturbably good-natured wearers of rags, of both sexes, that could not be shaken off, nor driven away, nor out-walked, nor escaped. They offered us counterfeit coins, they insisted on showing us the way to places we were familiar with, they begged incessantly. They persistently got between us and the views, and all sentimental reflections on the noble part of their city. For myself, I believe that their ancestors, the classic Greeks, were no better than they in manners and apparel, but they might have been more picturesque.

One might spend many charmed days among the noble ruins of old Agrigentum. There is one of the most nearly perfect Greek temples in existence, the so-called temple of Concord, the interior, or *cella*, of which was once used for a Christian church. There is not another so well preserved except the temple of Theseus at Athens. Its thirty-six columns are all standing. It is pure Doric, but wants the grace and charm of the Doric temple of Neptune at Pæstum. More picturesque and poetic is the temple of Juno Lacinia, on more elevated ground, with only half of its great columns standing, but very impressive, whether we see the blue sky through it at a distance, or stand within it and look out upon the smiling sea, and the wonderful landscape. These are only two of many grand edifices which were built along the cliff and overlooked the high city wall, and must have presented from the sea a magnificent spectacle. The most gigantic of their buildings, which is now a vast field of impressive ruins, was the temple of Zeus, begun in the fifth century B. C., and never finished. It had thirty-eight huge half-columns, each twenty feet in circumference. The drums of some of these half columns lie here, and the flutings are large enough to admit a man standing in each. Prone on the ground lies one of the colossal Atlantes, which stood within the temple, a figure twenty-five feet high built up of blocks cut with considerable skill. It has been reconstructed from the collected fragments. A great portion of the stones of the temple have been carted off to construct the Mole, but there is still a large area covered with huge fragments. The temple was one of the largest of antiquity, three hundred and sixty-three feet long, and a hundred and eighty-two feet broad. On this plateau, as I have said, are other standing columns, and remains of other temples, the gray rocks are cut into tombs, which attest the successive presence, triumph, and mortality of Greeks, Romans, Christians, Saracens, the whole presenting a most impressive lesson of the passing show of this world. We, the heirs of all the virtues and of some of the arts, sit amid these gray ruins, under a sky as blue as ever it was, in sight of a sea tossing and flashing as when it bore the little barks of the Greek adventurers, or the triremes of the Roman masters, watch the green lizards gliding over the stones, and hear the whistles of a locomotive which dares to disturb this desert silence. Girgenti is, I suppose, for the sixth or eighth time in its history, entering upon a new career of life and prosperity.

In passing by rail to the east coast of the island, from Girgenti to Catania, or around the highest passable portions of the island, we were almost elevated enough to overlook the whole of Sicily. We were much of the way amid sulphur mines, and above the region of the olive, the orange, the fig and the grape. I can believe that the apple grows on these uplands, but I saw no trees. Indeed the aspect of the country was generally wild and inhospitable, but for wide and noble mountain views the ride was memorable.

It was near the mountain crag on which stands the lofty city of Castelgiovanni that we had our first sight of Ætna, and thenceforward nearly all the way to Catania we kept its noble bulk in view, a vast long sloping peak of snow, lifted over 10,000 feet in the air, and glowing rosy red in the light of the setting sun, as we swept down to the coast. We begin to understand now that Sicily is built merely to show off Ætna; it is the great fact of the island, the *raison d'être* of the rest.

All this region, and all Sicily for that matter, is classic ground, the legendary playground of all the poets, long before the historians appeared, the scene of very many of the most beautiful myths. Beyond us, over the mountain, is the Lake Pergusa, a mere miasmatic pond, which was in Ovid's day set about with lofty trees, having flowery banks and clear blue water, the charming place whence Pluto carried off Proserpine.

Catania is a very satisfactory city to the Sicilians, because it is busy and big (nearly 90,000 people) and thriving, but the romantic traveler does not care much for its long and regular common-place streets, although one of the longest is named Strada Lincoln. It is built on an old lava stream, which here descended to the sea, and is in summer so hot that an English inhabitant — the most truthful man in the place — told me that the lava rocks down by the shore are so heated that eggs laid on them (not by the hen) become perfectly cooked. The houses are mostly built of lava, and these with the lava beds about the city so absorb the heat of a long summer day that the radiation at night is almost intolerable.

Catania detained us only long enough to make a day's excursion up the side of Ætna, and to visit the old convent of Saint Benedetto, the largest religious house I have ever seen. We went there to see the arrested stream of lava behind the noble gardens, a stately terrace of a garden, sweet with fruits and flowers, where the old monks used to walk about and think of the sins of other people, in sight of great Ætna. The stream of lava, from the disastrous eruption of 1669 was, as is well known, arrested at this spot and turned aside, so that it spared the convent, and most of the town, by a display of the veil of Santa Agatha at the critical moment at this spot. The hot current went away to the southwest, descending into the sea and partially filling up the harbor. I saw the chapel of Santa Agatha in the cathedral, but not her veil, which is rarely shown. In the chapel is the silver sarcophagus with her remains. This is carried in procession through the town once a year, in February. The Santa Agatha suffered martyrdom in the year 262, rather than yield to the dishonorable proposals of the Roman Decius.

The other object of interest in the cathedral is a monument to the composer Bellini, who was a native of this place. The monument has for inscription the musical notes of the beginnings of favorite airs from his operas. In the museum in one of the apartments of the suppressed convent — and a very interesting museum it is for antique fragments — you may see carefully preserved the coffin in which the remains of Bellini were brought from Paris. On the square in front of the cathedral is an antique elephant in lava, bearing on his back an obelisk of Egyptian granite. Whether this is the elephant that the Catanians captured from the people of Syracuse when the latter made war on them by aid of an elephant, long ago, I do not know. But these people of Catania did capture an elephant from the soldiers of Syracuse, and have had the beast as their coat of arms ever since.

In the great eruption of 1669, which spread ruin all over this part of the island, Monti Rossi were upheaved on the side of Ætna, two round peaks 3,110 feet above the sea. We drove up the slope twelve miles to Nicolosi, in order to ascend Monti Rossi, and have a near view of the giant volcano, of which I shall have more to say, personally, when I come to speak of Taormina. The whole country is lava, the houses, villages, walls, fields. Vast fields are merely wastes of contorted lava, which, cooled in all sorts of grotesque shapes, might have suggested Doré's drawings of the "Inferno." Amid it the uncouth cactus flourishes. But on vast areas, also, the lava has crumbled into the richest soil, which supports plantations of oranges and lemons, and fields of grain. This soil is now black, and only beginning to show the green of the spring.

By and by it will all bloom. I suppose there is not a more fertile slope in the world than this of Ætna to the sea, and it is literally true that the snow-fields of the volcano rise out of vineyards, and groves of orange and lemon.

No region, I should say, is more interesting to the geologist than this. We had a driver with the distinguished name of Pasquale Syracuse, who had probably been with scientific people. He pointed out the effects of the lava eruptions as we passed along. In reply to a question if a certain conformation of rocks was due to the eruption of 1669, he said, "Oh, no, that is from the *diluvio universale*." We felt on firm ground again with vestiges of the Deluge.

Monti Rossi are twin peaks, heaps of soft ashes and scoria, very difficult to climb, scoria and crumbling rock, blotched with brick-red color, and full of shining black crystals. From the summit we had a view of hundreds of like mounds of extinct craters on the side of the mountain, scars of old eruptions. The volcano always has a little torch of smoke above its crown of snow, but it has a habit of breaking out not on the top but anywhere along its blistered sides. The scene was grand; great fields of snow above us; around, the black desolation of lava fields, the cultivated soil not yet started into life, farther down the slope the fruit-bearing trees, and the far-curving shore with its villages and the deep blue sea.

CHAPTER XI.

TAORMINA.

WHEN you are on the east coast of Sicily you are in the most poetic locality of the classic world. Not in Attica itself are there clustered more Hellenic myths. It is the land where one understands Theocritus, and finds the sources of the inspiration of Ovid. Here, as scarcely anywhere else, unite the loveliness and the terror of nature's idyllic shores and flowery slopes, dominated by the mysterious majesty of Ætna, the giant volcano with its eternal snow-crown and pennant of smoke, vast Ætna, so full of beauty and of destruction, warming into life on its fertile sides the golden orchards, and the purple vineyards, which ever and anon it overwhelmed and laid waste with its subterranean fires. It was this eternal possibility of sudden wrath and ruin out of such passionate beauty — as calamity so often follows in the train of a lovely woman — that made, that makes, this land so fascinating to every poet. Beauty, I suppose, must always be a dear purchase in this world.

I do not know that Proserpine was carried off from a flowery margin of a lake in these hills, for I did not see the lake, but there is good evidence of the troubled loves of Acis and Galatea, and the interference of Polyphemus. The story of how the lovers were united, and flowed down to the sea, escaping in happy immortal death — the common escape for all of us, if we do escape into happiness — the persecution of the Giant, does not depend altogether upon the testimony of Ovid or Theocritus. For does not one see still the river Acis, and the fountain of the charming nymph — too tender a morsel for the Cyclops, who had his lair in the caves of Ætna?

The rail from Catania to Taormina runs along the curved shore of the sea through a succession of lemon groves — in blossom at this time of the year, and in yellow fruit also — and a way bordered with wild flowers, cactus, and geraniums. We skirted the bay which Virgil describes, the Portus Ulysses, and looked down on a ruined castle of the thirteenth century, perched on a low rock headland, a castle that Normans and Aragonese and Saracens fought over year after year. We passed along the high cliffs under which the Carthaginians under Himilco defeated the Syracusans in the fourth century, and suddenly came in sight of one of the most interesting places in the world to the boy who loves his Virgil. Off that point of land rise out of the sea the seven basaltic rocks — one of them two hundred feet high — the Faraglioni or *Scogli dé Ciclopi*. The blue sea dashes and foams about them as in the days when the Greek adventurer first saw them. They are the very rocks which Polyphemus hurled after Ulysses and his little ships, when that crafty sailor escaped from the hospitable giant whose eye he had put out. I looked up the long slope hoping to see the cave where Polyphemus lived, and entertained the guests whose usual fate it was never to issue from their night-quarters. I did not discover the cave, but I saw the steep slope down which the enraged Cyclops, roaring with the pain of his extinguished eye, and guiding his steps by an uprooted pine tree grasped in his hand, pursued his insidious and lost guests.

Only a little beyond this, rising still more from the sea, we come upon the sloping plateau where Acireale stands, crossing the Acis, and the flowery mead haunted aforetime by Galatea. Acireale is a very lovely town built upon a lava stream, overlooking the sea and commanding a superb view of snowy Ætna. All this region has been repeatedly overflowed by lava and shaken by earthquakes, and it is difficult to tell exactly how it looked in the days of Polyphemus and Galatea. It is now a garden of bloom and color and beauty.

Travelers visit on this road, several miles up the slope of Ætna, above Giarre, but we did not, the remains of a monstrous chestnut tree, called *di Cento Cavalli*, because a hundred horses of a troop were once sheltered under it. It is, however, not one tree but a group (said to have common roots); but there is a tree near it said by the guide books to measure seventy-six feet in circumference. These trees are no doubt one thousand years old.

The road continues through a country of great fertility and of great beauty, the mountain on one side and the sea-plain on the other. The plains are very malarious, and probably have been so from old times. We crossed the stony bed of the ancient river Acesines, called the Alcántara, and had below us the remains of the oldest Greek settlement in Sicily, made by Theocles and a colony from Sybaris in B. C. 735. Here on this long, curving promontory, now a lemon plantation, and the site of a poverty-stricken fishing village, was old Naxos. The peasants, digging in the fields, still turn up coins and remains of this primeval city. It was a convenient landing place for colonists and adventurers, but always open to attack, and very early in their history its citizens climbed up the heights of Taormina, above it, for security. They called it Tauromenium — the old coins have a bull on one side — and there was their acropolis.

Taormina, above the cape of that name, lies on the edge of a rocky cliff, nearly four hundred feet above the sea, and we consumed nearly an hour in reaching it up the ziz-zag carriage road, which offers a succession of charming prospects. In this lofty and most picturesque of towns I lingered two weeks, finding it more difficult as the perfect days went by to tear myself away; but if I were to write of it for two weeks I should fail to possess you of its many charms. I have come to no other place where one a little tired and willing to rest in the winter season could be so perfectly at peace and so fed with varied beauty. The climate is all that one could wish, mild and free of snow, and the situation is so elevated that the air is inspiring. One can do, what he can in so few southern winter resorts, climb about the hills and walk with no feeling of languor. Of course there are now and then days of sirocco, or enervating south wind, but not many. It is as yet, also, a somewhat primitive place, and not melancholy with invalids or insufferable with unintelligent tourists. The natural beauty of the place is supplemented by classical and historical associations, and one lives here two lives, without any wearying effort of the imagination or bodily fatigue.

I stayed first at a hotel on the main street of the town, the windows and balconies of which overlook the precipitous slopes of the hill, the curving coast, and the great expanse of blue water, but I liked better the quarters I had afterwards at the Timeo, a little inn on the hill under the Greek theatre. It takes its name from one of the most distinguished of the Greek historians before our era, Timæus, who was born at Taormina. The accommodations were simple but very good, and the people who kept it were kindness itself. Nothing adds more to the pleasure of a traveler's stay in any place than courtesy and civility and good temper on the part of the hosts. Everybody gets fond of the obliging keepers of the Timeo.

To sit on the terrace in front of the inn is one of the supreme satisfactions in life. It is one of the places from which you would never care to stir. Absorbed in the restful beauty of the scene, I imagine one might in time lose the power to stir, give up ambition and the desire to get other people's property and the offices already held by the "honest and capable," and let the world pass without a sigh.

This view is similar to that from the Greek theatre above it. But from the hill of the theatre above we also have a view northward up the strait toward Messina, with its many lofty headlands, covered with towns and towers, and off upon the high, purple-colored mountains of Calabria, and over a vaster expanse of the Mediterranean. But the prospect from the inn would suffice any glutton of scenery.

On the left and below is the indented, curving coast as the sea follows and flows along it, giving its sands a dozen shades of green, blue and purple, a coast of fruit plantations, towers and graceful points, stretching southward to the long, dim promontory that hides Syracuse from us. We look immediately underneath upon old Naxos, and upon the precipitous side of the cliff upon the edge of which the town of Taormina lies along, a town of mediæval aspect, with old decorated palaces, and towers of the Norman time, and Saracenic features. To the right and hanging over the town is a high peak, the Castello, a half-ruined stronghold. In classic times this was the acropolis of the city. When Dionysius besieged the town, B. C. 394, he made a bold attempt on this fortress at night, at the head of his soldiers, but it is said that, incumbered by his armor, he was hurled down the rocks, and nearly killed. The night was stormy, and I believe there was sleet and ice on the steep. Two years afterwards he made another attempt and captured the place. Still higher and behind it on a peak two thousand feet high, is Mola — for the possession of which Greeks, Romans, and Saracens have contended by force and strategy — a picturesque succession of shabby houses, glued together like the cells of a wasp nest. The inhabitants are poor as poverty, and sturdy beggars. It was our lot when we were there, seated on the ruins of its fortress and drinking a bottle of Monte Venere wine which the keeper of the osteria brought out, and of which he drank half to the health of Garibaldi and ourselves, but for which we paid, it was our lot, I say, to be approached by a bevy of girls in holiday attire, to beg a contribution to the festa of some saint, or virgin, soon to come off. We had a levee of all the town as we sat there enjoying the magnificent prospect, every person anxious to do enough for us to entitle him or her to a copper coin. We were asked repeatedly by boys, men, and women if we did not wish to see the "Universale," which seemed to be the one object of interest and treasure of the town. We consented at last to view the wonder, and were taken down to the little plaza by the church, where the curé and the tavern keeper together produced a folio volume and opened it with a flourish of pride. It was one volume of a Universal Atlas, published in Holland in the last century. A dense crowd gathered about it to help us examine it, and seemed perfectly familiar with its contents, explaining as the leaves were turned, "Asia," "Napoli," "Sicilia," etc., as the different lands and cities hove in view. When the exhibition was over the landlord demanded a fee, and followed us with disparaging remarks because we refused. We thought we were quits in paying him for the wine he had so hospitably drunk.

Still farther to the right is Monte Venere, nearly 3,000 feet above the sea. There the town is shut in on the west by this shapely peak, a contrast to the limitless prospect seaward. But the chief and distinguished feature in the landscape is Ætna, which rises up into the blue sky, beyond the towers and mountains, beyond the slopes verdant with olives, oranges, and vines, beyond the fields of lava and the reddish crumbling rocks, Ætna with its great fields of snow, hard and shining, the dome-like volcano, remote, in an accessible majesty, over 10,000 feet above the classic and smiling shore.

I do not know any other place in Europe where so much is combined in one prospect, the sea, the shore, the towns, the fertile fields, the peaks crowned with ruins, the slopes of verdure, fields and hills of classic and historic charm, all dominated by the king of volcanoes, shining and terrible. Where else shall we find in one sweep of the eye so much of beauty and of grandeur?

And this prospect the ancient Greeks had as they sat in the circular seats hewn out of the hill, and looked over the low stage of their theatre. This was the background of their tragedy and comedy. The spectators in the higher range of seats commanded a wide extent of sea, and the slopes and snow of Ætna.

This theatre is called a Greek theatre, and the stage is said to be in the most perfect condition of any extant. It has been, however, so wholly remodeled by the Romans as to have very little of the Greek left about it, except the ranks of amphitheatre seats. The stage is wholly Roman, built over and raised upon the Greek construction. And the whole (always excepting the seats) has been so torn away for other buildings, and built over, that it is unsatisfactory as a classic study. Yet nothing can be finer than the view through its broken arches and columnar spaces. And there is no place where one may more satisfactorily dream away his days than in this theatre. Its beauties are very well known. One day I counted twenty amateur artists, of both sexes, sketching in the ruins. The town itself has great charm for the artist. Indeed I do not know any place of its size that has more architectural surprises, fascinating street glimpses, lovely old windows and doorways, bits of towers and decayed palaces, fountains and old gateways. An artist, in any time of day and light, need never want subjects for his pencil. In the centre of the town is an old square with a bell tower that was very pretty before the people modernized one side of it with paint and a clock face. On one side is a rubbishy church that has on the balustrade of the steps four plaster figures cut off at the waist and planted on posts, surrounded by substantial red flames in plaster, like some species of human aloes. These, male and female, are martyrs or people in purgatory, I cannot tell which. But by the placid expression of their faces they appear to enjoy the purifying flames.

In the old tower are a couple of bells which strike every quarter of an hour day and night, loud harsh strokes. Each time they strike the quarter they strike the hour also — for instance, for 10.45 they make three strokes for the quarters and ten for the hour. There is another tower close by that has also spasms of bell ringing. At twelve o'clock at night I counted it striking 100 times, at four in the morning 50 times, and so on. A person who seemed to me a fiend used to climb up that tower and violently ring the bells at all hours, ringing for several moments at a time. There were also three or four other bells in convents and churches that also struck all the hours and were always on the swing for some religious or chronological purpose, so that the town was always in a clamor enough to distract a stranger. I lodged at first in the Hôtel Bella Veduta, close under the big tower. You enter this hotel through an archway into a lovely court and terrace, the walls set about with antique marble heads, inscriptions, and fragments of sculpture, and the whole beautiful with vines, and roses, and semi-tropical plants. From its terrace is a wonderful view. From the terrace of my room, also, I enjoyed a wonderful view over the sea, and of the Greek theatre and its height. This was all very well in the daytime, but at night when we had nothing to do but to lie awake and count the heavy strokes of the bells every quarter of an hour, it was otherwise. Nobody, when his attention is called to it, can go to sleep in fifteen minutes. He simply lies in dreadful expectation of the next strokes of the hammer.

The people of Taormina are as picturesque as their town. I suppose the old Greeks wore these sheep-skins and these rags, and no doubt the Greek maidens walked thus erectly with jars, the pattern of the amphora, on their heads. No doubt they also had brown skins and large soft brown eyes, and looked half shyly at the passer-by, and held out their hands for coin. How straight they are, and how firmly and freely they step out. When I see a group of them emerging from an archway or coming down the street, balancing the water-jar, or the load of stone, or other heavy burden, on the head, chatting and laughing gayly with apparent thought of nothing but the sunshine and the free air, I wonder how much fashion and an emancipating education would do for them.

My companions insist that the scene must have been very different when the real old Greeks thronged the streets on holidays and in gay flowing robes climbed the hill to the theatre to hear one of the tragedies of Sophocles. It may be. But I find the pictures of Theocritus still true. I doubt, indeed, if the shepherds and shepherdesses of his day were any comelier and any cleaner than these their descendants. Indeed, Ovid and Theocritus no doubt wrote of a poetic age before their time, as our poets write now of the golden days of the past.

I saw in the streets, day after day, pictures that only

TAORMINA.

need distance to be as fascinating as any the Greek poets made. Up a broad lane by the city wall is a fountain, coming out of the old aqueduct. The wall whence it issues into a stone basin is painted, and the pink color is subdued by time. There are always girls there in picturesque attire, filling their jars and gossiping. I saw a group of them one evening at sunset, while up the lane towards the fountain trooped a flock of goats driven by children, and the scene, girls, goats, children, jars, and fountain, was exactly such as Theocritus would have sketched.

The prisons that I have observed in Sicily are on the most frequented streets. Commonly the grated windows have blinds with the wooden slats so arranged that the prisoner can neither see out nor be seen from the sidewalk. But the prison at Taormina is more friendly. The prisoners at their gratings can gossip with anybody who passes by, and the prison is on the chief street. We noticed at the window, day after day, a pretty woman, with soft sweet eyes, and olive complexion. So far as I could conjecture, she would have been handsome if she had been washed. Generally she held in her arms a young child, a girl of some three years old. It was her sole amusement to watch the passers-by, and get an occasional word from them, and perhaps a copper from a stranger. I believe the prisoners are not over-fed in these places, and a bit of money is welcome. The young woman was one of the prettiest young women I have ever seen in jail, and her face was altogether most pleasing, showing good temper and a winning, lovely disposition. If appearances go for anything, there were several women outside with whom she might have changed places to the profit of the world. We do not, in fact, in our imperfect civilization, select our people for the jails with much discrimination. This sweet girl was sentenced to two years in prison, and had already been immured twenty months. I was curious to inquire what peccadillo had deprived the world of her society, and I learned that her only offense was stabbing her husband, who after all was not killed, but ran away. I did not learn the story, but I have no doubt that the husband deserved all that he got, and probably if the law could take proper cognizance of such offenses as his, he would have been shut up, and his ill-treated gentle wife would have been presented with a medal. We were obliged to come away and leave her looking pretty, out of her bars.

When you are in Taormina you ought, at least once, to get up at dawn and go on the hill above the theatre, and see the sunrise. The performance could be improved in some respects, for the sun here comes out of the sea off the lower point of Italy, and a sunrise at sea is apt to be tame. But you cannot elsewhere see it rise and throw its first rays on Mt. Ætna with an effect so fine. It happened the morning I stood on the hill near the signal station that there was an arrangement of clouds which made an iridescent light on the Mediterranean, and gave an unspeakable splendor to the sea and to all the Calabrian coast. Before that was developed, however, the earliest ray of the sun struck the white dome of Ætna and made it as pink as a garden rose. The color rapidly spread down the sides of snow until there was a ruby dome instead of the white mass we were familiar with. The shadows of night fell down also from the slopes, and gave place to a purple, which grew deeper and deeper in the valleys and on the orange groves, until the wave of morning passed over, and we had again the everlasting beauty of green and brown slopes, and fields of white snow under the deep blue sky.

CHAPTER XII.

SYRACUSE.

THE impression is general that the chief attractions of Syracuse are the Ear of Dionysius, and the exploit of Archimedes in firing the sails of the Roman fleet with his burning-glass. These "historic facts," which have as much basis as many others which go to make up a person's historical information, the traveler will speedily replace by more substantial interests. The so-called Ear of Dionysius is only an arbitrary localization of the sixteenth century, and the story of the feat of Archimedes grows "thin" when one overlooks the small bay called the Buon Consiglio, or Bay of Good Counsel, near the Capuchin convent, where it is said to have been performed. One seeks in vain for the tomb of the great mathematician, though a more modern Roman one is shown for his. There is, however, in the present city a square named for him, in the pavement of which stones are laid in circles, squares, and triangles, supposed to represent the famous mathematical figures which the old Ben Franklin of Sicily used to draw in the sand.

Syracuse (or Siracusa, as it is called to-day) was the largest and most important of the Hellenic cities.

Strabo says it was twenty miles in circumference. Against its impregnable walls the power of Athens was dashed to pieces in B. C. 413, and the city of the arts lost there the prestige and leadership which it never recovered. For a period of about nine centuries, down to the year 212, when the city was plundered of its valuables, and reduced to a provincial town by the Romans under Marcellus, Syracuse, with varied fortune, was always a city great in war, and distinguished in arts and letters. It was many times attacked and robbed thereafter, but it did not wholly lose its importance till the year 828, when the Saracens reduced it to insignificance. Of all the cities of the ancient world that have had a continued existence, after a fashion, Syracuse is now the most desolate, impressive, and melancholy waste. Even Girgenti is hardly so swept of remains of power and prosperity. The city of the Middle Ages and of to-day occupies only the small walled and fortified island of Ortygia, which was not a fifth part, though it was the oldest portion, of the ancient city, which is reckoned to have had half a million inhabitants.

The railway ride down the coast from Catania offers a succession of lovely sea views, but passes much of the way over low land which is extolled of old as the richest grain-bearing part of the island, and is now very productive of malaria. Especially unwholesome, I should say, is the neighborhood of the shallow, waterfowl haunted lake of Lentini, the largest body of water in Sicily. The most famous of the old towns we touched is Agosta (now called Augusta), and beyond this we ran along the Megarean bay. At Megara was an old Phœnician settlement, and some interesting relics of a civilization before the Greek occupation have recently been found there. I saw some rude terra cotta heads from there, upon the faces of which is that curious indefinable smile that is the characteristic of nearly all the statuary discovered by General di Cesnola in Cyprus. We saw also on a hill to the right the ancient town of Melilli, where the Hyblæan honey so loved of the poets was made. We were not fortunate with the honey of Hyblæ that we ate at Syracuse. I was assured that delicious honey was procurable, but that which was served us as Hyblæan may have been as old as any remains in the city, but it seemed to be a decoction of bees-wax and stale molasses, and I doubt if any bee was ever concerned in its manufacture.

The railway skirts the high promontory and rocky plateau upon which the larger portions of the old city stood, follows the ancient sea wall, and comes to a station on the main line about three-quarters of a mile from the present city, to reach which we pass a neck of land, cross two or three bridges, and drive under arched gateways that are of Spanish construction.

The island of Ortygia hangs like a pendant to the promontory, and is shaped like a duck. To the north of it a bay makes in forming the Little Harbor, a very small harbor for the historic associations it carries. On the west of the island is the spacious Great

Harbor, where the Athenian fleet was hemmed in and destroyed. The present city has an imposing appearance from the heights to the north of it or from the harbor, but within it is neither clean nor interesting. When you have seen the gigantic fragments of a partially excavated temple of Apollo — the oldest structure on the island — looked at the great fluted Doric columns and ancient walls, the remains of the temple of Minerva, which form a part, and the most interesting part, of the cathedral; strolled along the Passegio Aretusa, the favorite promenade that runs above a pretty garden along the harbor, and sat and meditated by the fountain of Arethusa, you have done your duty as a tourist. This fountain, which is spoken of with contempt by some modern travelers, I found inviting and even poetic. To be sure it is a deep circular walled pit — something like the bear-pit at Berne — but it is clean, its water bubbles up abundantly, and the Egyptain papyrus plant flourishes in it. Those who say that this is not a natural fountain by the sea, but is an opening of one of the ancient conduits which pass under the little harbor, and brought fresh water from the plateau of Achradina, would destroy the legend of Arethusa. But it is as well settled as such a fact can be, that when Arethusa, the nymph of Elis, was pursued by a river-god named Alpheus, she was changed by Diana into a fountain on this spot. When the weather is clear you can see Mt. Ætna from the Arethusian promenade. Indeed this noble volcano exercises a sort of sovereignty over all this.

coast. From the terrace roof of our hotel it appeared to great advantage at sunrise, though scarcely so majestic and deeply rosy as when seen from the Greek theatre at Taormina. It is one of the few objects that can coax the weary traveler out of his bed at dawn.

We found in Syracuse another Sicilian hotel worthy of mention. This is the Locanda del Sole. It is only about half as dear as the Vittoria, which we tried first, but it is a little worse. We did not understand at first why there were no bells in any part of the dirty house, but we soon discovered that there was nothing to be had if we could have rung for it. It is a very old and not uninteresting sort of barracks, and its rambling terraces give good views of the harbor and of Ætna. The rooms, too, are adorned with quaint old prints which give it an old-time air. It can be fairly said of its management that the attendance is as good as the food. I do not know how long it would take to starve a person to death there, or to disgust him with victuals to that extent that death would seem preferable to dining, but we touched close upon the probable limit of endurance in five days. It was a lengthy campaign of a morning to get a simple early breakfast. It was a work of time, in the first place, to find anybody to serve it. When the one waiter was discovered and coaxed into the dining-room, I ordered coffee and the usual accompaniments. In about fifteen minutes he brought in a pot of muddy liquid, and a cup. I suggested then, that, in reason, a spoon ought to go with it. A spoon was found after some search — sugar also I got by importunity. The procuring of milk was a longer process. Evidently the goat had to be hunted up. By the time the goat came to terms, the coffee was cold. I then brought up the subject of bread. That was sent out for and delivered. Butter also was called for, not that I wanted it or could eat it when it came, but because butter is a conventional thing to have for breakfast. This butter was a sort of poor cheese gone astray. The last article to be got was a knife. The knives were generally very good, or would have been if they had been cleaned. By patience after this you could have a red mullet and an egg, and some sour oranges. All the oranges in Sicily are sour. The reason given for this, however, is that all the good ones are shipped to America. The reason given in America why all the Sicily oranges are sour is that the good ones are kept at home. When the traveler reaches Malta and Tangier he will learn what an orange really is. I do not know that I can say anything more in favor of the Hôtel Sole, except that the proprietors were as indifferent to our departure as to our comfort while we stayed. We left at ten o'clock at night to take the boat for Malta. We procured a facchino outside to move our luggage, and not a soul connected with the hotel was visible. The landlord had exhausted himself in making out our bills. There was some difficulty in separating our several accounts, and when the landlord at last brought a sheet of paper on which the various items were set in order and the figures were properly arranged, he regarded his work with justifiable pride and exclaimed "it is *un conto magnifico.*" We agreed with him that in some respects the account was magnificent.

The old city consisted of five distinct parts. The first was the island of Ortygia, the oldest. The other four, on the main-land, were Achradina, occupying a plateau of limestone rock to the north of the island; Tyche; Neapolis; and Epipolæ, the highest point of the city. Dionysius surrounded the main-land city by a complete wall, which was built between the years 402 and 385 B. C. To visit the various portions of the vast area covered by the old city requires two or three days. Any description of it would not be intelligible to the reader without a detailed map.

The best thing the traveler can do first is to drive to the northwest some five miles up to the highest point of Epipolæ, take a seat on the ruins of Fort Euryalus, or Mongibellesi, and study the scene with Thucydides in hand. There you have the whole interesting locality in view, and by the aid of the historian you can follow the famous campaign which was so disastrous to the Athenians, and trace the operations of the conquering Roman general, Marcellus, 200 years later. The view of the Great Harbor, and of the walled city on it, of the vast marshy plain west of the harbor, through which the river Anapo runs, across which the despairing Athenians attempted to retreat, and of the rock-strewn site of the main-land cities, is exceedingly impressive. Perhaps nothing at Syracuse is so impressive as this general view over a now almost desolate stony waste, that was once the scene of a splendid civilization. But there are some details that must be mentioned.

Fort Euryalus, on its rock eminence, the vastest and most nearly perfect Greek fortress extant, gives one a new idea of the military genius of this wonderful people. The inclosure and the fort towers are a heap of ruins, but the extensive and spacious subterranean passages and galleries, hewn out of the solid rock, rooms for the magazines, for the stabling of horses and the shelter of the soldiers, and passages communicating with the city of Epipolæ, attest the skill and enterprise of those who made them. For me they much surpass in interest the famous rock-galleries at Gibraltar, and I think they were of more use in their day.

Without any attempt, which would only confuse the reader, to locate the places I shall name, I will speak of a few of the remains of antiquity which we visited. The Greek theatre, in the quarter of Neapolis, one of the largest of the kind, and well preserved in most of its seats and the ground plan of its stage, is hewn out of the rock of the hill, in semi-circular form. Like all Greek theatres I have seen, a magnificent view is commanded from its seats. Back of it on the hill are streets of rock tombs. It was only a step from the play-house to the grave, and this juxtaposition perhaps proves that the Greeks did not associate gloomy ideas with death. This old theatre is a sunny, pleasing lounging place for an idle man, who can at his leisure conjure up the drama and the spectators of more than two thousand years ago. Your imagination is assisted by several Greek inscriptions, and the names are still to be read of King Hiero and of the queens Philistis and Nereis. Of Philistis I believe nothing is certainly known except her head on the loveliest Greek coin extant, but she is supposed to have been the wife of Hiero II. If this was a good portrait of her on the coin, she was the handsomest type of a pure woman whose features art has transmitted to us from antiquity. The head in its graceful drapery strikingly resembles one of the most lovely of all the representations of the Virgin Mary, and I should not wonder if some Christian artist made the face on this coin his model. Gorgo and Praxinoe, two lively Syracusan gossips in Alexandria, immortalized by Theocritus, might have sat in these seats.

The Roman amphitheatre was built in the time of Augustus, and is a very good specimen of Roman work, massive, and intended for a more brutal amusement than the Greeks indulged in, the parent of the national pastime of Spain. Near this amphitheatre is the so-called altar of Hiero II., a stone platform over six hundred feet long, with steps on every side, on which it is thought were sacrificed four hundred and fifty oxen annually, to commemorate the expulsion of the tyrant Thrasybulus. It looks rather like the platform of an enormous temple.

SYRACUSE.

The objects which will most surprise and delight the visitor to Syracuse are the ancient quarries, called Latomiæ, perpendicular excavations of one hundred feet or more in the solid rock of the plateau, out of which the stone was taken to build the city. The principal are the Latomia del Paradiso, the Cappuccini, the Casale, and the St. Venere. These vary in extent and in beauty, but all have the same general character. The larger have an area of several acres. When you descend into one of them you find yourself in the most luxuriant and sweet-smelling garden you can imagine. The high and evenly-cut walls are hung with ivy which spreads in great masses of green from gigantic stems. The rich soil of the bottom makes to flourish the orange and the lemon and a wilderness of graceful plants and ever-blooming flowers. The air is vocal with the songs of birds. Out of this paradise of scents and color one looks up to a sky as blue as sapphire. The excavations are irregular. Here a single column of rock has been left by the quarryman; here a passage has been opened into another enormous apartment, vaster and more impressive than any cathedral. Here the rock has been cut under and we are in a vast vaulted chamber, the ceiling of which has acquired by some chemical change a pink tinge, as if it had been decorated for a ball room. Indeed a superb ball was given not many years ago in one of these cyclop chambers.

These ancient quarries have been used in past times for various purposes, for prisons and for burial places, before they were turned into gardens. In the largest, the Cappuccini, it is supposed that the seven thousand captive Athenians were confined in 413 B. C., until they perished of alternate cold and heat and thirst and hunger; it was then a horrible pit of death, impossible to be conceived from its present smiling aspect. Of the seven thousand, the few survivors were sold as slaves, although it is said that all those were set at liberty who could recite the verses of Euripides.

The Paradiso is more wild and gloomy than the other quarries, although not so beautiful, but it is more famous because it contains the Ear of Dionysius. This Ear is one of the historic frauds. The story was that Dionysius had the rock hewn in the form of an ear, so that by stationing himself in a proper place, he could hear what the prisoners below said, and enjoy their lamentations. There is a winding and lofty excavation in one part of the quarry not unlike the passage of a giant ear, and from above there is a gallery leading down to a small chamber communicating with it. It is evident, however, that in making this singular carved hall, the quarrymen were only following a particular vein of stone. The grotto has extraordinary acoustic properties. A whisper made at the entrance can be heard in the remote chamber above, and the cavern gives back the most remarkable echoes and reverberations. The slamming of the wooden door at the entrance produces a sound resembling thunder or the discharge of artillery, and the tearing of a bit of paper at the same place sounds like the crack of a revolver.

It was Caravaggio, who was down this way in the sixteenth century to execute some sacred pictures for the churches, who named this grotto the Ear of Dionysius.

Those who have a taste for looking about in catacombs will find here the most extensive in the world. They are, I believe, miles in extent, and their passages are much broader and more agreeable than those at Rome. Arched rooms, with loculi on all sides for bodies, and small chapels abound in them. It is thought that they were begun and used as burial places by the Greeks, and continued by the Romans and early Christians. Not many years ago a German professor and a party of students were lost and perished in these labyrinths. Since then daylight has been let in, in various places from above. We followed the guide about among the tombs for a while, but a very little of catacombs is enough for me.

One of the most interesting of the modern sites is the church of St. Giovanni, for underneath it is the oldest church in Sicily, called the crypt of St. Marcian, the friend and contemporary of St. Paul. In this damp and gloomy subterranean chapel, rock-hewn, it is said that St. Marcian was martyred, and that we see his tomb here. Here, also, we were shown the altar at which St. Paul officiated during his sojourn of three days at Syracuse. On the walls are some remains of quaint old frescoes. I do not vouch for all this, since it is probable that the crypt is of the fourth century.

We made the last day of our stay an excursion up the swift and turbulent river Anapo, to visit the Cyane fountain. We crossed the Great Harbor and ran aground in our big, clumsy boat long before we came to the mouth of the river, so that the boatmen had to jump overboard and push the boat over the bar into the stream. The river is narrow as well as swift, and bordered by high banks of mud. Sometimes we could row, oftener we poled, and a considerable part of the way the men got ashore and towed us with a rope, as the Egyptian boatmen "track." There was much in this whole awkward, lazy proceeding to remind us of the Orient, and not the least reminiscences of it were the peculiar minor songs of the laborers that came to us from over the flats. Throughout eastern Sicily one hears this peculiar singing, by which the Eastern origin of the people is shown. For an hour or two we could see nothing in this ditch, and but for the fact that we knew we were passing through classic ground there was not much to keep up our spirits.

At length the banks fell away, and we came to the open marshy land, over which we could see Syracuse and Ætna, and our eyes were delighted with the luxuriant and lofty papyrus plants. This plant, which is almost extinct in Egypt, grows, I believe, nowhere else in Europe. One account is that the Arabs introduced it here, another that one of the Ptolemies sent it over as a present to some fellow king. It flourishes splendidly, and is a very beautiful object. The straight stalk shoots up from six to fifteen feet, and is crowned by a feathering top. A group of these classic plants is very graceful. The papyrus paper is made from

SYRACUSE.   131

the stalks, which are cut in thin slices, laid close together, and with slices laid transversely. This soft, fibrous substance is then passed between rollers and dried. The result exactly resembles the Egyptian papyrus.

The fountain of Cyane, from which this full stream issues, is a bubbling pool some fifty feet in diameter, and perhaps thirty feet in depth. In its ordinary condition it is very clear, and the fish can be seen at the bottom of it. It is related that the nymph Cyane was metamorphosed into this fountain by Pluto when she opposed his carrying off Proserpine, and it was down this watery hole that he dragged his prey into the infernal regions. The pool is very pretty, set about as it is by the graceful papyrus. But I think the present infernal region lies all about it in the malarious meadows. Our guide somewhat resented the imputation of unhealthfulness which we put upon all this region, and to refute it related the story of an American lady who came ill to Syracuse. "She hired a villa on the hill, by the Cappuccini convent, bought a cow and had plenty of milk, got well in a few weeks, and went back to America and married a species of poet."

A milk diet, and union with a "species of poet," is better than being converted into a fountain.

CHAPTER XIII

MALTA.

THERE are three picturesque things, at least, in the island of Malta; the scarlet coats of the soldiers; the crimson fields of clover; and the black *faldetta* of the women.

First place to the dames. On first sight of the women of Malta, gliding about the streets in black, you think they have thrown their skirts over their heads. But they have not. The *faldetta* is a combination of hood and cape. Take a black silk apron, gather it close at the top with several runnings and put a whalebone through one side at the edge, so as to form a hood. This sort of hood is then thrown over the head, the "gathers" coming at one side, drawn so closely that it makes a curve, and the apron falling obliquely across the back. It can be drawn across the face so as to conceal everything except the eyes. And the large eyes of soft brown are the last things you or the women would wish to conceal. The costume is a relic of the Saracenic days, and is one of the many signs of Moorish descent.

This is a very clumsy description of a most fascinating garment. It gives a piquant interest even to an ugly woman — and Providence for our sins still permits ugly women — but it adds a charm to a pretty woman that is quite bewildering. Mind, this is not my opinion that I venture to give, but that of European ladies whom I have consulted. Perhaps I might not have noticed them otherwise.

All the Maltese ladies, as well as the common people, wear the faldetta to church, though on other occasions European hats are gaining ground with the higher classes. I am speaking at length of this costume because groups of these figures in the street or thronging the churches are the feature of the town. The faldetta is always worn with a black skirt, but some bright color is often worn about the neck, or for the bodice, together with heavy gold necklaces, and the glimpse of this half-hidden warmth of color that the faldetta permits in contrast with the prevailing black is very effective. It is perhaps the most coquettish devotional garment ever invented by the contradictory nature of the sex. I have given much reflection (while we are waiting here for a steamer to Gibraltar) to the reason of its peculiar charm, and I think it lies in this, that it gives to its wearer the mystifying appearance of a demure nun and a dangerous adventuress. How much the large, soft brown eyes and the clear, creamy Moorish complexion have to do with it is a scientific question. When one of the knights of Malta saw one of these ladies of oriental suggestion glide out of the church from her devotions, and permit the faldetta, as she passed him at the church door, to disclose one flash of her entreating eyes, if he did not follow her at least with his own eyes, he was not the gallant combination of priest and soldier that I have supposed him to be. But I am getting beyond my depth. What I wish to say is that if the sex wish to look both devout and fascinating, the faldetta is the best invention of their genius. I am told, however, that it is not a comfortable garment in a warm climate, and that the wearing it tends to produce baldness. And when we get to a bald woman it is time to change the subject.

The scarlet troops go along with the giant fortifications. I do not know much about either, but for my entertainment I prefer the scarlet coats of this sort of soldier to the red legs of the French variety. With a white pith hat they are very effective, and the rosy, manly British soldier is a decided contrast to the scraggy, undersized Frenchman engaged in that occupation. Certainly these fellows make a fine appearance in review — there are now some five or six regiments on the island, besides a battalion in blue with the Maltese cross on the shoulder, recruited entirely from natives. And the regimental bands are excellent. It is a great treat to hear some good music, both in the streets and in the churches, after being so long in Italy.

I can understand of the two anachronisms the soldier better than the fortifications, but these fortifications impress me, and if I were required to take (not as a gift but by force) some city, I should not begin on this La Valetta, the capital of the island. La Valetta, which was founded and fortified by the grand master of that name, is on a high, long, rocky peninsula, an arm of the sea on either side, crowned with solid houses, half its streets stairways; it frowns down on you on all its water sides, and on the land side, a mass of grim masonry and natural rock. I've been looking about a good deal, and I cannot find a spot, a gateway, a defile, or fosse, or angle, or whatever you call it, that is not swept by some murderous guns. It is all bastions, and batteries, and ramparts, and on the land side gates with covered ways, and so guarded by monstrous works that no amount of men, without a pass from the governor, could get in.

The main harbor, deep and long and winding, has in it several little bays where vessels lie, vessels of war, troop ships from India, with sailors in white apparel, and steamers from all the Mediterranean ports. The day I came in there was an American corvette lying there, sent for aught I know during Mr. Blaine's administration, to spy out what we could do with John Bull in case he trod on the tail of the Monroe Doctrine. But I was glad to see the dear old flag all the same, and felt a sense of absolute security as long as it stayed here. It has now gone to protect Leghorn. This harbor is not only very impressive with its surrounding fortifications, but it is gay with hundreds of small boats, not the clumsy tubs of Italian waters, but sharp and slender craft, apt to be painted green and adorned with pictures, and with high, blade-like prows at each end. They suggest, but do not resemble, the gondolas of Venice, when seen at a distance, as they are propelled by oars that are pushed by the boatman, who stands erect, face to the prow. This is much better for the chest than pulling, and I wish our college crews would adopt this style. They could not make as good speed in a race as they do in their shells, but they would display their fine figures to much better advantage to the spectators.

And now about the clover. Malta is an island large enough to have twenty-seven cities and villages on it. The total population is something about 150,000, of whom some 70,000 are in La Valetta. It is an uneven but not a lofty island, and is pretty much all limestone rock. When you look over it it seems to be nearly all stone walls, fencing in small fields, — in fact it beats western Massachusetts for stone walls. It is absolutely denuded of trees, except the fruit trees in gardens, and a few planted here and there for ornament. The prevailing hue of the island is therefore gray — the rocks, the towns, the stone walls. Imagine, therefore, in this gray setting everywhere patches of most brilliant crimson. This is the clover (called here *sulla*) now in full flower. Its stalk is much longer and stouter than our red clover, its leaves are larger, and the flower is on a long spike, each petal by itself, and the petals not grouped in the form of a bee-hive like ours. But the flower is beautiful, and anything more brilliant than these crimson fields contrasted with the gray stone and the deep green of the wheat you will not see elsewhere.

In this English free port, there is, by the way, a duty on wheat — I suppose to protect its growth here. For

MALTA. 137

all the island is so rocky it is very fertile, growing various grains and vegetables, and even some cotton, and producing the most luscious oranges, fine lemons, figs, nespoli (the Japanese medlar), etc. One sees now and then, near a palace, and in the lovely garden of the governor, and in others, abundance of flowers, and semi-tropical trees and shrubs. In the governor's garden the oranges and lemons are now in full bloom, and the odor is almost overpowering.

As we drove out the day before Good Friday, to Citta Vecchia, the old city of the knights, the first capital of the island, and in its centre, I noticed the flags at half-mast, and asked our Maltese driver why.

" Don't you know dat? God died to-day."

" Not till to-morrow."

" Well, he begin to-day."

The island is strongly Roman Catholic, and very devout so far as ceremonies go. The Maltese have the reputation of being the most evasive, lying swindlers and cheats in the Mediterranean. So far as I have come in contact with the natives, they sustain their reputation, — of course I should except, on sight, the women of the faldetta, unless they are trying with their brown eyes to coax you to buy lace. Our driver was a typical specimen of the most perfectly exasperating falseness and impudence, and it was owing to his mutiny that we did not see the grotto where Calypso was not able to console herself after the departure of Ulysses. But we saw the grotto of St. Paul.

I should have preferred to see the grotto of Calypso.

Because if there ever was such a man as Schliemann, and he is correct in his notion that there was a poet Homer, and if there is historic ground for a belief in a hero named Ulysses, then it cannot be proved that the island of Malta or Melite is not identical with the island of Ogygia mentioned by Homer as the summer residence of Calypso. And if I could have seen her grotto (which is perfectly plain to be seen, with a fair day and a decent driver) it would have gone far in my mind towards the identification of Mr. Schliemann.

But everybody knows that St. Paul was in Melite and that he stayed here three years. But I confess that a cave cut out of the soft rock under the church of St. Paul, at Citta Vecchia, in the centre of the island, as shown to me, did not serve to bring much nearer the presence of the great Apostle to the Gentiles. I have seen so many caves of this sort. Here is the cave where he prayed for three years, and adjoining is the chapel, also in the rock, where he "said mass."

We drove some three miles over to the bay where St. Paul landed, when he was shipwrecked. It is a lovely little indentation in the coast, the entrance partially closed by St. Paul's Island. It was here, somewhere on the sand, that the fire was built for the shipwrecked passengers, out of which the viper came that fastened on the apostle's hand. It would have been much more convenient for tourists if the cave had been placed near the bay. Baedeker (whose guide-book for southern Italy and Sicily I advise everybody to shun, as wholly inadequate and inaccurate) says in one edition that St. Paul landed here B. C. 56, and converted some of the inhabitants to Christianity. This would go to prove that Paul was, like some of our Unitarians, a Christian before and without reference to Christ. Probably some orthodox person pointed out this peculiarity to Baedeker, for in a subsequent edition he lands Paul here A. D. 61. Somewhere here on the north side of the island he doubtless did come on shore, and the tempest could not have selected for him a lovelier bay than this. The grotto of Calypso is in another little bay just over the high ridge. Perhaps it was owing to the piety and not the " cussedness " of our Maltese driver that he was willing to show us the site of the miracle of St. Paul and not the scene of the wiles of the nymph, who no doubt fascinated Ulysses by wearing a *faldetta*. At any rate one of the chief charms of the island is the story of St. Paul.

The romantic interest, however, is in the evidences of the presence of the heroic Knights of St. John of Malta, and the vestiges of the magnificence of their Grand Masters. The best fish, by the way, put on our table, fried, a little larger than the red mullet, with a delicate white meat, is called the Grand Master, a delicate compliment to the Order.

It is in the highly stucco-decorated cathedral here that you see the chapels of the Grand Masters, and a few of their tombs with statues as odious, in the Bernini style, as anything in Westminster Abbey. The pavement is composed of slabs of marble, mosaic, and often lovely in color and design, marking the tombs of the knights. This pavement gives a solid richness to the otherwise tawdry church of St. John. But it is in the armory hall in the governor's palace that you will see the relics and trophies of the bravest and purest military defenders of Christianity, the order in which the proud humility of the Christian blazed forth, in that strange commingling of the cassock of the priest with the mail of the soldier. About this hall, and in the passage to it, stand the figures of knights in armor. The French plundered the armory, when Napoleon was on his thieving expedition to Egypt, but many curious and rich things are left, fine suits of armor inlaid, and hundreds of ingenious murderous weapons. There are cannon, twelve feet long and not much bigger than a grizzly bear rifle, loading at the breech, 300 years old; an air gun as old; a cannon, 500 years old, brought from Rhodes, made of ropes twisted and cemented, and covered outside with leather, having a thin copper coating inside. Here is a great quantity of old majolica brought from the hospital of St. John in Jerusalem, and from Rhodes, the relics of the order when it had its seat, successively, in the city of David, and the city of the Colossus. Here is the original bull, signed and sealed, by which, in 1113, Pope Pascal took the order of the Knights under his protection, and here is the charter of the Emperor Charles V., founding the order of the Knights of Malta, at Malta, in 1530. More interesting than anything else, perhaps, is the long trumpet that sounded the retreat on that disastrous day in Rhodes, in December, 1522, after the most heroic defence that a few ever made against a host of foes. I liked also, very much, the armor of one of the old Knights who is called the Spanish giant. He was seven feet six inches in height, and his armor is proportioned to such a stature. I took up his ordinary hat, not the one with a visor, just a mere iron pot, weighing twenty-seven pounds, but did not put it on. It is, like the ordinary English tall hat, made to last for a generation.

We were shown also the portraits of the Grand Masters and the state carriage in which they used to drive. It has an additional interest because Napoleon used it when he occupied Malta, and, Philistine that he was, daubed over the gilded body of it with paint.

On the night of April 8th was a procession of images, representing the Passion and the crucifixion, as one sees it in Seville in Holy Week. But it did not recall the splendid ceremonies and parades of the Knights of Malta. Indeed a more discouraged procession I have never seen. You may see its like in Holy Week anywhere in Southern Italy, Sicily, and Spain, and it would not be worth a paragraph but for the orientalism that pervaded it. The narrow and steep streets through which it made its way about sundown were crowded, and little effort was made to clear a way for it. One thinks of a procession as an organized, progressive movement. With the idea of a procession in mind it is difficult to give the reader a notion of this proceeding.

First appeared two nonchalant vagabonds, one with a fife, the other with a drum. They sauntered along, the fifer flourishing now and then a few vagrant minor notes, with no attempt at a tune, and the drummer now and then striking his skin in a desultory manner. The piping was exactly the lazy, oriental flourish, in mournful minor, one hears at the head of a wedding procession in Cairo, and the two players strolled on and stopped now and then to look behind them as musicians do in Egypt. If any procession existed, it was lost in the rear. At length appeared men in brown linen robes with hoods, the hoods drawn over the heads, having peep-holes for the eyes, carrying dirty lanterns, walking wide apart on each side of the street, and each man at the distance of a rod from the one behind him. The crowd filled up the intervening spaces, and it was very difficult to pick out the procession. Then came small boys, handsome fellows, prettily dressed, also at distances of a rod apart, carrying the nails, the dice, the crown of thorns, and the other emblems of the crucifixion. Soon appeared in view a platform borne on the shoulders of slow-moving men. On the platform was a life-size figure of Christ in the agony of the garden. Other men in masks and now and then a priest straggled on. The procession often stood dead still; when it moved it was at a snail's pace, and even when it did move little was to be seen of it except when a platform came in sight. There were eight of these platforms with figures — Christ scourged, Christ crowned with thorns, Christ falling under the weight of the cross, St. Veronica with the handkerchief, etc. All the figures were painfully hideous. The only time when the procession was compacted and recognizable as a procession was at the passing of the crucifixion. This was a large platform with Christ on the cross, the three women standing by the cross and the figures looming up in a wild manner in the deepening twilight. Before it walked one of the fine regimental bands of the island, playing a mournful march, and it was followed by chanting priests. The body of Christ lying under a canopy was followed by chanting boys. As the chief piece, the crucifixion, came into the main street, trumpets were blown, supposed to be the trumpets of the Roman soldiery. The last scene was a gigantic empty cross, and Mary seated disconsolate at its foot. Once again, as this distracted procession groped its way through the crowd, I heard the discouraged notes of the fife, and it did not need the picturesque *faldettas* of the Sarcenic-looking women who thronged the sidewalk, and cast up their soft eyes to the sad images, to impress me with the Moorish tone given to this Christian ceremony.

CHAPTER XIV.

GIBRALTAR AND TANGIER.

On the 14th of April, four days' sail from Malta on the steamer Mizapore, we sighted the Pillars of Hercules, two lofty rocks, apparently some ten miles apart, — the gateway to a new world. The wind was west and the day showery. These historic monuments gained imperiousness from the thunderous clouds that concealed their summits, and left something of their majesty to the imagination. They frown at each other across the highway of commerce and discovery, a symbol of Spanish and English distrust. In order to command the strait one power should hold both headlands. But since the English cannot be dislodged from Gibraltar, the Spaniards have seized the opposite rock, the high headland of Ceuta, the Punta de Africa, fortified it and garrisoned it, and converted it into an important military prison. Ceuta was the point from which the Moors embarked for the conquest of Spain, and the Spaniards now hold it *in terrorem* over Morocco. But the Moors, who have little desire to reconstruct the world, do not fret over its occupation, as the Spaniards do over the sight of the English flag on Gibraltar.

The Mizapore had come from Sydney, and her passengers, with a sprinkling of travelers picked up at Bombay, returning East Indians, olive-skinned nurses with heavy silver anklets, and lithe Lascars, — just enough to add picturesqueness to the ship, — were mostly Australians, going "home" for the first time in their lives; loyally English, exceedingly curious to see the old country, but entirely un-English in manner and speech, having a provincial (or was it democratic?) manner, not agreeable, I noticed, to the real English on board, and wanting both the polish and the individual assertion, amounting almost to indifference to people not born on the great island, — the sort of bitter-sweet which makes the English traveler usually the most interesting of companions.

Statisticians could have proved that the death-rate was high on the Mizapore, for we had two funerals in our short passage. One was that of a returning Indian officer, who succumbed to consumption the night we left Malta, and the other that of a baby. Among the passengers was another Indian officer, who had been eager to join his wife and child at Malta and take them home. Mother and child were at the dock, but the child was ill, and the happy reunion was followed by a day of anxiety. On the second day, the body of the child, after a brief prayer, was pushed out of the same funeral opening, on the middle deck, where the dead officer had been launched, and two more were contributed to the myriads who make the smiling Mediterranean one of the most populous of graveyards.

The isolated rock of Gibraltar, presenting perpendicular points to the east and north about fourteen hundred feet sheer above the sea, slopes away in a series of terraces to the west, where the straggling town lies, and helps, with the opposite coast of Algesiras, to form a small harbor, little protected by the low hills on the west of it, open to the southwest and the southeast, and swept by the current of air which draws over the flat land north of the rock, — the neutral ground between the rock and Spanish territory. The west wind was blowing freshly as we rounded into the bay, and the hundreds of vessels in the harbor were bobbing about like corks. It was no easy matter to get into one of the little boats that came off to take us to the landing, and we formed a very poor opinion of the harbor of Gibraltar as a place of shelter. Nor, although we were hospitably received, and given a ticket that permitted us to land and remain five days on the rock, with a warning not to be caught outside the gates at the sundown gun, could we get up much enthusiasm for the commonplace town. We endeavored to appreciate its military position and the labor that has been expended in cutting galleries and tunnels in the rock, and mounting big guns which peep out of embrasures and threaten Spain. I could not see that the strait was commanded against the passage of vessels; most of the armament is on the land side, and the rock is no doubt impregnable to any Spanish attempt, and a perpetual offense to Spanish pride. It looks insolent and dominating, both from land and sea. From a spacious chamber hewn out of the rock hundreds of feet above the water, on the north side; a chamber furnished with long, down-slanting, wicked-looking guns, ready with a turn of their carriage wheels to poke their cold noses out of the embrasures; a chamber in which the officers of the establishment give lunches to their lady friends; a cool retreat, where the artillery of love is just now more dangerous than that of war, because love is a repeating and revolving arm, that never needs to be reloaded, and is often deadly when it is empty, — from this banqueting hall, that might become lurid with smoke and saltpetre, we looked down upon the narrow neck of sandy flat that separates England from Spain. Immediately at the foot of the rock is the burial-ground of the English troops; beyond that, barracks, and then a line of British soldiers, slowly pacing forward and backward; beyond the soldiers, a strip of neutral sand, perhaps three hundred yards in width; and beyond that, a line of Spanish sentinels, also pacing forward and backward in hostile show, and behind them barracks again, and the town of San Roque on rising ground. And thus stand Spain and England, in this day of grace and Christianity, watching each other in mutual distrust, while their peoples meet in the friendship of trade and social intercourse.

The most prominent object in San Roque is the new Bull Ring, a vast stone structure like the Coliseum, —

a sign of the progress in civilization of the people of the Peninsula.

There are several pleasant villas nestled among the rocks on the southeast exposure, and the Alameda runs along to the southeast from the main town through flowering gardens and sweet-scented trees, — a cheerful promenade and drive when wind and dust are laid. Beyond, dwelling in caves in the east end of the rock, is said to be a remnant of the old and very respectable colony of tailless and harmless apes, who obey a leader, and seem, having discarded the tail as vulgar, to be trying to develop into citizens and voters. They have only reached the bandit stage of civilization of the region, and rob the gardens by way of varying their diet of sweet roots and the fruit of the cactus. There seems to be here an opportunity of encouraging the development theory, and a tempting field for Positivist missionaries. Our scientific age is not living up to its opportunities. Why should we grope about in the past to prove that men once had tails, when we have here an almost brother, who shows by coming out of the tail period that he is waiting for the higher education? Why should we not take hold of him, — not by the organ we would once have taken hold of him, — and lift him up?

Such thoughts come to the perplexed traveler, as he sees and hears, in the narrow street by the hotel, another rudimentary institution, — the drum and fife corps of Old England, piping and pounding out that barbarous and soul-stirring music which inspires the courage of the living, drowns the cries of the wounded, and is a requiem for the dead. I have never heard the drum and fife played with such vigor, vim, exactness of time, and faith, and, let me add, with such pride. These stalwart musicians gloried in their profession, and their magnificent vaunting of the power of England and the advantage of the trade of war seemed to me irresistible, as a recruiting argument. Certainly, I followed them about as long as I could, without enlisting, and was never tired of watching the drummers toss their sticks in air and catch them without missing a note, nor of feeling the thrill imparted by their vigor, nor of sympathizing with the swelling efforts of the fifers to split the ears of the town, nor of studying, as a scientific problem, the elevating effect upon the mind of well-regulated noise. This is, surely, the perfection of martial obstreperousness; and I scarcely wonder that soldiers, for a shilling a day and pretty girls for nothing, are willing to follow the English drum-beat round the world; and I do not wonder at all at the military prowess of the Briton. With such incentives, it would seem to be easy to kill a Frenchman, or an Egyptian, or a Chinaman, or to do anything except to sit on this sun-and-wind-beaten rock, and wait for the hidalgos to come and take it.

It seems, on the map, an easy voyage across the sunny strait to Tangier. The high coast of old Africa looks inviting, and the distance is not more than thirty miles. We went on board the steam-tug Hercules at noon. Getting on board was not agreeable, for the exposed harbor was exceedingly rough; all the vessels at anchor were as active as dancers in a jig, and the small boats bobbed about like chips on the heaving, chopping waves. The steam-tug, neither clean nor commodious, is a cattle and passenger boat. A deck passage for both is imperative, because the small cabin in the stern is a loathsome hole, in which the motion and smells forbid any human being to abide. The passengers stowed themselves about the deck seats under the bulwarks and on the hatchway, and a few of the first class on a platform raised above the engine. It was a choice assortment of traders and vagabonds, Moors, Jews, disconsolate women and children, and half a dozen English and Americans. In the teeth of a head wind we bore away for Point Tarifa, — a frontier fortress, which I suppose gave us the blessed word "tariff," — now a city of crumbling walls, and the sweetest oranges and most gracious and complaisant women in Spain, — according to the guide-book. The women wear the mantilla drawn over the head, so as to conceal all the face except one destructive eye, and the place is said to retain more Moorish characteristics than any other in Andalusia. In front of it is a fortified rocky island with a lighthouse. When we ran past this we were in the open strait, and nobody paid much attention to the scenery. The wind seemed to freshen, and when the boat struck the inward flowing current, which the captain said was seven knots an hour, she began to climb over the waves and sink between them, and bob about in a most confusing manner. To meet the wind and the current, her nose was pointed straight out to the Atlantic, and for weary hours we appeared to be going to America, while we were actually drifting nearer the African coast. In this battle with waves and wind, the waves had the best of it, and every few moments spray and volumes of water dashed aboard, drenching us all, even the occupants of the upper platform. It was almost impossible to keep a seat, or even to hang on to the hatchway. Most of the passengers gave up all effort, and sprawled about on the deck in any position chance gave them. I was particularly interested in a Jewish family, a man and his wife and a boy and girl of twelve and fourteen, who had established themselves on the floor in front of the cabin hatchway. The children, rolled up in blankets and locked in each other's arms, seemed to be sleeping, regardless of the tumult. But the quiet did not long continue. Father and mother soon ceased to take the least interest in their offspring, and rocked about the deck in utter misery. The children began to moan and writhe and twist under their blankets, and then to howl and kick, until they had rid themselves of half their clothing. Deathly sick, and apparently enraged at such treatment, they kicked and screamed, but never unclasped themselves from each other's arms. It would have been pitiful, if the misery had not been so nearly universal. The sun shone in bright mockery of our calamity, the west wind blew with fresh inspiration, the salt water soaked and blinded us, and the nasty little tug plunged about like an unbroken colt. We were five hours on this voyage of thirty miles; and when the vessel at last floated in calm water, behind the breakwater in the harbor of Tangier, it seemed as if an age separated us from Europe.

The harbor is shallow, and is open to the northeast. We anchored some distance from the shore, and were at once surrounded (who does not recall the familiar Oriental scene?) by a fleet of clumsy boats, and the usual hordes of eager, excited boatmen swarmed on board, — Moors in gowns and turbans, — who seized upon our baggage as if we had been captives, and fought for the possession of our persons. Amid pulling, hauling, shouting, screaming, swearing, and wild gesticulation, we found ourselves transferred to a small boat, and on the way to the landing. Boats were dashing about in all directions, with frantic splashing of oars and reckless steering; collisions were imminent; everybody was shouting as if crazy; and in all the tumult there was laughing, chaffing, and abundant good-humor. Half-way to shore our boat stuck in the sand, and overboard went the chattering crew, pushing, pulling, and howling, till we reached the landing pier, when there was another scramble out of the boat and a rush along the shaky scaffolding. The most helpful people these, — the whole population is eager to take a hand in disposing of us; and the moment we touch Africa a couple of dozen of men and boys have seized upon our trunks, bags, and bundles, and have rushed away with them through the gate and into the city. It looks like a robbery; in New York it would be; but this is not a civilized land, and we shall find every piece of baggage at our hotel, with a man guarding it, recounting the exhausting labor of carrying it, and demanding four times the pay he expects to get.

The hurry is over, the tumult subsides, and as we walk leisurely on there begins to fall upon us the peace of the Orient. At the gate sit, in monumental calm, four officers of the customs, in spotless white raiment of silk and linen, who gravely return our salute. We ascend through a straight street, roughly paved and not too clean, lined with shops displaying the tempting stuffs of Eastern ingenuity, — the shops of workers in metal, leather, slippers, horse furniture, and bricabrac, — and emerge, by the gate into the market-place under the wall, into a scene wholly oriental: groups of camels squatting in the dust, moving their ungainly necks in a serpent-like undulation, or standing, weary, in their patient ugliness; donkeys loaded with sticks, grass, and vegetables; on mats spread on the ground heaps of wheat, beans, salads, oranges, and all sorts of grimy provisions; water-sellers; money-changers, with piles of debased copper, and scales to weigh it; half-naked children tumbling about in the dirt, negroes, stately Moors in tattered gowns, wild-looking camel drivers, women enveloped in single pieces of white cloth, draped about the body and drawn over the head. We make our way, amid this swarm, up a hill gullied by the water, through a narrow lane thick-set with gigantic aloes and cacti, to the hotel Ville de France,— a spacious and very comfortable French house, backed and flanked by splendid gardens of flowers and fruit.

Outside and above the town, higher than any part of it except the castle hill, which is on the sea-bluff on the right entrance of the harbor, the hotel occupies a commanding position, and offers a lovely prospect. On its left, toward the north, the ground slopes gently up to a wide grassy plain, the level of the sea-bluff, along which are the picturesque cottages and plantations of the foreign embassies, lying amid gardens in the full sun, but fanned by the ocean breeze. From a window in one side of the room I occupied, I looked over the garden, blooming with roses, geraniums, acacias, oranges, to the sandy curve of the harbor and the blue-green of its shallow water, and the opening into a plain in the direction of Tetuan; and from a window on the other side, over the white town to the blue sea and the dim mountain coast of Spain. No lovelier and more restful prospect exists. When the traveler reaches the hotel of M. Brugeaud, opens the windows to let in the odors of the garden, and gazes out on the smiling prospect of land and sea, he feels that he has come to a place of rest. It is one of the few spots in the world where the wanderer loses his unrest and all desire to go farther. The town, which is shabby enough as we walk through it, is picturesque from this point. It shines like silver, under the sun; all the whitewashed, flat-roofed houses contrasting with the blue water beyond; a couple of mosque towers, green, looking as if tiled, but probably painted; and flags of all nations flying here and there on roofs that climb above their humbler neighbors.

Sunday is the best market-day. When I awoke at dawn I heard the throb of the darabuka drum in the place below, and the innumerable hum of traffic; and looking out I saw that the Soko was swarming like an ant-hill. When we descended into the motley throng, the business of the day was in full blast. The scene is familiar to every Eastern traveler, but it has an untiring fascination. The beggars followed us about; the snake-charmers and story-tellers had already formed rings of delighted spectators: women clad in coarse white stuff, with children slung on their backs; stately, handsome Moorish merchants in cool, gauzy robes; comely urchins in rags begging and offering to act as guides; sellers of unattractive goods crying their merchandise; camels roaring, and donkeys braying, and dervishes posturing, — the picture shifted like the bits in a kaleidoscope. Here was a fantastic dervish arrogating to himself the title of Shereef of Beggars, with a variegated turban, his dress thickly hung with ornaments, and four rings on each finger. Here were the unpleasant Riffs from the country, men in dirty embroidered robes, with the heads all shaved except one long curl on one side, — a lock left for Lord Mahomet to pull the wearer up to heaven. The high civilization and lack of self-consciousness of these people are shown by the fact that everybody may wear any dress he chooses, or none, and attract no attention.

In the town it was Sunday, also, and just as lively. The Jews form a considerable portion of the population, and are in appearance the most decent and thrifty. We were admitted to several Jewish houses, built with open courts, in the Moorish style, which were exceedingly neat and comfortable. The women, who have a reputation for beauty, are of light complexion, — much lighter than the men, — and many of them have fine eyes, and all the national fondness for jewelry. Notwithstanding their wealth and orderly behavior, the Jews are liked by nobody, and the Moorish merchants, who are no more scrupulous than other traders, always regard the Jew as dishonest. In no Oriental community does the Jew rise above this prejudice.

On a street corner was a roulette table in full operation, whirled by an honest man from Malaga, who coveted our good opinion, without expecting us to join his game; supposing that, as foreigners, we looked down, as he did, upon these ignoble surroundings.

"You ought to be very good here," I said, "with three Sabbaths, — the Moslem Friday, the Jewish Saturday, and the Christian Sunday."

"Oh, yes," replied the devout Spaniard, giving the wheel a whirl; "but Moors no keep Sunday. And" (said suddenly, as if it were a new thought) "Christians no keep it, neither! Jews *must* keep it; 'bliged by their law."

We left this introducer of Christian ways whirling his wheel and gathering in the stray coppers. How much sin it is to gamble with the Moorish copper is a question. Having need to fill my pocket with it to satisfy the beggars, I received from a money-changer a large bowlful of it in exchange for a *peseta*, a silver piece worth twenty cents.

Tangier, for climate, scenery, novel entertainment, is a delightful winter residence. In two weeks, at any rate, we did not tire of it, and every day became more in love with the easy terms of existence there. The broken country in the direction of Cape Spartel is inviting both to the foot-pad and the horseman, and the embassies, when they are not paying their annual visit to Morocco, the capital, must offer some good society. We went one day to the plantation of the American consul, some two miles out on the road to Cape Spartel, which is laid out on one side of a glen; sheltered from the prevailing wind, but open to the ocean breezes. Here in a pretty Oriental cottage, with an extensive garden, blooming the winter through with flowers of every sort, fragrant with the orange, the banana, the pepper, and the acacia trees, one might forget that snow and ice and "blizzards" and politics and all the discomforts of civilization in the temperate zone exist.

Tangier, notwithstanding its openness to the world, is still a place of civility and repose. Oriental costume is the rule; the streets are dirty, the people are amiable, the oranges are sweet, the climate is lovely. The *laissez-aller* of the town is attractive, and the shopmen and beggars have something of the politeness of the grave Moors. I used to be attended often in my strolls by a charming boy, in a ragged gown, handsome, and with the breeding of a prince. He had picked up a little French and a little English, broken fragments, which were melodious in his mouth, and he aspired to be a guide and earn a few daily coppers. He assumed an air of protection, and kept off the more clamorous beggars and the rabble of urchins that are willing to accompany the stranger all day in his walks. His gracious, deferential, and superior manner was guided by a sure instinct, which enabled him to keep the narrow line between haughtiness and servility, and to remain near me without compromising his dignity, when he was bluntly told that his company was no longer wanted.

"You know Mark Twal?" he asked, by way of scraping acquaintance, on his first appearance.

"Yes, I know Mark Twain very well. Do you?"

"Yaas; he friend to me. I guide to him. He vely good man, Mark Twal."

"Why, you young rascal, you were n't born when he was in Tangier, sixteen years ago."

"Oh, yaas, born enough. Me know him. He vely good man."

"What makes you think him a good man?"

"Oh, he vely good man; plenty backsheesh. You go castle?" And the handsome boy made a dive, and routed the increasing throng of beggars; and then returned to my side, with the easy but high-bred manner of an established friendship, and strolled along with the air of a citizen of the place pointing out the objects of interest to a stranger.

We climbed up to the castle — the shabby acropolis of the city — by a steep, cactus-lined road along the wall in the rear, and entered by a gate into the sprawling official quarter of the town. This is no doubt the site of the old city of Tândja — the " city protected by the Lord ; " and it is apparently still left to the Lord's protection. It has no traces of the Portuguese or the English occupation, although it was held by the Portuguese from 1485 to 1662, when it fell to Charles II. through his Portuguese wife, and occasioned the English no end of trouble and expense for twenty-two years, as may be read in the diary of Samuel Pepys, Esq., who was one of the commissioners of Tangier, and became its treasurer, an office which was " a good fortune beyond all imagination," and no doubt assisted that diligent naval administrator to set up his coach. It is a great loss to us that Mr. Pepys, who went to Tangier in August, 1683, with Lord Dartmouth, did not continue his entries in his Diary during his travels in Morocco and Spain. His open "Journal," which may have been of service to his contemporaries, contains little that is characteristic of the man or the city. Mr. Evelyn also built hopes of service to art and archæology upon the expected visit, and wrote to him reminding him to inquire about medals and inscriptions to be found at Tangier. He was also to inquire about the *citriæ* or *cedar* trees, that of old grew at the foot of Mt. Atlas, " and were heretofore *in delicijs* for their politure and natural maculations, to that degree, as to be sold for their weight in gold." Of this wood Cicero had a table that cost him ten thousand sesterces, "and one of the Ptolemies had yet another of a far greater price, in so much as when they used to reproach their wives for their luxury and excess in pearle and paint, they could retort, and *turn the tables* on their husbands."

This quarter now, like most oriental official residences, is little but a shell of shabby houses and dirty courts. Remains of better days are visible in a few fine ornamented Moorish arches and entrances, and in the iridescent tiles in the court of the Governor's house. Adjoining this — so close is justice to the royal house in the Orient — is the prison. It consists, so far as we could see, of one large room, filthy enough to please the most conservative anti-prison reformer, and crowded with an unambitious lot of criminals, who earn their food by making and selling baskets. Viewed as a place of security, I should judge it more easy to get out of it than to get in. At the castle gate overlooking the town, we sat a long time on the rocks with the beggars and donkey boys and swarms of children, and other idlers, who always have leisure for a sun-bath in this land of "to-morrow." The idleness of these people is certainly contagious. The most active traveler soon regards the day well spent if he has succeeded in accomplishing nothing in it — nothing except to take impressions of repose and content. We were enabled to make the whole idle group supremely happy at the expense of a handful of coppers, whose purchasing power in this case was enormous. They were exchanged with some vendors of confectionery, for white candy which is carried about on a stick, to which it is attached and hangs like strings of maccaroni, and is broken off in bits to suit the smallest coin. These coins would have no value in our eyes if they were not stamped on one side with the Seal of Solomon.

CHAPTER XV.

ACROSS AFRICA.

WHEN we determined to cross the Dark Continent, we wisely chose one of the narrowest parts of it. This feat has become so common in these days that one feels like apologizing for engaging in it, and still more for describing it. But it may mitigate the offense by confessing, in advance, that our adventure involves neither perils nor geographical surprises, and did not have for its object the opening of new channels for the cottons and Christianity of Manchester or Lowell.

We selected for our passage that portion of Morocco which lies between Cape Spartel and the Bay of Tetuan; but as we were already at the city of Tangier, it would have been mere bravado to begin our journey at the lighthouse on the cape. We saved a ride of two hours by starting from Tangier. The mule path from Tangier to Cape Spartel is over breezy downs, through Moslem cemeteries and fields of cactus and hedges of aloes, and winds along the side of Mount Washington, with the broad expanse of the Atlantic always in view. The accomplished linguist who acted as guide informed us that Mount

Washington takes its name from the fact that the women of the vicinity resort to the streams that flow from it to do their washing. It is certain that the landscape owes much of its picturesqueness to the women who are pounding clothes and chattering on every stream, or strolling along the white paths in easy-going groups. Draped in flowing white garments, with shawls drawn obliquely across the face, these dark-eyed, creamy-skinned daughters of the desert, loitering along the highway in clusters perpetually shifting as they go, embody much of the grace, the leisure, and the mystery of the Orient.

No sooner does one land in Africa than he passes into a sphere of tranquillity, and enjoys a state of rest and calm to which all parts of Europe are strangers. The haste and flurry of life fall off, like an irksome garment shed on a hot day; time is of no more account; and worry is impossible amidst a population which moves with dignified slowness, and defers all unnecessary exertion till to-morrow. Whatever may be the bustle of arrival, the clamor of boatmen, the indescribable noise and tumult and vociferation of the swarm that assails the stranger, seizes his property with a hundred hands, and threatens to scatter it all over Morocco; whatever may be the tumult of the market-place, with its camels, and donkeys, and dervishes, and conjurers, and beggars in clouds, sellers of lentils and greens, and bundles of stick for firewood, grain, sugar-candy, dates, oranges, pottery, and "truck" of all sorts powdered with dust; whatever may be the importunity of sellers, and the eagerness to act as guides of bright-eyed boys, who have a smattering of half a dozen languages, and often, as I have said, the courtly manner of young princes, there is, nevertheless, in all this noise and rout a sense of underlying calm, of absence of hurry, very grateful to Europeans, whose nerves, in the development of civilization, have all worked out upon the surface. There is even something soothing in the ceaseless and monotonous tom-tom of the drums, and the skirmishing and plaintive attempts of the flutes to suggest the minor air they are too lazy to play, and in the spasmodic and die-away ejaculations of the musicians, who sit upon the ground, worrying away at the tunes that are a thousand years old, and will be played with the same industrious idleness a thousand years hence. It requires less energy for the performers to go on with this sort of music than to stop.

It was difficult to summon resolution enough to break this contagious spell of repose, and make the journey to Tetuan. For the trip is not an easy one, and can always be performed better to-morrow than to-day. Tetuan is forty-five English miles from Tangier. The road is a model one for Morocco, and there is no decent halting-place on the way for the night. It is necessary, therefore, to push through between sunrise and sunset. With a good road and good horses this would be no hardship. But the government refuses to make the one, and circumstances denied us the other.

It was the time of the year for the annual pilgrimage of the European legations to the court of the emperor at Morocco. Each legation travels across the desert with considerable state and pomp, requiring for its train a large number of riding animals and beasts of burden, horses, mules, and camels. These caravans move very slowly, and consume nearly a month in the journey, making usually not more than fifteen miles a day on the march. As the legations remain at the court several weeks, about three months are spent in the trip. The caravans are furnished with tents and all the luxuries attainable, and, the march being slow, the excursion is much liked by the ladies of the different legations. The novelty of the desert journey and the visit to the thoroughly Oriental city of Morocco are pleasing inducements, but not the least of the attractions are the presents expected from the Emperor to the individuals of the suites, in return for the costly gifts of arms and goods which the European governments send the Emperor by the legations. The Emperor's presents are not always judiciously chosen. Last year one of the attachés of the Spanish legation so wormed himself into the favor of the Emperor that he received a couple of superb pearl necklaces, of great value. On his return, the thrifty Spaniard, instead of giving one or both to his wife, turned them both into hard cash in the market. My informant, a Portuguese lady, who made the journey, received from the Morocco sultan a mule.

The expense of these costly expeditions, so **far as**

transport is concerned, is borne, I was told, by the Morocco government; that is to say, the poor people have to be taxed for them. Their fitting-out sweeps off from Tangier and the region all the good saddle horses and mules. The English and some other legations had already gone, and the Italian was about to start. I saw at the Italian camp, outside the city, many fine horses and mules; the requisition for them made it impossible for us to procure decent riding animals for Tetuan. As we have only a consul-general in Morocco, the American government is not represented in these pilgrimages. If our government had any care for deserving travelers, it would furnish us the means of visiting the interesting city of Morocco in style befitting the citizens of the republic.

The government undertakes only to secure the safety of foreign travelers to Tetuan who are under escort of a soldier. This arrangement gives the soldier a dollar a day, which is paid by the traveler, throws around the latter the panoply of the law, and adds a certain state to his movements. The necessity of putting ourselves under the protection of the army was pleasing to us, and we commissioned our landlord to furnish us a man of war for our caravan. Our host assured us that he had procured the best beasts and equipments for our cavalcade, and we awoke early on the morning of our start, with excited anticipations of state and show.

When I glanced out of my windows at dawn, the view disclosed was exquisitely lovely. The comfortable hotel of M. Brugeaud, where we stayed, is on a hill outside the Bab-el-Sok, or gate of the marketplace, and above that busy exchange. One of my windows looked out on the garden, and the other upon the town and harbor. The garden is an orderly wilderness, a series of terraces of fruit-bearing trees, — oranges, lemons, figs, and palms; of flowering shrubs, — acacias, geraniums, carnations, pepper-trees, and rose-bushes, heavy with the weight of every form and color of this queen of the flowers. As soon as I had opened my window there came in a flood of sweet odors and a gush of bird notes. On the seats under the gigantic, wide-spreading sycamore that shades the front terrace were lounging three or four turbaned idlers, praising Allah, I hope, for the freshness of the morning, while they waited the advent of their prey, the foreigner.

From the seaward window the prospect was wide, varied, and most charming. Indeed, I scarcely know anywhere so pleasing a morning picture. The flat-topped roofs of the white-housed town, the even lines broken by a few pointed towers and minarets, and rising on the left to the ancient portions and castle, with the Alcazar; the little harbor, green and blue in patches, in the early light, with half a dozen sailing vessels and a steamer or two; to the left, the open Mediterranean and the high coast of Spain, and to the right the sand-hills of Morocco, rising by gradations and lofty mountains, over which the dawn was reddening, — this picture, for outline, repose, and Oriental suggestion, can hardly be equaled elsewhere. I think one might be content to spend a winter amid the color and perfume of this garden, with such a view to rest his tired senses. Already, as I looked, the life of the place was beginning to stir: trains of camels were wending their way up the hill into the country; donkeys, with bundles of fagots and country produce, driven by women, or lazily bestrode by bare-legged men, were drifting into the market-place, where the crowd began to swarm, and buzz, and shift about like the occupants of an ant-hill; and I could hear the confused murmur and stir of beggars, and traffickers, and sluggards, unrolling themselves from their bundles of rags, in which they had slept beside their patient beasts. It was a market-day, and before I was dressed the idle business of the day had begun, and a circle was already formed about the snake-charmer, called together by the throb of the rude drum. If the Orientals go to rest with the sun, they rise with it.

It was five o'clock when we descended to the courtyard to mount. The cavalcade was ready: the beasts nodding with their heads against the wall, — mules and donkeys appear to be always asleep, — and our attendants squatting about in angles of the inclosure, not in the least impatient to go, wrapped in their burnouses against the fresh morning air. Whatever notion I may have formed of this outfit, I must have been disappointed. There were three mules for our party; a horse to carry the guide and the baggage; a footman, a tall, handsome-featured, bare-legged Arab, to run along and "whack" the mules; and the Morocco soldier, with his barbed steed. The mules were small, ill-conditioned beasts, with rickety saddles; the one I mounted was intended to be of a mouse color, but he had not been cleaned since he was a mule.

The soldier, however, came up to my ideas of military grandeur in Morocco. Seated on the ground, he was a mere bundle of dingy white garments, the capote of his burnous drawn over his turban. Gun he had none, and we felt wronged by the absence of this long and showy weapon. The idea of a soldier without arms seemed to us undignified. No doubt our safety was increased, but our pride of appearance was touched. His steed was a piebald animal resembling those hairless purple horses that you may see performing at an English country fair. When our soldier rose, we perceived that he was bare-legged, but wore ruined slippers; and when he climbed into his broad saddle, elevated on a pile of rugs, we noticed with rising spirits that his gown protruded, and the red end of a sword scabbard showed out of his garb of peace. This bundle of soiled rags on horseback, and armed symbol of peace and good will to men, slowly led the way out of the court-yard and down the cactus-covered hill, never looking behind him, and we meekly followed in his train. I think it was the sorriest cavalcade that ever crossed Africa. The west wind was blowing softly and sweet, the air was full of life, the sea sparkled, the white town glistened, as we rode down through the now swarming market-place, and through the narrow, ill-paved streets of the city, in search of adventure. I do not know why it was that our man of war reminded me of the mounted trooper who sits immovable at the Life Guards gate in Westminster. Both figures are my ideal of a soldier. Neither is of the slightest use, except to assert the presence of the law, and both, I presume, are harmless. Our Life Guardsman moved on at a snail's pace, till we were free of the town, over the wide sandy beach of the harbor, and turned southward into a broad valley that winds among the low hills.

There are old Roman remains on the bay opposite the city, and a bridge of the solid architecture of the Roman period. Probably the ancient conquerors built roads and kept open good highways through this fertile country, but now there is not a road worthy of the name in all Morocco. If good roads are a sure sign of civilization, then Morocco is no more civilized than some parts of our own country. Perhaps the Moorish government is not altogether to blame for this want, though it is certainly unwilling to spend anything on highways or on the streets of the cities. For there is no popular demand for roads; if roads were made, it would be long before the people procured vehicles to run on them; they prefer the ancient method of transport by asses and camels. The way to Tetuan is exactly such a way as used to be made over our Western prairies, when every traveler found a path to suit himself, avoiding the corn and wheat fields, and describing a circuit to get over the marshy streams; that is, there are lines of wandering foot-paths, some of them deeply worn by ages of travel. In the rainy season the donkeys and camels make new paths, diverging here and there for firmer footing, so that the country is gridironed by chance roads.

The scene is animated as we advance. We meet hundreds of country people, in groups of twos and threes and dozens, with laden donkeys, on their way to town; all the women, however ugly and shabby and bare-legged, making a pretense of drawing their shawls over their faces as we pass. There are wide expanses of wheat, green and waving; flocks of sheep and herds of goats are grazing on the downs, and large numbers of the small cattle of the country, — the sort that takes nineteen to make a dozen, — such as are shipped to Gibraltar for beef. You may see them transferred from small boats to the steamers in the shallow harbor of Tangier, swung on board by a rope around the horns.

The land is vocal with the singing of innumerable birds; a very pretty warbler is a brown bird, the size of a meadow lark, with a peaked top-knot; flocks of ravens are circling about; and here and there in the fields stands a tall black and white bird, with red legs, a species of stork, the *signana* in Spanish. These domestic birds have their homes on the huts of a struggling Arab village, high up on a hill, which we pass,— thatched huts of brown earth, half hidden in the vast fields of luxuriant cactus.

After we pass this town on its high perch, the country is still largely cultivated, animated with the sounds of labor and the presence of flocks and herds, but there are no signs of habitations. Where do the people live who own these flocks and cultivate the ground? The absence of fences, or boundary hedges, and of houses, makes the picture a strange one to Western eyes. For hours we saw only two or three brown hovels.

The country is rolling, like a Western prairie, but the soil is stony, and before us, to the south, are lines of serrated mountains. We pass over miles of the monotonous route, where the only verdure consists of stiff patches of palmetto, varied occasionally by yellow broom and gorse in bloom, and again interminable oleanders, budding, but not yet in flower, which grow as profusely as alders on the banks of our meadow brooks. Two weeks later their crimson blossoms, contrasted with the vivid yellow of the gorse, must make a brilliant show.

Is that a caravan wandering over the plain before us? As we approach, the procession resolves itself into a couple of dozen of camels, without loads, and with only two drivers, leisurely returning to Tetuan. The beasts are shambling along in their ungainly fashion; craning their long necks, nipping bits of grass, strolling about in a dozen paths, in no order of march. They do not march, but flow along, changing places, falling behind, and moving ahead, like figures in a kaleidoscope. I have noticed that a group of Orientals on the road saunters along in the same shifting order. The ancients of days lift up their supercilious heads, and disdainfully regard us as we pass by.

Notwithstanding that large tracts of the stony land are neglected, we are never long out of sight of cattle, sheep, and people, and cultivated fields. Occasionally there are olive-trees, but for the most part the land is treeless. From the slopes, however, come the cheerful notes of labor: workmen are calling to each other, or singing the plaintive minor songs of Egypt. Plowing is going on. The plow is the primitive stick of wood, with an iron point, that only scratches up the soil on the surface. The motive power is a couple of small bulls, yoked wide apart, — the yoke in front of the horns, instead of on the neck; and progress is made by as much noise and clamor as is needed to move a house by rollers and handspikes elsewhere.

The man of war rides through all this with imperturbable gravity and slowness. Much of the way has been fair trotting-ground; it is necessary to make speed when we can, but the soldier is moving under the accumulated weight of three thousand years of leisure. When I urge him to advance, and push my mule upon him, — an effort which causes me much pounding and exhortation, — the Old Tortoise will raise his lumpy bulk in the saddle, lean forward like an old woman, and lift himself in his stirrups so as not to feel the jar: whereupon his steed will swing into a slow jog, which, slow as it is, seems very distasteful to our brave defender. At such times the red point of his scabbard sticks up behind in a military manner, lifting his burnous, the bundle of clothes is animated by motion, and, as I urge on my mule with whacks and ejaculations of encouragement, we present for a moment a martial appearance. But it is only for a moment. The seat of this hardy defender of his country, protected as it is by piles of rugs, is not inured to this sort of violent campaigning, and he soon subsides into a walk. It is only by taking the lead, and forcing the train to follow my forced pace, that we get over the ground at all.

We have been several hours in the saddle, the sun is hot, the morning breeze has ceased, the scenery has become monotonous, when our spirits are raised by the sight of the Foudak, where we are to take our luncheon and midday rest, — a white building on the side of the mountain, in the jaws of the pass we are to scramble through. It seems very near, but we ride an hour and a half, through hot gullies and stony ravines and over steep paths, before we reach it. After five hours of this sort of work we are quite willing to throw ourselves on the ground under the scant shade afforded by a fine old ilex-tree at midday.

Our halting-place was not the Foudak, which is half a mile beyond, but the spring, which is the resort of all the people and the cattle of the region. The place is wild and rugged, and not picturesque, but the view from it over the rolling country we had traversed, and the mountains beyond, was fine. This might be made, with a little trouble, a pleasant resting-place, and one would think that on a highway so frequented as this some pains would be taken to make it comfortable. It is, however, like every Oriental place of the sort, shabby and dirty.

The Fondak itself, which has no water near it, is worse, although natives, and Spanish men and women, who are no more fastidious, do spend one night there. The Fondak would be called in New England a cow-yard. It is simply a large, square inclosure, built of stone, and whitewashed. Within are some open arches, that afford a slight shelter to man and beast in stormy weather. A couple of the arches are inclosed, forming dark chambers, where we are told people sleep. Like the rest of the place, these rooms are full of vermin, filth, and fleas. This is, and has been, I suppose, for ages, the only sort of resting-place between two large cities that have daily communication, and considerable commerce. We met, on our return, a gay cavalcade, Spanish ladies and gentlemen, going down to visit the consul at Tetuan, who had spent the night in this khan; also a company of Jews, among them some very handsome women, who had also passed the night in that filthy place. Oriental and Spanish women can do this sort of thing, and still look pretty, — look even like the painted rose.

It was two hours and a half after midday when we aroused our nodding train, and the Life Guardsman put himself again valiantly in the advance. The beasts had not been fed. It is a piece of Oriental cruelty to let working animals toil all day without food. The path was as rugged as it could be, and be a path, like the bed of a mountain torrent, up and down sharp hills and through desert ravines. The old bridle path up Mount Washington in its best days was not so bad. We went on miles and miles, stumbling and sliding over the rocks; and I had always before me that hateful bundle of soldier, with his capote down over his head, having only this one trait of a great soldier, that he was as silent as a fish. The only exclamation he made all the afternoon was when we came to the summit of a sharp ridge. Turning in his saddle, and pointing forward, he cried out, "Tetuan!" And there, over the intervening mountains, like a vision in the sky, was the fair town of our pilgrimage, lifted up on a mountain ridge, a long, white streak, white as chalk, and beyond it the sapphire blue sea. Even at this distance — and we must have been over fifteen miles away — the walls and houses of the town shone dazzling white, and hung in the sky like a city dropped out of heaven. Not so glorious for situation as the New Jerusalem, doubtless, but more glorious than the old Jerusalem from any point of view I ever beheld it. We were so elevated that the sea beyond it seemed close to its walls, and we did not know then that between the city and the sea lay a flat plain, at least six miles across.

Inspired by this glorious picture, we felt that we were almost at our journey's end: but the sight was like a cup of cool water presented to the lips of a thirsty traveler, and then withdrawn. The city disappeared as we plunged down the steep path, and it was weary hours before we saw it again.

The sun was getting low when we emerged into a windy plain, cultivated, and traversed by a considerable stream. Here were signs of life again: laborers on foot and on donkeys were moving over the plain, and groups of women and girls in white garments, idling by the stream, told us that we were near habitations. On the spur of a mountain opposite appeared the white houses of a Moorish village. We must be near Tetuan at last. On this plain was fought the last battle between the Spaniards and the Moors, in the war of 1860-61, and before the capture of Tetuan. I urged the Old Turtle over it at a livelier gait, much against his will. We crossed a substantial bridge with Moorish arches, turned the spur of the mountain that we had been approaching for hours, and again beheld Tetuan, a long, white mass on its hill, apparently close at hand. In a few moments we should enter its white gates, and, thanks to the protection of our dollar-a-day Moslem knight, be safe from the numerous wild boars, monkeys, hyenas, jackals, gazelles, and ostriches promised us as sure to be encountered on the way, by the guide-book, — none of which, owing to our protector, had put in an appearance. The plain on which we had now entered, a rich bottom land, watered by a winding river, and inclosed on every side by high mountains, seemed one continuous wheat field, — an emerald in a gray setting. Here and there on the hills to the right were white villas, and at the southern end the white town rose beautified in the slanting rays of the sun.

The plain proved of vaster extent than we supposed. Our road along the hillside was far from level. We descended into gorges and emerged again, we caught sight of the town and lost it again and again, until, in our weariness, it seemed a very will-o'-the-wisp of a city, shown to us and removed by the enchantment of a genius. It was over an hour and a half from the time of striking the plain that the road became so cut up and utterly abominable that we knew we must be near a large city. We were now involved in cactus lanes, and splashing along through muddy pools; crowded and jostled by laborers and donkeys, and herds of cattle and sheep being driven inside the walls for the night. Within the outer wall of all these Oriental cities and the first row of houses is usually a vacant space for the herding of cattle.

Ascending the last slippery slope, we found ourselves under the high city wall. Behind and above the town on the hill rose a harmless-looking citadel. On our left, projecting from the wall, was what is called a battery, which looked like a school-house with guns in the second story. We followed the wall to the right, and entered by a great gate, in which a lot of loafers playing soldier were lounging. They hailed us and ran after us, demanding an entrance fee; but we took no heed of their necessities, pushed on through the herds of cattle, entered, and crossed the big market square of the city, surrounded by shabby buildings and resembling a stock-yard, — a place humming with Oriental life, with whose fantastic squalor and picturesqueness all travelers in the East are familiar. We turned from this square into a narrow street, into other and yet other narrow streets, lined with little shops and dens where human beings labor and sleep, into a region swarming with life, swimming in grease, and over cobble-stone pavements slippery with refuse, into the quarter of the Jews, and alighted at the house of Isaac Nahon, Jew by religion, British vice-consul by title, keeper of a house of entertainment by occupation. O Tetuan, Tetuan, we said, that shone so white and pure in the distance, what a whited sepulchre you are!

But the street and the house of Isaac were clean. We were admitted (the mules, for a wonder, staying outside) into a house thoroughly Moorish in design, — a court in the centre, open up to the stars above, upon which all the rooms in all the stories looked. From the gallery on the second floor, upon which our rooms opened, we talked with the family in the court below, and held communication with the kitchen. Our rooms were long, narrow, and high, with little windows at one end (for these houses are built to exclude the sun), Moorish-arch doorways and hangings, and the walls ornamented with strips of the painted wood, cut in Arabic designs, for the manufacture of which Tetuan has a reputation. In the morning I was surprised to see how much light came in at my diminutive window, but the secret of it was explained when I looked out. All the houses are whitewashed; all the flat roofs, every inch of them, are whitewashed; and this reflected glare of the sun makes every room luminous to which a ray of light is admitted.

The charm of Tetuan, which is a city of about twenty-five thousand inhabitants, exists somewhat in the imagination. Only a little over half the people are Moors; there are resident here several hundred Spaniards, and some eight thousand Jews. But Tetuan is the city of Barbary most romantically connected with Spain. In every city of Andalusia is a street called Tetuan. Tetuan was in fact founded by the Moors when they were finally expelled from Granada by the religious zeal of Ferdinand and Isabella, — a loss of skillful artificers and chivalrous poetical people from which Granada has never recovered. The only things in Granada worthy of the traveler's interest are the reminiscences of the Moors. It is always said that the expelled Moors, who carried away with them such wealth as they could save from the rapacious Spaniards, and endeavored to reproduce their luxurious houses in Tetuan, expected some day to return to Granada and the Alhambra. We are told that their descendants to-day cherish the same hope, and that they preserve the title-deeds to their Spanish possessions, and the keys to their houses in Granada. I think the latter part of the statement is apocryphal. It is hardly probable that keys would be preserved hundreds of years, in the hope of using them, to houses that have not existed for centuries; and it is doubtful if the intelligent Moors of Morocco have to-day any higher ambition than getting what they can out of the government, escaping taxation, and living at ease.

When one sees the beggars and the commonplace and shabby condition of Spanish Granada, and regrets the expulsion of the Moors, he may perhaps give a new turn to his reflections by visiting Tetuan. What have the Moors done since they left Granada? Have they not retrograded in every art and refinement of life? Had the race not culminated in the splendor of the Alhambra? Had not the Moorish civilization run its natural career, and come near to its close at the time of the conquest? What have the Moors ever done since, anywhere, that has been of the least service to the world? Moors and Spaniards alike went into a decline after the brilliant epoch of the conquest and of discovery; and if Spain recovers, it will be owing wholly to the actual contact with modern civilization, which has been wanting to the Moors. If, when the Moors departed, the stately and luxurious Alhambra could have been locked up, saved from the destruction and the neglect of the Spaniards, and preserved to modern curiosity and intelligence, the traveler might be content, and regret neither the expulsion of the Moslems nor the occupation of the Christians.

The street where we lodged was, as I have said, clean; but it was very narrow, and the line of high whitewashed houses on either side, presenting a surface of solid wall broken only by small grated windows, was entirely Moorish in its character. Few other portions of the compact city were so clean. It was market-day, the day we spent in Tetuan, and the best occasion for seeing the country people and the life of the place. The open squares and streets of shops swarmed with buyers and sellers and calm waiters on Providence. The crowd had a certain picturesqueness, but it wanted the color of many Oriental populations, for the uniform dress is white, or dirty white and dirty brown, and of very coarse material. The exceptions are the Jews, who wear, as in Tangier, black skullcaps, and the few Moorish gentlemen and rich shopkeepers, whose voluminous turbans and amply flowing robes of spotless silk and linen present the true Oriental type of luxurious magnificence.

The guide-books are always beseeching the traveler to admire the Jewesses of Tangier and Tetuan. As these women go unveiled, it is easy to do so. They use color in their street apparel, a sort of broad embroidered bands worn longitudinally on the dress. Those past youth are usually rather gross in form and face, but the young women have regular features,— some of them a faultless form, fine eyes, and a good complexion; and all of them are many shades lighter than the men. A really handsome woman, however, is usually such a surprise to the traveler in Africa, as she is in Southern Spain, that he is apt to fall into an extravagance of gratitude for the sight. The Moorish women may be equally alluring, but they cover all of the face except the eyes. I noticed here, as I had noticed on the plain the evening before, that the women wore short leggins of red leather. These are survivals of the Roman *fasciæ*, and are exactly such as were worn by the Moorish women of Granada, as may be seen in a curious bas-relief representing the baptism of Moslem women, after the conquest, in the chapel of Ferdinand and Isabella, at Granada.

Tetuan has not many good shops, though it has in one quarter a nest of narrow streets lined with tiny rooms, just big enough to hold the dealer and his stuffs, and roofed over by trellises covered with grapevines, which will pass for a bazaar. It is a cool and agreeable retreat out of the glare of the sun and the dust and clamor of the market-squares, and it is a pleasure to sit down and bargain with a coolly dressed, regular-featured Moslem, who is in no haste to sell, and whose courtesy is rather that of the gentleman than the shop-keeper. These dealers have intercourse with Rabat, Fez, Timbuctoo, and other towns in the interior, and can offer you barbarous embroideries and other curiosities. Tetuan is famous, also, as a manufactory of red and yellow bags of the soft leather which takes its name of morocco from this country in which it is made. Part of the traffic on market-day is done by auctioneers, who carry their goods upon their arms, and push about in the crowd, asking for bids. They repeat continually their last offer, and sell only when their price is obtained. If the original bidder desires to raise his bid and compete for the article, he must follow the auctioneer. I believe the fellows are quite honest in stating the latest offer.

Tetuan is no more pleasing interiorly than any other Oriental town. It is a mass of lanes, abominably paved, and presents to the sight-seer only dead walls, with here and there a door. But looking up the narrow streets, we saw, above the flat roofs, the sharp mountain peaks, which seemed in the clear air very near, and reminded us of the situation of Innsbruck in the Tyrol. One might walk the streets forever, and have no hint of the luxury and even magnificence of the dwellings masked by the dead walls. The opening of a door, and the passage of a winding entrance, tiled and decorated, may admit one to an earthly paradise, — a palace amid gardens sometimes occupying an entire square. By the courtesy of the Spanish consul, whose residence and garden are of considerable extent in the heart of the town, we were taken to see some of the best Moorish palaces. For spaciousness, elegance, and sumptuousness there is nothing comparable to them in Tangier. One was a specimen of the best old Moorish houses: open courts with fountains, surrounded by light colonnades, and galleries above; cool recessed apartments, open to the air and the sight of falling water, and yet shaded from the sun, — apartments with the dado of slightly lustred tiles, the walls painted in toned colors, the ceilings of carved old wood, gilded and softly colored, furnished with divans and luxurious rugs. The courtly old Moor who showed us his apartments and did not offer to show us his harem, looked as if he had passed a long and useful life in voluptuous repose. As we went about the house — time had been given, while we waited in the vestibule to warn the women — we could hear scurrying of slippered feet, and there was a great opening and shutting of doors, through the openings of which we saw curious female eyes peering at the foreigners. But the proprietor did not think it necessary to hide from our view the numerous female slaves, who had charge of the children, or who were engaged in other domestic work. The house contained many delightful pieces of the old wood-work, ancient inlaid doors and latticed windows. The charm of the house was completed by a large walled garden, delicious to the senses with the odors of the orange, the lemon, the jessamine and the rose, and marble ponds and fountains of sparkling water.

Another Moorish house that we visited was quite new, and built and occupied by the late finance minister of the Emperor, whose finances had thrived, whatever had happened to his master's. The house was equal in extent and stateliness to the old one, but lacked the subdued taste in decoration. It was over-gilded and over-splendid, and its noblest apartments were incongruously furnished with French clocks, French chairs, rows of mirrors, and staring rugs. Yet one of its long and gilded apartments, notwithstanding its somewhat oppressive luxury, would be a charming retreat in the warm season. Through its arches on one side we saw the open-pillared court and the fountain, while from a row of windows level to the floor, on the other side, we looked over the vast extent of green plain to the blue Mediterranean, from which a refreshing breeze entered this abode of luxury, the owner of which probably never troubled himself with the query, Is Life Worth Living?

We ascended the hillside to the citadel, which commands the town. The city spread out below us, and was larger than we thought it when looking at it from without; and the entire prospect was one of the most interesting to be beheld anywhere. The uniform flat roofs of the entire city and its dazzling whiteness were broken only by a few towers and a dozen minarets, some of them octagonal and covered with green tiles. We stood upon the end of a long spur of the Riff Mountains. Fertile plains spread away on either side, bounded by the blue sea and by bold serrated hills.

When we descended the steep and winding streets we had a fleeting vision of beauty. From a high window, just large enough to frame her face, looked out a Moorish woman, with dark eyes of fascination and perhaps of sin; for no woman of a well-regulated harem will show her face to a man. If she was as handsome as she was painted, she was a dangerous person. The native women of Tetuan, our guide said, are famous for their beauty, and the town lends itself to adventure. Over the flat roofs one can with ease and security go all over the city, and the Moorish girls not seldom evade the watch of doors and windows, and cross the house-tops at night to keep appointments with their lovers.

Still descending, we encountered in a narrow street, for contrast, a funeral procession. The body of a woman, scantily wrapped in a white cloth, and resting on a light, rude bier, was borne upon the shoulders of men, who advanced at a rapid pace. The bier was followed by a motley procession of men and women, chanting a lament in an unearthly, shrill, minor key. The haste, the shabbiness, the mournful notes, were fit to wring one's heart, breaking in as they did upon the careless life of the buzzing streets, and it was long before the sad refrain passed out of our memory.

The house of Nahon, the Jew, was a pleasant place of shelter, in our brief stay. Although it is Moorish in style, and the iridescent tiles of the interior doorways recall the skill of another race than the Jewish, there is a Hebrew atmosphere throughout. On the side of the doorways to two of our rooms, I discovered a tiny recess, not more than three inches long and an inch deep. It contained a little roll of parchment, transcribed with Hebrew, and I remembered the injunction of Jehovah to this ancient people: Write my words on thy doorposts.

With our dessert at dinner we were served with a new confection, — orange blossoms cooked in honey. Nothing could be more appetizing in the sound than this truly Oriental sweetmeat; it tasted like sweetened turpentine. The house of Nahon, like other houses in the city, distills a great quantity of orange-flower water from the blossoms. The oranges of Tetuan are very large, fine of skin and firm of flesh, and delicious. After eating the sour fruit of Southern Italy and Sicily, one appreciates the luscious oranges of Malta and Barbary.

We were off at an early hour for Tangier, for we had before us the endurance of eleven hours in the saddle, exclusive of the noon siesta, over a route which had lost its charm of novelty. The Life Guardsman, whom we had not seen since he came in the morning after our arrival to kiss our hands, — a truly knightly hint for backsheesh, — turned up, smiling, after a day of repose from the actual hardships of war on the first day. But to our disgust, when he mounted and led the way out of town, we saw that his fiery military ardor had abated. He no longer wore his sword, — our sole dignity of appearance, — but had given it to the mule driver to carry. I had the curiosity to examine this weapon of war, upon which we had relied. It took the united and prolonged effort of the guide and myself to draw it from its scabbard, in which it was firmly rusted. I do not suppose it had been drawn before in all the wars our brave trooper had engaged in. With the sword in the hands of the mule driver, our martial appearance fell to zero.

We were five hours in reaching the Fondak. The Turtle had evidently made up his mind that his carcass should not be jolted by a trot in returning. The only new objects we saw during the morning were a species of bird, that kept close to the cattle in the plain where the natives were plowing. The Arabs call them cow-birds, because they always attend the cattle, as the crocodile-birds do the Egyptian saurians.

Before setting out, after our halt of one hour and a half at the Fondak, I insisted that the mules, who had drank nothing since morning, should be watered. The soldier refused to permit it, and moved off. I asked the reason, and was told that the beasts were too warm, and that they could be watered in the river, which was just ahead. Knowing that Orientals seldom give the true reason for anything, I asked again. The reply was that the water in the spring was too low, but they would get water directly. I could not see how the mules would be any cooler with more travel in the heat, but I was obliged to yield, although my animal was evidently distressed for drink. It was over an hour and a half before we reached the river, and there the animals had to drink from a stagnant pool. Why this cruelty was practiced, I could not understand.

When we set out from the Fondak we took a different route from the one we had come by. I inquired the reason, and the answer was that this route was shorter and better. It was the track I had noticed as diverging from ours, on the morning we left Tangier. I then asked where it led, and was told that it went to Tetuan, but that it was a longer and more difficult road! This was Orientalism, pure and simple. This return route, we found, was in fact an hour longer; it was hilly and stony, with hardly a rod of it that we could trot over. I have no doubt that our protector took this long and rough way out of revenge, because I had pushed his pace on the journey out, and because it was impossible to move over it faster than a walk.

I was never so tired of anything as I was of that soldier's back. But there is an end to everything, says the proverb, except the tongue of woman, and before sunset we came out upon the vast and lovely plain near Tangier. The western sky was flecked with light clouds of burnished crimson and gold. The broad fields of wheat waved green in many shifting shades, interspersed with patches of a yellow bloom, in the slanting rays. It was a marvelous effect of color. Long shadows were cast over the plain by the flocks of sheep, goats, and cattle, and the slowly moving groups of peasants, returning from labor to the Arab village on the hill, upon the roofs of which the storks were already perched for evening meditation. Good-by, lazy, picturesque Africa!

As we rounded the last ridge, there were the sea beach, the sands of gold burning in the light, the waves white-capped and racing before an eastern breeze, and, beyond, the purple mountains of Spain.

CHAPTER XVI.

ALONG THE SPANISH COAST.

To reach Cadiz from Tangier, it is usually necessary to go to Gibraltar, thus making two voyages on the strait. We thought ourselves fortunate, therefore, when a Spanish steamer came into port, one evening, bound for Cadiz. Passage was taken, and we were on board at seven o'clock in the morning. The steamer was a small tug-propeller, with a weak engine, an inclination to roll and pitch simultaneously, with that peculiar corkscrew motion that landsmen loathe, and absolutely no accommodation for passengers except a chance to lie on deck, or sit on the hatchway and hang on with both hands. It was a charming day; the wind west, the sky blue, with scattered white clouds sailing in it, and the coasts of Africa and Europe in sharp outline. When we got away into the strait, and began to feel the long swell of the Atlantic, nothing could be more inviting than the fair, indented Spanish coast, — the blue water lapping the white sand ridges, the shining cities and towers, the rolling hills behind; and yet, as we turned to look upon receding Africa, the green bluffs and white houses of Tangier, the mass of mountains rising into the snowy heights of the Atlas, we felt reluctance to leave it. Our reluctance was indulged. The dirty little tug, discouraged by the Atlantic waves, had no heart to drive on, but staggered about like a footman in a plowed field, unable to make more than five miles an hour. All day long we loafed along the charming coast of Spain, the sport of the waves, which tossed us and flung us; laughed at by the merry breeze, which dashed us with spray; cheered by the sun and the blue sky; wearied beyond endurance with trying to keep our seats on the slanting hatchway; diverted by the historic pageant, points, bays, watch-towers, and towns famous in wars and adventure. And we had time to study the shore; for "passing a given point" was not the forte of the little Pablo. It was often a matter of doubt whether we, or some town or point of which we were abreast, were going ahead. In this way we loitered along the low sandy lines of Cape Trafalgar, where the dashing Nelson, at a quarter past one o'clock on the 21st of October, 1805, received his death-wound. Inland a few miles is the Laguna de Janda, near which, in 711, Tarik, in a single battle, won Spain for the Moslems. All this coast has been fought over. Farther along to the west is the knoll of Barrosa, where the allied English and Spaniards barely escaped defeat in 1811. We are long in sight of San Fernandino, which we mistake for Cadiz, — a gay-looking city, straggling along the shore, distinguished by a great observatory, the southernmost on the continent of Europe. Abreast of it is La Isla de Leon, an island which masqueraded under half a dozen classic names, and is believed to be the place where the fat cattle which Hercules stole were fed. A different breed of bulls is bred on it now, for the ring. The island gets its name from the Ponce de Leon family, to whom it was for a time granted in the fifteenth century. The marshes here are celebrated for the production of salt, and delicious small crabs, — a most obliging animal, which grows its claws again after the epicures have torn them off and cast the crab adrift.

We stayed here, loitering over the waves, long enough for a crab to grow new claws. Cadiz was at last in sight, brilliant white over the blue sea, conspicuous with its hundred *miradores*. We thought our long agony was over. We drew near to Cadiz, we sailed along it, we kept on and on and sailed by it, and appeared to be making for another city across the bay, which we began to think must be the real Cadiz. But the fact was that we were beating entirely around the city to get into the channel that enters the harbor on the west side. For Cadiz is on a rocky peninsula, the shape of a ham, curving out into the ocean, and its harbor is on the narrow isthmus. This peninsula rises from ten to fifty feet above the sea, and white Cadiz, lapped by the blue sea on every side, is like the diamond setting of a ring in turquoise. Nothing certainly could be more brilliant than the coast picture as we saw it that afternoon: the white, jutting city with its strong walls and bastions, the dancing, sparkling sea flecked with lanteen sails leaning from the breeze, and the white sand of the curving shore twinkling in the sun. It was all life and motion.

There were ten hours of pitch and toss before the sluggish little tug anchored in the inner harbor, within the breakwater behind the town; and we lay there an hour longer, waiting the pleasure of the lazy officials. At six o'clock a sail-boat came off, with a health officer and an inspector, and after we were found to be in good health we embarked on the boat and sailed about the harbor for half an hour longer, tacking back and forth, before we could make the landing. Besides our company of four, the only other passengers were a Jew commercial traveler and a Tangier Moor with a box of live chickens. We made friends with the customs officer, gave him an exact list of our luggage, hand-bags and all, explained that we had only the ordinary baggage of travelers, and thought our troubles were over when we stepped ashore. Desperately tired, and hungry after fasting all day, we inquired for hotel porters, and thanked the officer for his courtesy. The dock loafers picked up our luggage and carried it across the quay a few steps, and deposited it in a musty shed with grated windows. We followed and entered, when the polite official informed us that we could go now. "It is finish."

"What is finish?" we asked, in astonishment.

"Finish, the baggage; you can't have it till morning."

"Can't have it? We must have it. We cannot go to the hotel without it."

"Can't help that; too late; inspector gone home."

"That's not our fault," we said; "you kept us waiting in the harbor an hour; and we must have our hand-bags at least — our night clothes and brushes and combs. You can see there is nothing else in the bags. This is simply barbarous."

"You can have them in the morning."

"But can't we take out what we absolutely need from the bags?"

"Nothing;" and the official turned abruptly away, and left us amid a pushing, jeering crowd of Spanish spectators, who were bent on exhibiting the native courtesy to strangers. I inquired for the American consul, and went in search of him, leaving the ladies seated on their baggage in the musty room, near a grated window. The crowd increased about the door and windows, and during the hour I was absent the ladies were the objects of the most insulting remarks. I found that the customs officials had a reputation for extreme incivility and no disposition to oblige travelers. The consul was prompt in his offers of assistance, and set out at once to see what he could do, but had little hope of extricating us from our difficulties that night. But when I returned, the appeal to the consul had had some effect, for we were permitted to take a hand-bag each and depart. It was nearly nine o'clock before we reached our hotel. To make the vexatious story short, it occupied us all the morning to get our handful of baggage free. The inspector did not appear till ten o'clock, and I owed our late deliverance to a young

English resident of the town, who dispensed the necessary coin to the officials and various impudent hangers-on, who put in preposterous claims, and got our baggage away to the railway station. "Your troubles have just begun," said our young friend; "the Spaniards hate all strangers, and you will find little civility."

This little experience of our entry into Spain was so contrary to my preconceived notions of the behavior of the "politest nation in Europe" that I have departed from my usual habit in regard to such annoyances of travel, and set it down. We learned afterwards that the self-conscious and provincial Spaniard has a peculiar way of showing his superior breeding.

Cadiz, though old, looks modern in its complete suit of whitewash, which is spread over every building, from basement to summit. Its narrow streets, flanked by high buildings, are clean, and it is well lighted and paved and pleasing to the eye. But it does not attract the sight-seer. We saw enough of it from the high old tower, La Torre de la Vigia, whence we looked upon the entire town, smokeless, dustless, whitewashed, with its flat roofs and picturesque look-out towers. Indeed, the peculiarity of the city is in these towers, or miradores, of which there are h .ndreds rising from the lofty roofs all around, each one with a little turret on the side. In the days of her commercial prosperity the merchants of Cadiz used to ascend these to look out for their laden galleons returning from the West Indies. They have the air now of being unused, and merely ornamental; the merchants of Cadiz have little to expect from the Indies, and I doubt if they often climb into the miradores to see the sunsets.

When the traveler has walked in the spick-span-clean streets, shaded by tall balconied houses in endless perspective, peeped into the *patios*, the centre courts of the houses, where flowers and fountains suggest family groups and the guitar, and strolled about the sea ramparts to inhale the sea breeze, he will have little to detain him in Cadiz. It boasts two cathedrals, both despoiled, and both renovated and unattractive. An idle man might sit a good while on the sea wall and angle for red mullet with a long cane, and enjoy it, watching meantime his fellow fishers the gulls. We went to the suppressed Capuchin convent to see the last picture Murillo painted, — the admirably composed and harmoniously colored Marriage of St. Catherine. The artist was on a scaffold finishing this picture — that was in 1682 — when he fell and received injuries from which he died shortly after in Seville. In the same chapel is another work of this master, St. Francis receiving the Stigmata, — a charming piece.

We left Cadiz without reluctance, yet I confess I look back upon it with some longing; it is so white and shining and historically resplendent. I wish the Romans or the Phœnicians were still there, or even the Moors. I cannot be reconciled that this sea-blown picturesque town is not more attractive. We went out by rail through interminable salt marshes, where the salt is stacked up like the white tents of encamping soldiers; keeping at first by the sea, and then still over level and barren plains, to ground slightly rolling, past Jerez, with its great whitewashed sheds, which are the famous *botegas*, or wine vaults, where the sherry is manipulated and refined; and so on, approaching the Guadalquivir over land as flat as a floor and extensive as a Western prairie, and as treeless, we came at evening to the last station before reaching Seville, eight miles distant, the poetically named Two Sisters, embowered in great orange gardens. The night was mild; we could see faintly the twinkle of dark shining leaves and golden fruit, and all the air was heavy with the perfume of the blossoms. It was the odor of the Spain of our fancy.

CHAPTER XVII.

A RIDE IN SPAIN.

WE were at Jerez, which is still pronounced as if the name began with an H, as it used to be when it began with an X; the universal substitution of J for X is the Spanish spelling reform of the last twenty years, — we were at Jerez, and wanted to go across the mountains to Ronda. My companion was an Oxford scholar, who was traveling from Oxford through the Church of England towards those fresh religious pastures which the modern faith of so many of the clergy of England expects to find in a future, when the creeds shall be adjusted to the changing religious perspective.

We were agreed to take a short ride across a region of Spain not much vexed by tourists, in search of the characteristic and the picturesque. The difficulty was to find means of conveyance; for Jerez was undergoing its annual three days' fair, and animals were not to be had for money, the only spring of movement or attention to a traveler's wants in Spain. The town was crowded and excited, the hotels charged double price, — as the Spanish hotels do on the least provocation, — and the owners of horses and mules were coining money, transporting people to the fair-ground, the races, and the bull-fight. The races on Saturday and Monday, and especially the bull-fights on Sunday, were the absorbing attractions of the week.

Jerez, which is dear to the world as the depot and factory where the Manzanilla and kindred sorts of grape-juice are manipulated, seasoned, and colored, and fortified into the various kinds of sherry, is ordinarily as dull and uninteresting, as modern and whitewashed, as most other Spanish towns. We had read in the guide-books a great deal about the *couleur locale* of this and that city of the Peninsula. Observation has taught us that the *couleur locale* of Spain is "whitewash." Houses, within and without, are whitewashed; churches are whitewashed; walls, and monuments, and fountained courts are whitewashed; heaps of stone on the highway for repairing the roads are whitewashed; everything, except the cactus hedges, the treeless hills, and the bulls, is whitewashed. Whenever the private owners of a delicious bit of old Moorish ornamental work in stucco can have their own way, they whitewash it.

It was Sunday in Jerez. In all the Sunday-schools the good children were saying, "What a sweet Sabbath day for a bull-fight!" The bull-fight was not to take place till the afternoon, — so carefully do these devout people separate their religion from their amusements. In this land, girls and boys are taken at a tender age to the bull-fights, in order that they may be accustomed early to the characteristic national pastime, and not be disgusted with the cowardly cruelty and the degrading spectacle when they arrive at years of discretion. Train up a girl in the way she should go, and when she is at the most effective fair age she will not depart from the arena so long as there is a noble bull to be tortured, and a two dollar and a half hack of a horse to be ripped open by his horns.

Our acquaintances in Jerez tried to convince us that our proper way to Ronda was the great railway circuit round by Gobantes, and thence by diligence. We replied that the one way we wished specially to avoid was the one by Gobantes. We adhered to this blind purpose, and failing to procure horses we took places in the old diligence for Arcos, and on Monday afternoon, at four o'clock, mounted our seats beside the driver, and set out over the arid plain of Caulina; leaving on our right the once magnificent monastery, the Cartuja, famous in old time for its fine cloisters and *patios*, or courts, its unrivaled collection of pictures by Zurbaran, its rich vineyards, and its breeding ground for Andalusian horses, — a properly conducted monastery could not well be celebrated for much more.

Our driver was a compact little man, round-faced and clean shaven, — as most of the Spaniards are, — taciturn to his kind, but very communicative to himself and to his horses. We had a team of five horses, two at the wheel and three leaders abreast, the latter driven without reins. I noticed that the two reins were attached only to the outside of the bits of the wheel horses ; the control of the team depended largely upon the driver's whip and the power of his lungs. The whip was always swinging and cracking in the air, and the driver called to his horses almost incessantly, and occasionally made them long addresses, which they appeared to understand. The harnesses were monstrous constructions of heavy, broad leather straps, ropes, and big collars ; the drawing-traces were ropes ; each animal had upon his headstall a string of bells. The diligence was a lumbering, rickety vehicle, which swayed and creaked. As soon as we were under way, with bells jingling, whip cracking, coach creaking ; the inside passengers, among whom was a smart *gendarme*, chattering ; the driver conversing with his cattle ; the dust rising in thick clouds that almost hid from view the hedges of cactus and aloes along the road, and made the crowd of laden donkeys, carriages, and big wagons like phantoms in a dusty dream, — when, I say, we thus got under way, at a speed, with all this noise and tumult, of probably little less than three miles an hour, we felt that we were actually in Spain. We had sixteen miles to go, and we made the distance in about five hours.

The road was a straight white line across the arid plain, a good specimen of the treeless, sun-baked wastes of Andalusia. Beyond were low hills, equally denuded of foliage ; but when, after a weary pull, we ascended among them, more green appeared, and large fields of grain, but sadly stunted and burned up by the long drought. We soon, also, came upon olive orchards among the rolling hills, but the general aspect of the country was desolate. Beyond the hills, however, we saw glorious mountains, and one majestic dome of rock, which I took to be the Pico de S. Cristoval, towering above the others. In the transparent air it seemed very near. The road, it must be said, was exceedingly well made, carried round curves, through cuts in the hills, and over embankments, like the graded track of a railway. Where roads are made at all, they seem to be thorough pieces of work, very different from our make-shift and ungraded highways for wagons.

At regular intervals on our route we encountered a couple of *gendarmes* posted by the roadside, a civil force to which I shall have occasion to refer again. We found two of them at the half-way posada, where we stopped to breathe and let the passengers "wine," — a good example of the Spanish inn of the country. This inn is principally a stable; but a part of the stable is partitioned off for the family, and another part for the refreshment room. Above seems to be a low garret. It appeared to be altogether a very decent place, for a stable, and the proprietor and his wife and daughters were civil. Spain is still the land of riding, and not of driving. After leaving the environs of Jerez, we encountered no wagon, but scores of travelers on mules, donkeys, and horses. A very good specimen of its *caballero* dismounted at the inn, — a resolute, square-riding man, on a powerful white horse, who rode as if he were mortised into his "Mexican" saddle, an embroidered *manta* strapped behind, and a gun in its leather case hanging perpendicularly behind the saddle.

There were no houses along the road, and only here and there one on a hillside, whitewashed, and commonly with a whitewashed wall about the premises. I suppose that those were *haciendas*, and that in English an *hacienda* would be a stable for mules and cattle, with family apartments above it.

All the region for miles and miles around Arcos is thickly planted with olives, which give a pleasing aspect to this hilly country. It was late twilight when we came clattering into the ancient town, and were set down at the house where the diligence stopped, which seemed to be presided over by three old women. We were surrounded at once by a curious and helpful population, all eager to seize our pieces of luggage and bear them to parts unknown. The driver, who was our friend, appeared to be having a conference with the old women as to whether they should have the plucking of us, or would send us to the regular posada, to which we wished to go. In the growing darkness it was impossible to see where we were, or where the posada was, and it required all our vigilance to keep track of our luggage. After a great deal of confusion, we found ourselves transferred, bag and baggage, to the posada, which was almost exactly opposite, in debt to half the loafers of Arcos for their valuable assistance. The posada, the best in the place, showed no sign of light or life. We entered the stables, and made our way up a stone staircase to the hotel apartments. No obsequious landlord or landlady welcomed us, but we at last discovered a tall, sour-faced maid-of-all-work, haughty and dirty, who condescended to show us a couple of clean but utterly bare little rooms, and undertook to get us something to eat. We felt humbly obliged. The stranger in Spain, at most inns and elsewhere, is treated as if the most acceptable thing he could do would be to take himself speedily out of the country. Our apartments were furnished with Spartan simplicity; the guest is allowed a washbowl, but no pitcher, and the water given him in the bowl is supposed to be quite enough for his needs; but the bed, though the mattress is made of uncomfortable lumps of wool, is scrupulously clean. Our repast was all that we could expect. The person who is fond of tasteless beans will find Spain a paradise. In this land of olives, those served on the table are bitter and disagreeable, and the oil, in which everything is cooked, is uniformly rancid. But it should be confessed that the oil is better than the butter, when the latter luxury is attainable. Something seems to be the matter with the cows. I do not wonder that the Spaniards are at table a temperate and abstemious race. It is no merit to be abstemious, with such food and cooking. The wine at Arcos, however, was a sort of Manzanilla, that made us regard any food with favor. It was a medicinal draught, with a very strong flavor of camomile; a very useful sort, I believe, in the manipulation of the market sherry, and exceedingly wholesome. So long as a man can drink this wine, he will not die. I should recommend the total abstinence society to introduce it into our country.

Cheered by our repast, we walked out to see the town. The moon was at the full; the night was lovely. On such a night a whitewashed town shines with dazzling splendor, and Arcos is picturesque even in daylight, especially in its situation. It lies on lofty hills above the river Guadalete, and in old times, before the final conquest, was a famous fortress. The horses bred in the plain below, and their fearless riders, gallop along in the spirited ballads of the time. It is called Arcos de la Frontera, because of its frontier position after it was taken from the Moors. During the wars of Granada it was in the possession of that gallant soldier, Roderigo Ponce de Leon, Marquis of Cadiz, whose wife, the high-spirited marchioness, was once beleaguered there by the Moors, when the most immense of grandees, Don Juan de Guzman, the Duke of Medina Sidonia, came to her rescue, and saved Arcos to the Christians, — a most gallant and Christian act on the part of the duke, for he and the marquis were hereditary enemies. We could make out by moonlight the convent and the tower that crown the two hills of the town, and from the esplanade in front of the Gothic cathedral we enjoyed a broad view over the plain of the Guadalete. The town must have been, in the old days, almost impregnable in its situation. We could fancy the fair marchioness of Cadiz on such a night, centuries ago, looking down from her watch-tower upon the Moorish camp, and expecting the rescue at the hands of Medina Sidonia.

The pensive night should have brought out the romance of Arcos, but, save the tinkling of a guitar here and there indoors, there was little sign of what is supposed to be the universal occupation of Spain. I fear that the lovers do not go about much at night-time with their guitars. Lovers we saw, at least youths in the attitude of lovers; but they trusted to their own natural powers of persuasion. The attitude of a lover in Spain is to stand motionless, hour after hour, at a heavily grated window. We saw one slim gallant in the position, when we set out on our walk, and an hour after he maintained the same impassioned, patient embrace of the iron grating. It would seem to be a safe sort of courtship, and as intoxicating as talking with a nun through the grille of her cell.

We had bargained the night before for a muleteer, two mules, and a horse for the baggage, and the sour-faced maid roused us at four o'clock in the morning. It is needless to say that the muleteer had the profitable end of the bargain, for the traveler has to pay for the privilege of associating with the proud and haughty Spaniard, — and all Spaniards are proud and haughty. I ought to except our friendly driver of the diligence, who seemed to feel a responsibility for our getting on safely. He came to our room before we went to bed, and shook hands with us, and patted us on the shoulder with something like affection, which was not all the offspring of the piece of silver we had given him.

His good-humored face expressed the most cordial interest in a fortunate journey for us. We could not exchange an intelligible word, for the few pure Castilian words we had picked up were not current with him; but I doubt if our mutual sympathy would not have been marred and less perfect if we could have talked with him.

To mount we came down into the stable, the perfume of which is "convenient" to all parts of the house, and found our cavalcade ready. Our mules were stout, lazy-going animals with comfortable saddles. The sun was scarcely free of the horizon when we descended the stony streets into the ravine between the two hills of the town. Early as it was, the morning market was already an active scene, bright with piles of oranges and heads of fresh green lettuce. All operations were suspended to see us pass down the valley, and our exit was hailed with mingled cries of admiration and derision.

The morning was lovely, the grass and foliage sparkled with dew, birds sang jubilantly in the hedges, and we set out with an exhilarated feeling of adventure and discovery. As we descended into and crossed the rich plain, and the river Guadalete, the town rose behind us in most picturesque magnificence on its hills, with its white houses conspicuous in the sun, grouped about the sheltering cathedral, and presided over by the ancient tower. Paths led in all directions through the vast plantation of olives. Most of the trees were very old, — the olive does not reach its best bearing till it is past thirty years, — gnarled and twisted, and many of them were mere skeletons of bark and decayed wood, not simply hollow, but showing the daylight through them, so that it was a marvel that they could stand. Yet they not only stood, — withered, tough, and ugly as the Spanish beggars, — but supported vigorous green branches. The trees were now in full blossom, and made a very pleasing show. Across this sweet valley of bloom and color and promise, the tortula (turtle-doves) were calling to each other in the accents of love and spring, and all the plain was vocal with the notes of the cuckoo. It was now the 2d of May. I do not know the habits of the bird in Spain, but I was reminded of the old English rhyme: —

> In April,
> Come he will;
> In May,
> Sing all day;
> In June,
> Change his tune;
> In July,
> Away he fly;
> In August,
> Go he must.

The country people whom we met urging their donkeys towards town saluted us gravely and without curiosity. "The salutation," said my companion, "reminds me of the saying of a — a — What was it he said, and where did he say it?" It reminded me of the same thing. All the landscape and the scene seemed the simulacrum of an old romance, the echo of an early dream.

As we mounted out of the plain, the country became still lovelier: it was still covered with olives; great wheat fields were brilliantly sown with scarlet poppies; the cactus hedges were in full blossom, of red and yellow; and the lustrous dark green aloes sent up splendid central spikes, twelve feet high.

Crossing a stony ridge, we entered extensive groves of cork-trees, large misshapen boles, often larger where the branches diverge than near the roots; bulging, distorted trunks, looking like a hospital of invalid trees. The donkeys we have met were laden with cork bark, and most of the trees had been stripped, some recently. The inner, remaining bark of these torn and abused veterans had a dull red color, that contrasted finely with the dark green of the branches. All the morning the mountain range we had marked at Jerez was in sight, and just ahead of us, and above all, hovered the rock dome, the purple height of St. Cristoval. After hours of travel towards it, it seemed just as distant as when we started.

Dwellings were scarce on the way: only here and there a white farm-house embowered in a plantation of trees. Usually, the houses had one door and no windows, at most a square opening to admit the air; and the centre room of the dwelling, to which the door gave access, was a mule stable. And it is only right that the donkey, who abounds in this region, should have the best place, for all the carriage and transport devolve on him. Herds of fine cattle were frequent, and springs and streams of clear water were abundant.

We passed one small salt-work, with a few vats. During the day we had been joined by several horsemen, who jogged on with us for some hours, and at last turned southward among the mountains, at a clear spring, with a large stone reservoir of solid construction. Before noon we were near El Bosco, or El Bosque, the village where we were to lunch, and its neighborhood was marked, as is the approach to all large places of Eastern origin, by worse roads, walls, cactus hedges, and a general Oriental appearance. But El Bosco is not Oriental. It is simply a clean, rudely-paved town of low whitewashed houses, without an architectural or other object of interest. We strolled into the parish church while our lunch was preparing, and found a bare interior, a few rubbishy images and pictures, and a discouraged priest, who said naïvely that the people were so poor that it was impossible to make the church like the cathedral at Seville.

At the clean posada, over the stable, we were served with a very good lunch, by a big, motherly, Connecticut sort of woman, who took such an interest in us that she showed us her large beds, and urged us to stay all night. We had bread, and eggs, and fried meat, and milk, and wine, and coffee, — everything the land afforded. The bread, after the fashion of this region, is made in small, white, and hard loaves, with twisted handles to carry them by, and on each loaf is plainly stamped its weight. If it is sold by weight, it must be expensive. The wine was a Manzanilla of an excellent quality, not nearly so strong of camomile as the Arcos sort. The motherly old Connecticut woman charged us thirty reals for our entertainment, which being translated is the large sum of a dollar and a half. That came of our reckless draught on the resources of the country. A Spaniard would have lunched for about two reals, and taken it out in bread and green beans.

An hour after leaving El Bosco, we came in sight of the secluded mountain town, Puerto Santa Maria. The road was more rugged and stony, and the country grew wilder at every step. We were, in fact, entering the fastnesses of the Serrania de Ronda, that jumble of mountains and hiding-places and obscure passes, renowned in the wars of the Conquest for border forays, retreats, and pursuits, and desperate hand-to-hand encounters of the Moorish and Christian chivalry, and in later days as the resort of the bandit and the contrabandista. On the water-course in the deep narrow gorge at our left were two or three small cloth factories, and long strips of the coarse brown fabric were spread on the rocks to dry.

Puerto Santa Maria is a white town of perhaps two or three thousand inhabitants, built on a ledge at the foot of Saint Cristoval. The centre of the town was a large open field of fruit trees and pasture, the houses ranged around it in an elliptical form. Perhaps this place was a survival of old communal times. The town was evidently poor enough, — poorer than El Bosco. I did not see a pane of window glass in the whole place. Glass is a scarce luxury in all this region.

We mounted through the town, and rose rapidly round the mountain side, ascending by an exceedingly steep and rough highway, which had once been well paved with large blocks of stone, laid sometimes, so sharp was the ascent, in steps. I do not know whether this solid path for horses was the work of Moors, or of Spaniards after the Conquest, but it is utterly neglected now. We had ascended into wide-spreading forests of stately oaks and ilexes, with an undergrowth of shrubs and gay wild-flowers. Occasionally a level bit of road gave us charming glimpses of open forest glades. On one side we looked down into the deepening gorge and over a jumble of mountains, and on the other up to the gray buttresses and walls of Saint Cristoval. We were on historic ground, which had been the scene and witness of one of the most stirring and bloody episodes of the wars of the Conquest.

It was in the year of grace 1483, after the overwhelming disaster to the Spanish knights in the mountains of Malaga, that Muley Abul Hassan, King of Granada, who had regained the city, and denounced his son, Boabdil el Chico, as a renegade, planned a plundering raid that should carry alarm and desolation into the fertile plains of Andalusia. He chose for its head old Bexir, the gray and crafty alcaide of Malaga. The rendezvous of the expedition was Ronda, the most pestilent nest of Moslem depredators. The fierce inhabitants of this belligerent city were then in command of Hamet Zeli, surnamed El Zegri, of the warlike tribe of the Zagories, a proud and daring warrior, an old campaigner, who knew every pass and cleft in the Serrania. His immediate attendants were a legion of fierce African Moors, mercenary troops, of the tribe of Gomeres. Trained to the hardships of rapid marches and sudden onsets, mounted on the swift and strong horses bred in the rich pasturage of the valley of Ronda, this cavalry was the terror of Andalusia.

The summons of Bexir to the foray were responded to by all the border chivalry, and soon a force of fifteen hundred horse and four thousand foot assembled within the walls of Ronda. In secret the preparations were made; in silence, and without tap of drum or clash of cymbal, the splendid host sallied out of Ronda, and entered one of the savage defiles of the Serrania. Many of the warriors had insultingly arrayed themselves in the rich armor of the Christian knights slain in the massacre of the mountains of Malaga, and some rode the Andalusian steeds captured in that disaster.

So craftily had Bexir concerted his plans and movements that he was confident of surprising the Christian towns. But, unfortunately for him, some Christian scouts, or marauders, hovering about in hope of picking up cattle or prisoners for the Christian market, saw the march of the host, and speedily spread the news in every direction. Among those who were warned was the Marquis of Cadiz and Luiz Fernandez Puerto Carrero, in command at Ecija. The result is well known. The Moors descended, in fancied security, into the plain of Utrera, and separated into bands for pillage. The hastily collected army of Christians took them by surprise in the rear, on the banks of the river Lopera, and there occurred, on the 17th of September, 1483, the famous battle of Lopera, in which the Moslem host was cut to pieces, and pursued with slaughter into the recesses of the hills. A large body of them fled southward to the Guadalete, where they were encountered and destroyed by the valiant Ponce de Leon, Marquis of Cadiz. But few Moors escaped the savage pursuit and slaughter. Great quantities of Christian armor, captured at the Malaga massacre, were retaken, and the marquis encountered and slew the Moor who rode the horse that belonged to his brother Beltran, one of the victims of the mountain slaughter.

Hamet el Zegri, the alcaide of Ronda, was raiding over the plain of Utrera gathering cattle, when he heard the noise of the fight on the Lopera and dashed thither with his handful of Gomeres. He was too late; his comrades were slain or scattered, and the Christians held all the passes of his retreat. There was in his little band, however, a renegade Christian, who knew a circuitous route through the enemy's country by which a pass in the Serrania could be gained; and under promise of a purse of gold if he conducted El Zegri in safety, and the threat of being cleaved to his saddle-bow if he betrayed him, the renegade guided the troop round about through the plain to a pass in the hills. At midnight they dodged under the walls of Arcos, crossed the Guadalete, and, by the very way that we had been traveling all day, effected their retreat to the mountains. They followed this same wild path that we were now leisurely pursuing. "The day dawned," says Irving, from whose brilliant pages I have condensed this narration, " as they made their way up the savage defiles. Their comrades had been hunted up these very glens by the enemy. Every now and then they came to where there had been a partial fight, or a slaughter of the fugitives, and the rocks were red with blood, and strewed with mangled bodies. The alcaide of Ronda was almost frantic with rage, at seeing many of his bravest warriors lying stiff and stark, a prey to the hawks and vultures of the mountains. Now and then some wretched Moor would crawl out of a cave or glen, whither he had fled for refuge; for in the retreat many of the horsemen had abandoned their steeds, thrown away their armor, and clambered up the cliffs, where they could not be pursued by the Christian cavalry."

As we toiled, still upward, around the mountain side the view opened, the ravine beneath broadened into a valley, with green fields and occasionally a house or two, and from the cultivated spots in the far deep, sounds of laughter and of labor came to us. Flocks of sheep and goats were picking about in the scant, green patches on the slope where we rode, tended by vigilant boys. One of the bright-eyed urchins, who might become a Pizarro, if Spain now had any occasion for heroes, had a hot conflict with the little foxlike dog which accompanied us. I suspect the dog had been insulting the sheep, and the boy pursued the cur, breathing forth maledictions and hurling stones, up and down the rocks, and back and forth, for fifteen minutes. No steeps or sharp stones daunted the boy, who had stern death in his eye. The dog escaped, at last, with a wound in his breast, but my sympathies were altogether with the young shepherd. A good David has no doubt gone to waste in him. He had the gift of song, the wailing monotonous strain of the Orient. All day long the singing of men at the plow, or women in their houses, or children at play, was of the purely African sort.

The prospect opened more grandly as we rose. At one time we looked, through the openings in the mountains, westward beyond Jerez, and southward to the region of Gibraltar. The great valley, whose side we were ascending, was closed by a sharp divide that ran from St. Cristoval to the jagged range opposite; it was the height of the pass, and we climbed it with intense curiosity to see what it would reveal. Our anticipations were exceeded. We were by the barometer something like thirty-one hundred feet higher than Arcos, but the view was one belonging to a greater altitude, and such as one chances to see not often in life.

To the westward, the eye ranged over mountains to the sea beyond Cadiz, fully sixty miles away. At another time of day the water would not have been visible, but the sun struck it so that a long expanse of the Atlantic shone along the horizon with the brightness of silver. Before us, to the eastward, and precipitously below us, the prospect was more varied and striking. We looked into a great valley, but a valley diversified with sharp peaks of rock, and set about with high-running mountain ranges. In the middle foreground was a shattered mountain of stone; below it, on either hand, the green of trees and meadows; and beyond all, on a mountain plateau, what seemed to be the level walls and shining houses of a large city. We could scarcely believe that it was not, but the muleteer insisted that it was only a peculiar formation of rock, and the shifting light soon convinced us. Upon each side of this gorge before us, descending as if to a focus, swept the jagged rocks of the boundary ledges, broken into towers and bastions and pinnacles. It was a scene of mingled beauty and sublimity. As we stood there, a hawk sailed about, close to our heads.

As we descended several hundred feet by a treacherous path of loose stones, and turned the corner of a ledge, a still more wonderful sight greeted us. It was the city of Grazelema, directly beneath us; a town of ten thousand people, with compact white houses, tiled roofs of reddish-brown, irregular streets, two or three church spires, and a cathedral mass, lying in a stone bowl of the gray mountain, which towered behind it, and held the city from the valley below as if in a dish.

A RIDE IN SPAIN. 219

At the distance we stood above it, the green fields below seemed close to the city; but we found when we descended, next morning, that it is really high up above the valley. Grazelema was a surprise to us, and we declared that it alone was worth two days of mule-back to see. My companion, who had been a wide traveler in the known places of Europe, Asia, and Africa, but believed that he never before had been off the lines laid down by the ubiquitous Murray, was delighted to visit a place not mentioned in the guide-book.

The sun was still above the horizon when we rode down, down, through the clean and roughly paved streets of the city, and ran the gauntlet of stares and comments of a population unaccustomed to the sight of foreigners. But we had long ago ceased to expect civility in the demeanor of Spaniards toward strangers, and certainly did not expect it in a place so remote as Grazelema, where curiosity is added to dislike. The town is clean and apparently thriving, though what it thrives on, there among the rocks, and with no communication with the world except by mule paths, we could not imagine. Many of the houses had pretty balconies, gay with flowers; glass in the windows was more common than in other mountain towns we had passed; and here and there an open door gave view of a neat *patio*.

The national costume has pretty much vanished from Spain, but we saw some relics of it here in the dress of the men, especially the young bucks and *majos*, some of whom still affect the dress now usually seen only on the lower class. Its peculiarity is a short, plain jacket, a broad, red sash about the waist, and a round black felt hat, with a broad brim turned up about the low crown, like a saucer with a cup turned over in it.

The women, who were sitting in the door-ways, or taking the air in the streets, with the lace mantilla over the head and the incessant fan in hand, were the most comely we had seen. With well-made and elastic figures, regular and finely formed features, and large dark eyes, they have not the pasty skin of the Andalusian beauties; and their complexion is not a matter of powder and paint, but clear and light in hue, and only slightly olive, with the red blood of virtuous health shining through. I am delighted to pay these prepossessing women this compliment, in return for their attention to our unprepossessing cavalcade.

Our muleteer took us to the best posada in the city. From the neat and thriving appearance of the place we were led to expect excellent accommodations; much better, said our muleteer, than at El Bosco. I do not know what a Spaniard's notion of good quarters is, but this posada was not built for anything above the refinement and aspirations of a mule. We entered the usual stable, a place that would delight a farmer in search of fertilizers, and climbed up the broken stone stairs, through the reek, to the apartments above. After some search, we roused an ancient crone, who hospitably offered us the best the house afforded. The room that I obtained was a small chamber with a stone floor, and it did not take me long to make an inventory of the furniture. There was a cot bedstead with horse-blankets, but clean sheets, a tripod with a wash-bowl, and a chair. I forget: the room had a good coat of whitewash. The window was a small opening, without glass, and an iron grating outside; when I shut the wooden blind, the only method of closing the window, the room was totally dark.

When, after we were installed, we approached the kind old woman on the subject of something to eat, she seemed a little surprised that anything of that sort should be expected of an inn. There was no milk to be had at this time of night, nor in the morning: milk was only to be procured about noon. She could send out and buy some meat, if it was absolutely necessary, but it was late. As to bread, the old entertainer's face brightened up at once; bread, certainly; wine, yes; perhaps eggs; may be cheese. We were reminded of a dialogue, which Gautier quotes, in a Spanish inn: —

Traveler: "I should like to take something."

Landlord: "Take a chair."

Traveler: "I should like something more nourishing."

Landlord: "What have you brought with you?"

Traveler: "Nothing."

Landlord: "Well, the baker is down the street, there, and the butcher is just round the corner."

While our provident hostess was looking for a hen's

nest, we sallied out to view the town. It is as neat as whitewash can make it, has several large churches, a spacious public square, and better houses than one would expect to see here. The plaza was a genuine surprise for its size, smart appearance, and animation. The oblong centre, elevated slightly, and surrounded by a low parapet, is the place of promenade and of shows. At one end is a lofty church, and at the other a prosperous jail. This institution is contrived for the pleasure as well as the detention of criminals; the barred windows open upon the square, and the prisoners on the ground-floor were chatting with their friends. Our advent was received with marked attentions. The young *majos*, or loafers, decorated with the black saucer hat and red waist-scarf, who were lounging about the prison end of the square, or leaning against the door-posts, bestowed upon us scowling and suspicious glances; people crowded to the doors, to stare at us; women, seated before their houses, or promenading in groups of three or four, nudged each other and laughed; and a crowd of unmannerly boys followed us about, and inspected us with undisguised interest. As we crossed the plaza towards the church, we were struck by a few pebbles; but they were small pebbles, and the boys ran to a safe distance when we turned around. Perhaps they were only trying to attract our attention, and see what a new kind of human being would do when excited. Boys are much the same the world over, and we bore them no malice; indeed, we could not take in ill part a performance that seemed to entertain their haughty and courteous elders. Besides, we were by this time so accustomed to Spanish civility that we did not mind it. I have no doubt that if we had been familiar with the language, and dressed so as to pass for Spaniards, we should have been spared these delicate attentions. The people of a shop into which we stepped were certainly polite. It was the only shop in which we saw anything characteristic of the country. The articles for sale were blinders of mule bridles, and saddle cloths embroidered in worsted of vivid colors and staring patterns. The Spaniards are fond of this sort of decoration.

But the glory of this bright plaza is its situation. Above it, and almost overhanging it, is a mass of gray rock, nearly perpendicular, and rising, I should think, a thousand feet. Its color is superb; I have seen nowhere else such a mass of solid mountain of anything like this lovely gray color. It is gray, and yet upon its surface, in patches, is a light green lichen that serves to bring out the gray. The terrace above the town, to the right, is strewn with enormous bowlders. The mountain seems to threaten to crush the city, which it holds in one of its rocky bowls. Half-way up the side of the gray precipice is a large white church; a pilgrimage chapel, I suppose. I could see no path leading to it along the cliff, nor could I discern how it held itself there against the mass of rock, on which it seemed to hang like a bird-cage on the wall of a house. But of course it had a sufficiently broad ledge for a resting place.

It rained in the night, and it was still drizzling when our muleteer called us at five in the morning; but a day in this dark and foodless posada was not to be thought of. The landlady made us some beverage which in Spain, as well as in France, is called coffee, — it was six hours too early for milk, — into which we dipped our hard bread; and thus refreshed, after paying our hostess a dollar and forty cents for the pleasure of her society and our stable accommodations, we mounted, and rode down the slippery streets into the valley. We then saw in what a mere eagle's perch the city lay. The clouds soon broke away, hanging in heavy masses about the mountain peaks, and disclosing to us superb views, as we ascended the opposite hill. The road was bad, but the views and the country made amends. Our way all the morning lay through woods, openly planted, — great forests of oak, ilex, and cork. The mountain sides were gay with cistus, a shrub not unlike the oleander in appearance, with large white single blossoms having yellow stamens, — a show as beautiful as a laurel mountain side in New England in spring. Mingled with it were patches of the yellow gorse and broom, the poet's asphodel, and a hundred wild flowers besides. After a long climb, we emerged upon a large breezy plateau, like an English park, and, crossing this, descended by a steep path into a cultivated valley, and struck a well-graded highway leading into the basin of Ronda.

The muleteers we met on the way, and all the men and women whom we met during our ride, returned our salutation with the uniform phrase, "Va usted con Dios." Literally it is, "Go you with God," and I fancied it had a slightly different signification from "God go with you," or our "God be with you"— good-by. For does it not imply that it will be well with you if you go with God, and not otherwise, making your welfare depend upon your free choice?

The great highway was not yet finished, though parts of it were old, as if it had been a long time building, and was not used except for riding. I suppose the road is really in advance of the demands of the people, who seem not yet to have come to the wheel age; they are still in the horse age. We saw no wheeled vehicles in this region till we left Ronda, and then no private carriages; nothing but the diligence and big goods-wagons. Yet this highway is splendidly built, and graded as if for rails. It winds down through a lovely defile, wooded and watered by a clear stream. We jogged easily down for miles, until it emerged and swept down the mountain side in long curves, opening to us the valley, the rocky hill in the centre of the valley on which Ronda stands, and the mountains which hem it in on every side.

It was doubtless up this mountain defile that the shining and confident troops of the wary Bexir and the fierce Hamet el Zegri took their way that September morning, unconscious of the bloody reception that awaited them on the banks of the Lopera. It was from the cliffs yonder that the marauding scouts looked down and beheld the Moslem army, bearing the standards of the various towns and the pennons of the well-known commanders, clad in velvet and steel, and flaunting their caparisoned steeds and costly armor, stealing up this rocky way, without sound of drum or trumpet, or clash of cymbal. Already the fierce Gomeres of Ronda, curbing their prancing steeds, anticipated the descent into the rich plains of Andalusia, the scene of so many productive forays. Vanished is all this pageantry. Never more will these defiles brighten with a like warlike array. As we move along down the easy grade, the only cavalcade we meet is one of laden donkeys, and instead of a war-cry we hear only, Va usted con Dios.

The situation of Ronda is vaunted as one of the most picturesque in Europe. It is on the top of a long, sharp-backed mountain, cut off from the mountains around it by a deep valley. The prospect from it is extensive and fine, but its boldness seemed a trifle tame after the region we had passed. The peculiarity of the town is this: that the old Moorish quarter occupies the south end of the hill, and is cut off from the modern town by the Tajo, a gigantic rent in the rock, some two hundred feet wide, and three hundred and fifty feet deep. Across this chasm a noble modern bridge has been thrown. The old town was not only defended by this chasm, but there was no approach to it, up the precipices which surround it, except at the south end of the hill, which was guarded by a strong fort. Before the invention of artillery it was of course impregnable. The portion of the city built on the north part of the hill is higher, and commands the old town.

But no part of the town is now old. It is all thoroughly modern and uninteresting, and the place is only worth visiting on account of its historical associations and its picturesque situation. There are only two objects that will detain the sight-seer. One is the pretty Alameda and rose garden in the new town, from the parapet of which you look sheer down the precipice of rock, nearly a thousand feet, into the green valley, and off upon the lofty mountain peaks and wild passes to the west. It is a favorite place of promenade for the inhabitants at sunset; and although the day we were there was showery and cold, a number of idle cavaliers in long cloaks — which are still the country fashion in Spain — were pretending to enjoy it, and several priests, in broad-brimmed black hats, were promenading in twos and threes, like devout ravens. The other sight is the Tajo, or chasm. Under the pavement of the bridge itself is a city prison, and by leaning over the parapet the visitor can see the grated window out of which the prisoners look down, as he does, into the abyss. The place would seem to be a secure and cool summer residence. At the bottom of the chasm flows a considerable stream, which rises in the chasm itself, and is used now, as it was in the time of the Moors, to turn several little mills, which nestle under the rocks.

We descended into the Tajo, on both sides of the bridge, and slid about on the slippery stones and amid the city sewage with true antiquarian zeal. We looked at a dirty pool said to have been cut out of the solid rock by Christian slaves in 1342. Above it is a wooden door, opening to a staircase in the rock leading up to the house of the Moorish king, built in 1042. It was by this secret way that the inhabitants procured water when they were besieged. I suppose that it was this source of supply that the Marquis of Cadiz discovered and stopped, when he captured the city, in 1485.

The capture was a surprise. Apprehending no danger to his impregnable perch, old Hamet el Zegri, since the Christians were engaged in the siege of Malaga, had taken his Gomeres for a refreshing turn in Andalusia, and was returning from a satisfactory raid into the rich lands of the Duke of Medina Sidonia. As he came with droves of cattle and flocks of sheep through the Serrania and approached Ronda, he was startled by the roar of artillery. Spurring his horse to an eminence overlooking the plain, he beheld the Christian army encamped about the city, with the royal standard of King Ferdinand displayed, the devoted town enveloped in smoke, and shaken by the incessant discharge of the heavy guns. El Zegri smote his breast, and cried with rage, in vain; in vain he tried to cut his way through the beleaguerers with his fierce Gomeres; in vain he kindled watch-fires and summoned the mountaineers. The camp could not be forced, and the siege went on, its handful of warriors defending it with the heroism of desperation. The valiant alcaide was impotent to aid them. "Every thunder of the Christian ordnance," writes Irving, " seemed to batter against his heart. He saw tower after tower tumbling by day, and various parts of the city blazing at night." " They fired not merely stones from their ordnance," says a chronicler of the times, " but likewise great balls of iron, cast in moulds, which demolished everything they struck. They also threw balls of tow, steeped in pitch and oil, and gunpowder, which, when once on fire, were not to be extinguished, and which set the houses in flames. Great was the horror of the inhabitants: they knew not where to fly for refuge; their houses were in a blaze, or shattered by the ordnance; the streets were perilous from the falling ruins or bounding balls, which dashed to pieces everything they encountered. At night the city looked like a fiery furnace; the cries and the wailings of the women between the thunders of the ordnance reached even to the Moors on the opposite mountains, who answered them by yells of fury and despair."

I can believe all of that except that the women's screams could be heard on the distant mountains. However, Ronda fell, never more to be regained by the Moors, and the chains of the Christian captives, rescued from its dungeons, were hung upon the church of San Juan de los Reyes, in Toledo, where they may be seen to-day. Ronda is reputed a salubrious place, and productive of octogenarians. "The ladies," says the Guide Book, which is worthy to be called a guide to the female beauty of Spain, " are as fresh and ruddy as pippins." We did not see many of these pleasing pippins, but they doubtless all appear in full bloom once a year, at the annual May bull-fights. The bull-ring is an ancient building of stone, and superior in solidity to any other we have seen. The Rondañas pride themselves on their good apples and pears, rosy women, and superior horses, and the fair and bull-fights in the last of May have a more than local celebrity.

The inn-keepers of Spain are ready arithmeticians, and have nothing to learn in the way of their business except how to keep a hotel. In their bills they cleverly unite the European and American systems. They charge a round sum per day, and then embellish the account with ornamental extras; and their method of reckoning time is peculiar. We arrived at the Ronda posada at eleven o'clock one morning, and departed at nine o'clock the next morning. Our bill was made out for a day and a half. Breakfast is not included in "the day."

We attempted to reason with the landlord. I said:

"So you think that is right?"

"It is our custom."

"I am sorry. Not for myself. I don't mind it. I am a mere traveler, and shall soon pass away from Spain — if the hotels leave me money enough to get out of it. But I am sorry for Spain. For no country can rise in civilization whose people call twenty-two hours a day and a half."

The landlord gave a deprecatory shrug for the future of his country, and stretched out his hand for the money.

Ronda's communication with the world is by diligence to the railway at Gobantes, nearly thirty-five miles. A critical assembly of boys, loafers, and beggars is collected to see the start. The baggage is secured on top; the passengers take their places; we ascend the ladder to our seats in the coupé above the driver's box; the horses are brought out, — two horses, four horses, six horses, eight horses, half of them mules, clad in heavy harness, and all jingling bells; the conductor mounts to his seat, grasps the two reins of the wheel horses, and swings his long whip; the postilion, as the team starts, vaults into the saddle of the near leader without touching the stirrup, a cool light-weight in shirt-sleeves, with a short whip, and a horn slung at his side; the supplementary driver, who also has a short whip, runs beside the team to excite it for the start and then springs up beside the conductor. We are off; three whips cracking, bells jingling, conductor, postilion, and driver shouting, horn tooting, as we turn the street corners, and away we go at a pace of seven miles an hour over a smooth turnpike, on an exhilarating morning. There are few pleasures in life equal to this.

The gait struck at first is maintained without change, up grade and down grade, through cuttings, round long curves, over the rough stones of newly mended places, — a trot unbroken for an instant during the first stage of twelve miles. The postilion squarely sits his saddle, and directs the team; the conductor swings his long whip occasionally, but rarely utters an ejaculation; the business of the supplementary driver is to do the talking to the team. He talks incessantly, calls the horses by name, shouts peculiar wild cries of encouragement, makes long speeches. The conductor is too dignified a person to waste himself in this gabble; but on an unusual grade, over a newly stoned stretch, the voices of the three drivers are required, and the team is kept up to its slapping pace only by frantic appeals and talk enough to get a bill through Congress.

The road is superbly made. Every three miles there is a white station-house, in which the road-repairers live, with *Peonas Comineros* written over the door. The road-makers are in uniform. Red is a favorite color with them, — red sashes and red facings to their coats. Portions of them are at work all along the line. Other houses beside these stations are not seen. The country, wholly denuded of trees, is broken into rolling, irregular hills, cut with deep ravines, bristling with sharp, rocky peaks. We are always sweeping round curves, circling ravines, ascending long stretches of road, from which we have superb views of distant mountains. The soil is deep red; the hill-tops and ledges seaming the sides are of gray rock; the cultivated spots in high valleys are vivid green: and we get some splendid effects of color, patches of red, green, and gray, mingled in harmony by distance.

At La Cava, a whitewashed little village in a valley, we change horses; nine in the team, this stage. At the posada in one end of the stable we all take coffee, which is as good as you could expect in a stable. We change again at Peñas Rubia, or Red Rock, taking its name from a mountain of red stone that overlooks it. We change again at Teba. Except for these villages, the region we passed through is houseless.

At intervals of five miles along the route we encountered two *gendarmes*. They always stood in the same attitude, one on each side the road, facing the coach, and presenting arms. We saw them in this position a long distance off. They maintained the same immovable attitude as long as we were in sight. These men belong to the *Guardias civiles*, which is the most remarkable and effective body of police, perhaps, in the world. This guard was organized in 1844, and is composed of 20,000 foot and 5,000 horse guards, all picked men, selected from the army and the cadet college at Madrid, for high character as well as physical perfection. They are tall, well-made, fine-looking fellows, and remarkable for their *esprit de corps*. They wear a picturesque and becoming cocked hat, their uniform is blue, with buff belts and straps, and they carry the Remington rifle. Two of them are stationed in every small town and village, and in barracks on every highway, and squads in every large town. They patrol the roads, meet every train at every station, and perform the duties of police with such effect that robberies are rare and seldom undetected. It is due to this alert, well-disciplined, self-respecting body of men that order and security exist in Spain, and the country is safe for travelers. The body has a weekly periodical of its own; it is governed by minute and severe rules, and is animated by something of the spirit of devotion and knightly pride that characterized the soldiers of Loyola. We had encountered these men all the way from Arcos. We had met couples of them mounted in the most lonesome mountain passes and forests. They were always neat, always civil, alert. If Southern Italy and Sicily had such a body of guardians, the robbery and brigandage which disgrace people and government would cease.

At two o'clock we dashed into the insignificant little railway station of Gobantes. Our exciting ride was over. The lively postilion approached, hat in hand, for a peseta. The conductor gravely commended us to God. As we ate our lunch in a mean posada, our minds ran back over the region through which we had been whirled, mostly barren, except for the patches of wheat and vetch, now and then a small olive plantation, or a line of slender trees and bushes by some feeble stream. The prevailing impression was of a wide, open, windy sweep of desolate, treeless land. But for four days, at least, we had been in Spain.

CHAPTER XVIII.

THE ALHAMBRA.

FORTUNATELY for my readers and myself, detailed descriptions of the palaces of the Alhambra, and plaster casts of its courts and decorations, are so common that I am relieved of duty in that respect.

And thanks to Washington Irving, one inherits without effort all the romance of the place. He is in some sort the *genius loci ;* the guides show the apartments he occupied, and American travelers like to sit in the arched window of the hall of the ambassadors and look down into the valley of the Darro, or lounge by the fountain in the orange garden of Lindaraja, places where Irving liked to dream and to reproduce from old chronicles, or the lips of the gossips, the ancient Moorish legends ; his guide and romancer, Matteo Ximenes, who died only two years ago, is represented by his son, who calls himself the grandson of the Alhambra, as his father was its son, and is as proud of his connection with Irving as he is of the supposed family relation to Cardinal Ximenes ; the dwellers in the house of Tia Antonia like to tell that she lived there, because she was Irving's housekeeper ; and the neighborhood cherishes a certain tender interest in the charming little Dolores, because Irving was fond of the child, the Dolores who married the surgeon, and was years ago turned into dust.

I suspect that the elements of romance still exist among the inhabitants of the Alhambra precincts, if Irving were only here to idealize the plain and simple life. A certain freedom of vagabondage is gone, since the government has taken the once deserted palaces and gardens in charge, and swept and garnished them, locked up many apartments, and put the halls and crumbling towers in charge of custodians.

Within the Alhambra inclosure, that is, within the circuit of the walls of the hill, there is considerable unoccupied ground, and quite a little village of small houses and gardens. Whether their occupiers originally were "squatters" without title, I do not know, but the premises are now owned by private persons. The governor of the Alhambra, who has made many restorations within the palaces, occupies a house, a part of which is Moorish, and a portion of his establishment is devoted to the reproduction of the stucco decorations, and the manufacture of the models which are now seen in all parts of the world. It must be a very profitable trade. The governor's garden, is a narrow terrace, backed by the high walls of the inclosure of the old Vela tower. This wall is draped with ivy and rose climbers, and against it are trained orange and lemon-trees. Three of these orange-trees, the gardener says, are two centuries old. The effect of this wall of glistening green, enlivened by the globe of yellow fruit, and the roses, red, buff, pink, and crimson, is exquisite. The garden is in fact one of the loveliest places in the world. Thrust out, as it is, on the point of the rocky ledge of the Alhambra, it commands a prospect almost unparalleled. Looking over the low parapet, you have immediately beneath you the great Elm forest, farther down the wide-spread city, to the right the extensive Vega, a green plain through which you can trace the bed of the winding Genil, and on the left, beyond the mass of trees, and beyond the first range of purple mountains, the long sharp range of the Sierra Nevada, with its remote snow fields, like silver under the blue sky.

Looking down upon the Vega, and the hills some thirty miles away that hem it in, you can re-create the scene of the final siege before the capture of Granada. Through that pass the army of Ferdinand and Isabella poured into the plain. There they spread themselves over the smiling meadows, set up their shining camp, and planted their standards. There are the remains of the city of Santa Fé, which they raised as if by enchantment after the conflagration of their camp. There were the Moorish gardens, in which the Moslems fought, foot by foot, for the retention of their paradise. This tower of the Vela above us was the ancient watch-tower. There hangs the silver-toned bell which the Moslems rung as a signal to let on the waters for the gardens and the fountains, in the city below, the sound of which it is said could be heard as far as Loja, thirty miles off. The maiden who strikes it now is sure of a husband before the year is out, and of a good one if she rings loud enough. On certain *fête* days the women make it lively for the bell. On that tower floated the old Moorish standard, which was pulled down at the conquest, and there Ferdinand and Isabella, who watched in the plain below for this sign of surrender, saw with exulting hearts the unfolding of the banners of Castile and Aragon, which assured them that the coveted Alhambra was theirs.

Among the chief charms of the Alhambra are the groves and the waters. Outside the Alhambra walls are the slopes and ravines that were the gardens of the palace-fortress. We enter them from the city below, by an ancient gateway, and through three broad paths and roads that lead up to the entrance of the Alhambra inclosure. These gardens are now an immense grove of elm-trees, the originals of which were sent out from England by the Duke of Wellington. Whether the trees were thickly planted, or were self-sown, I do not know, but they stand now closely together, and form a forest thicket, making a dense shade. In the course of three quarters of a century they have become large trees, and standing in such thick array, have shot up to a great height. It is a magnificent grove. Falling down in cascades from the height of the Alhambra, the waters run in swift streams beside the roads and paths. The forest abounds in birds, and their singing mingled with the music of the leaping waters, and the sunlight sifted through the green canopy upon the tall stems and the undergrowth, make an enchanting scene. In the edge of this wood, under the walls of the inclosure, are the two hotels, the Washington Irving and the Siete Suelos, the latter so named from the Tower of Seven Stories above it. It was through this tower that Boabdil descended when he went to meet Ferdinand and surrender his kingdom.

The Alhambra promontory is one, and not the highest, of the spurs that make down into the plain between the rivers Darro and Genil. It was only a barren and rocky projection. The Moors by their taste and genius transformed it into the most luxurious and charming abode in the world. From the mountains by several conduits they brought down abundant waters. There were fountains along the hill-sides, there were fountains, ponds, and baths in every part of the palace and gardens, and the overflow descended into the gardens and the plain below in fertilizing streams. You can hear now, as you walk about the inclosure, the pleasant noise of water running under ground. Many of the conduits have become stopped up, and the palace fountains, which were always bubbling in Irving's time, and add the last charm to the lovely interiors, now only play on rare occasions. The Spaniards have had neither the taste nor the energy to keep open the channels that the Moors created with so much loving labor.

The inhabitants of the Alhambra grounds are of the humble sort, for the most part, although when the girls put on their black mantillas and walk out armed with the fan they are not to be distinguished from the ladies of the land. Here reside guides, and small artificers, and the poor who have a prescriptive right to dwell in and about marble halls. The race is not likely to run out, for the place swarms with children. A people are, I dare say, industrious, after the easy manner of Spaniards, and necessarily frugal, yet not without the enjoyments of existence in a place so wholesome by waters, and made so attractive by art: one hears at all times, and especially at twilight, the tinkle of the guitar and the gay chatter of the neighborhood.

I was fortunate enough to get established in these precincts shortly after my arrival, and escape the tourists (like myself) at the hotels, and the hotels themselves, which by their situation in the glen among the tall trees, and under the walls, are somewhat damp. I have pleasant rooms with an honest worker in silver and gold, who fabricates ladies' breastpins, and earrings, and other ornaments in imitation of some of the pretty devices on the walls of the Alhambra. Here I am furnished with such simple food and cooking as these economical people think sufficient for themselves, which I eat with more thankfulness that it is eaten within the Alhambra than I would muster to bestow upon it elsewhere. God has so constituted these happy people that they eat with relish a dish of disagreeable beans, cooked in oil not of the sweetest, two or three times a day during their natural lives. But beans served with kindness are better than — well, better than beans served without kindness. I am waited on at table by Narcissa, the pretty daughter of my host, who brings me daily my daily beans, for which I do not pray, with as sweet a smile as she offers the oranges and the dish of wild strawberries. Narcissa is, I do not doubt, as lovely a little maiden as Dolores was, and perhaps more prepossessing when she is decked in her holiday clothes. If women have any vanity of dress, I should say that Narcissa is artlessly pleased with her appearance; and why should she not be, for she is as fresh and winning as the vase of roses which she places every day upon the table. When the little maid is not about her household duties, she is always strumming a guitar. Every day a young professor of the art — I am sure that *he* cannot be her lover — comes to give her lessons, and I see him in the room below, with his hat on his head, and a cigarette in his mouth sitting opposite to her, performing his agreeable duty, playing always the same dance tune, the Fandango, day after day, in which she accompanies him in endless iteration. That tune is the air of Spain, common as the atmosphere, and it never seems to weary performers or listeners. The Spaniards, like the Moors, seem content in music with the simplest harmony, and never tire of repetition.

The guitar, however, is a different instrument in the hands of a master. I went the other evening to see a Gypsy dance, and to hear the king of the Gypsies play. The king, who wears the dress of an ordinary Spaniard, is a man of some forty-five years, very dark complexion, and, unlike any other of his race I have seen, with a fine head, and good features, and a commanding and dignified bearing. I had heard that he is the best guitar player in Europe, and that he has refused offers to go to the capitals. He certainly handled the instrument as I never saw it handled by anyone else, and made it sing and almost speak, in a sort of articulation of the airs he rendered, in a most remarkable manner. Most of the compositions he gave were *gitano* dances, but he played one piece of exquisite pathos and feeling. It was, he said, a *marche funebre*, *El ultimo Suspiro del Moro* (The Last Sigh of the Moor), a mournful and touching reminiscence of the departure of Boabdil from his lost capital, when he turned back from a sandy knoll on the other side of the Vega, to look his last upon the towers of the Alhambra.

The dancing of the Gypsy women, whom the king had called over from their quarters for the amusement of the strangers, was in no way remarkable. The dance consists largely in posturing, in a movement of the hips and the arms, while the feet execute the steps. Although much livelier than the Gawazee dance of Egypt, it is in essence the beguilement of the old serpent of the Nile, and is intended to be the seductive expression of passion. It is done with more abandon and less reserve in the Gypsy quarters. When it is performed with skill by women of some grace and beauty, it can be imagined that it would have a barbaric and passionate attraction. But the girls dancing before the king were all ugly and all clumsy.

Gypsy dancing, it may be said here, is practiced in low resorts — a shade under the *cafés chantant* of Paris — in Malaga, Seville, and most of the large Spanish towns, frequented by men, who sip their coffee and liquors at small tables, while the performance goes on upon the stage, in a lazy, monotonous, but indecorous manner. We went one evening in Seville to see an exhibition of National Dancing, gotten up for the instruction of foreigners, in a cheerful and well-lighted hall. The spectators occupied benches on two sides of the hall, and the performers were seated opposite. Most of the dances were *pas seuls* and *pas deux* of the ballet order, with the bolero and the cachuca very coquettishly and prettily executed, accompanied by the sharp rattle of castinets, the measured clapping of hands, and an occasional outburst of singing in the Arabic manner, and quavering ejaculations of encouragement — *a-ya, a-ya*. The music was minor and thoroughly Moorish in character, so that in spite of the ballet costumes of the dancers, the whole performance was full of Oriental suggestions. It would have been tiresome, on the whole, but for an incident which may or may not have been on the programme. On the bench with the girls was seated a woman of perhaps thirty-five years, who seemed to be the directress of the performance. Tall, with supple, slender figure, rich olive complexion, and large, dark, flashing eyes, there was no mistaking her *gitano* blood. You might have called her plain anywhere else, but as she watched the dancing with glowing eyes, clapped her hands, and swayed to the time of the lingering, enticing music, one could see that some excitement was growing within — it might be from reminiscence, it might be the flash of desire — until something like beauty lit up the expressive face. During the pauses in the dancing, the music still went on, and the clapping of hands, and the outbursts of singing and ejaculation, sometimes rising into a wailing, passionate chorus, as if it would sweep away all barriers and go headlong. The woman was not insensible to this sensuous invitation. Suddenly, as if impelled by a power within that she could no longer resist, she sprang up, and stood in her long gown, calm, with the calmness of one quivering with suppressed excitement. A partner stepped out before her, clad in the national short jacket, sash, and knee breeches, and the dance began, with lifted arms and slow, reluctant steps. Without spring, without elasticity, but in measured heaviness the dance began. I do not know how these light figures contrived to give the impression that they were borne down by a weight almost impossible to be lifted from the floor. Every movement seemed a lift against gravitation. The woman struggled with an intolerable languor, which yet was not so much languor as weight, as if her limbs weighed a ton, and could not respond to the music which every moment grew louder and more entreating. It was the heaviness of passion, that bound its victim to the earth. In all this symbolic dance, in which the story of courtship was told, the advancing, retreating, denying, accepting, her movements never lost this sense of weight and struggle. There was little gesticulation, none of the springing as in the cachuca, none of the quivering of the muscles of the body as in the dance of the Gawazee, but always the appearance of deep passion suppressed. And it was not alone the passion of the body but of the soul, for the notable thing was that this woman, who was always decorous, threw into every movement an expression of inward feeling, intense, passionate, subtle. The impulse was all from within. You regarded little the external performance, so impressed were you by the inward effort and longing. All real dancing — that is, not mere capering for exercise — is the expression of sentiment and emotion. This dancing, if one may make the distinction, so entirely was it from passion within, seemed rather the emotion itself seeking expression. This was the art that no dancing-master can teach, inherited, I doubt not, from her ancestors on the Ganges, but the art that none but a woman can inherit.

There are about six hundred Gypsies in Granada. There is one settlement on the Albaycin hill, the oldest Moorish quarter of Granada in the ravines above the Darro, and another in a ravine opening to the Genil. A few of them have rude huts of stone, but most of them live in caves hollowed out of the rock. The front and the door being whitewashed, these habitations look like houses in the distance, half concealed as they are by thick plantations of cactus. The whole mountain-side and the ravines are covered with an almost impenetrable growth of cactus, and the entrance to the caves is through lanes of the prickly shrub. The caves usually have two apartments, which may be from ten to fifteen feet square. The outer one is the living room, the kitchen, the workshop, where the basket-weaving or the blacksmithing, or some other trade, is carried on; the inner room, little more than a dark hole in the rock, is the sleeping chamber. The only light to both is from the door. Some of them, into which we went, were very neat, and the honest housewives were proud to show them, with the rows of blue and other decorated pottery hung on the walls for ornament, as the fashion is in all æsthetic homes. The Gypsies are most persistent beggars, and the traveler who ventures into their quarters has some difficulty in extricating himself from the swarm of young and old women and children, who obstruct his path, and seize hold of him, and clamor for money. In all the camp we saw but one beauty, a slender girl of perhaps seventeen, who danced with grace and Oriental suggestiveness. Her raven hair was arranged in heavy rings fastened down to the forehead (in a fashion affected now by Spanish ladies), and put up behind in a mass secured by a silver stiletto; her dark eyes flashed under a low brow, the very brow of beauty; nose and mouth and chin might be called regular, but had an individual piquancy, and her complexion was tawny, glowing with color. She was barefooted, and her scanty dress was in rags, — this wild beauty among the distorted cactus hedges was like a rose among thorns in a neglected garden; but I do not know how she would bear transplanting and taming.

To return to our Alhambra. My windows look out over a trellis of grape vines, into a little garden watered by one of the old Moorish conduits, where the fig and the pomegranate grow, but it is chiefly a garden of rose-bushes, trees almost, which flower in this month of the Madonna with the utmost luxuriance. Varieties that are commonly only grown in a hot-house, superb crimsons, with petals of velvet and a perfume that recalls the old-fashioned rose that grew by the New England door-step, make gay this little reserve, and fill the air with odor. Beyond, over the trees, and lifted up above purple, rocky hills, is the long range of the snowy Sierra Nevada. In the common light it is silver against the blue sky, but at morning and evening it takes a ruddy hue, and glows with a soft splendor. Just across the street is the church of Santa Maria, on the site of a mosque, with a tower hardly over-topping the tall poplars clustered about it, in which the bells are always jangling. And yonder is the convent of the Franciscans, where was placed for a time the body of Gonsalvo Fernandez de Cordova, the Great Captain, and where the coffins of Ferdinand and Isabella remained till they were removed to their present resting-place in the cathedral of Granada.

The Alhambra is a jumble of buildings, with irregular tiled roofs, and absolutely plain, rough, uncolored walls on the exterior, that give no indication of the beauty within. Thus the Moor in his palace fortress masked the splendor of his luxurious residence, as he concealed the beauties of his harem from vulgar eyes. What the chief entrance was, we have no means of knowing, for Charles V. pulled it down, together with a portion of the palace, to make room for his own palace, an enormous, heavy mass which obtrudes itself in the centre of the Alhambra inclosure. This pseudo-Roman and Bramante construction is the eye-sore of the grounds. The Emperor drained his treasury on it, and left it unfinished, and it is solid enough and ugly enough to resist earthquakes and the weather. Nothing could be in worse taste, and in less keeping with its surroundings. Within the vast pile is an arena for bull-fights. The Spaniard, who touched nothing after the conquest that he did not degrade it, replaced some of the tile-work in the halls and courts of the Alhambra with the rough and tasteless tiles of his own manufacture. He also roofed one of the lesser halls with heavy and vulgar ceiling. We can forgive his destruction and his neglect better than his restorations and substitutions.

The beautiful stucco decorations of the walls can be reproduced with an approach to the original, except as to color, for it is not difficult to take impressions and make accurate casts of the old work. The new work, however, is too sharp, and lacks the delicious tone that the old has acquired. The original stucco work, the designs of which are infinite in variety, and as exquisite as the finest laces, was colored in blue, red, green, yellow, and gilt. These colors have been reproduced in some restorations of the Alhambra, but the colors are too garish.

What is beyond imitation, and beyond copying, however, is the tiling on the dadoes. It is in endless variety of pleasing and never-wearying patterns, done in the solid primary colors, but all iridescent, shimmering in colors like an opal, or the feathers of the peacock. I go day after day to feast my eye on the splendor of this reflected light and sheen, and I wander from hall to hall, and tower to tower, in amazement at the fertility of invention that never repeated itself.

There are two or three incongruities in the decoration of the Alhambra which cannot escape observation. One of them is the rude, snub-nosed, heraldic lions that support the fountain basin in the court that takes its name from them. Another is three roof paintings in the Sala de Justicia, off the Court of Lyons. One of these paintings represents ten bearded Moors, seated in council; they are in the true costume of the Granada Moor, the features are Oriental in cast, but regular and noble, even beautiful, the figures are well drawn, and the colors are brilliant and fresh as any fresco of the best period of the art. There are other scenes of chivalry, of love, of hunting, with a background of trees, castles, and animals, but all the subjects are in honor of the Moor, whose royal shield is seen everywhere. In one a Moorish knight unhorses a Christian warrior. These paintings are said to be on leather, nailed to the ceilings. As the Moslem religion did not permit any carving, or any decoration in imitation of any living thing, how came these lions, and these paintings, in a Moorish palace, which is elsewhere devoid of even an imitation of flowers or any natural objects? It is suggested that the paintings were by an Italian artist in the fourteenth century, but why did the Moslems permit them? If they were executed after the conquest, in this hall where the pious Ferdinand and Isabella first heard mass, and where the cross was first erected after their entry, would not the subjects have been ecclesiastical? Certainly they would not have been in honor of the Moors. The lions may have been the work of Persians, who were Sunites, and made images, and used animal forms freely in decoration. But no Persian could ever have painted these pictures.

Another puzzle is the famous Alhambra Vase, considering the place where it was found. This noble piece of faience is over four feet in height, and of exquisite proportions. One handle is gone, and it is badly cracked. It is kept out of sight in a sort of lumber room, called the museum, lighted by one small window, and stands against the wall so that it cannot be seen to advantage. It is a treasure that should have a conspicuous exposure, well guarded, where all the world could study it. It is highly enameled and beautifully lustrous. The main color is a light blue — a cerulean color, of which the Arabs seem to have had the secret. The decorations are formed by this color, with gold and brown and white. The sides are different. On each side, however, are quaint figures of animals, the conventional Persian story. The whole of the decoration in its feeling and character is Persian; and I have no doubt in my own mind that the decorators were Persians. There is nothing else of the same character in the Alhambra halls or towers. I saw half a dozen wall tiles in the old Moorish *Cuarto Real*, in the city. They have a white ground with gold scroll work freely drawn, and have every appearance of being Persian work. It is to be noted that the iridescent tiles of the Moors have no resemblance to the superb glazed tiles of the Persians, and of the Saracens in Damascus and in Egypt, and that the Barbary Moors developed, both in stucco and in tiles, a perfectly distinct and independent sort of decoration. At least it seems so to me.

In what is called now The Court of Blessing, or sometimes the Court de la Alberca (of the Fish Pond) — at one end of which was the winter quarters of the palace, which Charles V. pulled down to make room for his hideous construction, and at the other the Hall of the Ambassadors — is a long tank set in marble, and the water in it, some five feet deep, beautifully reflects the surrounding colonnades, arches, and decorations. This pond is inhabited by gold fish, which "they say" are the lineal descendants of the fish that swam before the Moors. All I know is that some of the fish have the peculiarity of a tail with three partings, and these strange fish are as likely to be descended from the Moors as from Charles V., and everything in the Alhambra is attributed to one or the other. Some people believe that this pond was once the women's bath, but I cannot think that they ever, even when the Alhambra was most secluded, used so exposed a place, and, besides, the baths of the establishment are below. What is certain is, that Washington Irving used to swim here when he resided in the palace. The ladies' part of the Alhambra was probably that opening upon the Court of Lions, from which, through the exquisite Hall of the Two Sisters, we look through a double arched window, with a slender centre column, into the Garden of Lindaraja. This secluded garden is one of the most delightful retreats and lounging places in the whole Alhambra area. In the centre is a fountain with a large alabaster basin having an Arabic inscription; the garden is planted with box, and rose-trees, and myrtle, and violets, and against the wall in which are the windows of Irving's apartments are tall orange-trees now golden with fruit. This green and gold, seen through the colonnades and arches from the Fountain of the Lions, has a charming effect.

One cannot linger in these exquisite halls and courts, in which there is so much beauty and such desolation, or stroll about the circuit of towers, so stern and warlike outside, but decorated with such fairy work within, without attempting in his mind to re-create the splendid past. What must these halls and chambers have been before time frayed the stucco and earthquakes cracked the walls, when the colors were fresh and lustrous; when the walls were hung with the tapestries of the East and the embroideries of Timbuctoo, and the floors were soft with the carpets of Fez; when luxurious divans in the sculptured recesses invited to repose, and the senses were lulled by the perfumes of swinging lamps and the sound of tiny fountains from which the water ran away to the courts in marble conduits. It was a sensuous paradise, a foretaste of all that the Koran promises. When the Moor looked down from these lofty windows over the tree-tops to the busy quarters of the Albaycin, or across to the noble palace and gardens of the Generalife, and marked the security of his position, and the strength of his embattled walls, he might well deliver himself to a dream of unbroken voluptuous repose.

But the dream was broken forever by the advent of the Christian conquerors. The degradation of the Alhambra begins from the moment of the Christian occupation. Incongruities introduced by a people whose faith was not softened by a sense of beauty and harmony marred the perfection of the Moorish creation. In any other place one might be interested, if not excited by the pomp and pageantry of the chivalry of Spain which flowed through these halls, even if he did not join in the exultation with which the conquerors took possession of this wonder of the world. And now Ferdinand and Isabella, and Charles, and the Philips, have passed away as utterly as Abul Haja, Yusuf I., Ibn-l-Ahmar, and Muley Abul Hassan,

Zorayda and Lindaraja, Ayxa la Horra, and her son Boabdil, the Abencerrages, and the proud house of Nasir.

The conquerors are now only shades like the vanquished, and it has come to pass that the interest of the world in this former palace of enchantment is not in any marks the victors put upon it, but wholly in the reminiscences and relics of the race who were dispossessed. And yet in the hour of victory, in the moment of pride over the expulsion of the Moslem, Ferdinand and Isabella might have read, all over the walls, upon the royal shields, and on the capitals, the Arabic legend: *Wa la ghaliba illa Allah* — "God is the only Conqueror."

CHAPTER XIX.

THE BULL-FIGHT.

LET us begin tranquilly. We are going to kill a good many old horses, whose four feet were in the grave before they entered the ring, and we are going to torture them in their last hours on the way to the bone-yard; we are going to bait, and worry, and weaken by loss of blood, and finally slaughter a number of noble bulls; perhaps we shall break some *picador* ribs; we are about to enter the region of chivalry, and engage in the pastime most characteristic of and most esteemed by the Spanish people; we promise gore and carnage enough farther on, and we may be pardoned for a gentle and gentleman-and-lady-like introduction to the noble sport.

One afternoon, in Seville, we learned that there was to be a *funcion* at the Bull-Ring, given by amateurs, by a society of gentlemen Caballeros, whose object is the cultivation of horsemanship and the manly, national pastime. It was an entertainment given by the gentlemen of Seville to their lady friends, offering at the shrine of beauty the best fruit of a gallant civilization, and probably that which is most acceptable, just as the amateur Mendelssohn Society of New York gives its winter concerts to a refined and fashionable circle of friends. As admission was to be had only on special invitation of the members of the club, we had no expectation of participating, but we drove down to the amphitheatre with a praiseworthy curiosity to see the beauty of Seville, in holiday attire, flock in to the spectacle.

The Bull-Ring, which stands on the flat — all Seville is flat, and subject more or less to the overflow of the river — near the Guadalquivir, is an ample one, with a seating capacity of eleven thousand persons. It is built of stone, with wide interior corridors and entrance galleries to the different stories and private boxes, like the ancient Colosseum. Begun over a century ago, it is still rough and unfinished, but it answers all the substantial purposes of its erection. The upper galleries and rows of benches on the shady side are set apart for the gentry; while the tiers near the ring and all the sunny side are given up to the lower orders and the rabble, the seats being much less in price than the others.

Carriages blocked the space in front of the entrance, — the most aristocratic of which were a sort of private and not much glorified omnibus, drawn by a team of gayly caparisoned mules, — and into the gates poured a stream, principally of ladies in full toilet. It was evidently an occasion of the highest fashion, and one that exhausted and put on view the entire beauty and gentility of Seville. The regular bull-fights of late years appear to have lost caste somewhat with the more refined circles of society, and the stranger might attend a dozen and not see a tithe of the dress and display, or women of the upper rank, that were forthcoming at this amateur performance. This rare opportunity to admire the beauty of Spain, which is becoming, so far as national peculiarities are concerned, somewhat traditional, made us anxious to be admitted.

At length I plucked up courage and asked one of the gentlemen keeping the gate and taking tickets if there was any proper way by which a stranger could gain admittance. He replied, with great courtesy, that the only entrance would be by a member's ticket, but that, if I would wait a little till the rush was over, he would see what could be done. We amused ourselves with watching the gay throng trip past, in all the excitement of anticipation of the choice entertainment. At length the person upon whom my hopes depended beckoned to me, and said that he had been fortunate enough to secure a member's ticket, which was quite at my service, and he was evidently very glad to be able to oblige a stranger. The ticket bore the name of Don somebody, with a long title, and was evidently a piece of paper to be respected. I was required to write my name on it as his guest. When I read the document, I found that it virtually entitled me to all the privileges of the club for fourteen days. I had heard so much of Spanish courtesy and generosity, and unfortunately seen so little of it in streets and highways of travel, that I was glad to have my faith restored by this act of hospitality. Thanking my temporary friend as profusely as I was able, I was about to pass into the arena, when an expression on his face arrested my attention, and a good providence led me to ask, " How much may I give you for this ticket?" "Four dollars," was the prompt reply. I said I thought that was very little for a piece of paper conveying such privileges, paid the vulgar silver, thanked him anew for his favor, to which he replied, in effect, that I need n't mention it, with a gracious air of presenting me with the entire Bull-Ring, and I passed in among the select elect.

The ring had been contracted for action to about two thirds of its usual size, and the greater part of the seats, including all on the sunny side, were vacant. But the audience was, nevertheless, large, all the balconies and boxes, and most of the benches on the gentry side, being full, and the spectacle was exceedingly brilliant. How could it be otherwise, with three thousand ladies in full drawing-room toilet? The ladies of Spain, except in some remote towns in the mountain regions, have laid aside the national costume, and dress according to the dictates of Paris, preferring even the French fans to their own decorated with the incidents of the bull-fight and the serenade. In Seville, the black lace mantilla is still worn at church, and to some extent in the street; but the hat is the cover of the new fashion, more's the pity, and the high combs have gone altogether. I do not know why a woman, even a plain woman, should be so utterly fascinating in a mantilla, thrown over a high comb and falling gracefully over the shoulders, stepping daintily in high-heeled shoes with pointed toes, and moving her large fan with just that nonchalant air so accurately calculated to wound but not to kill. In the whole assembly I saw only one or two national costumes: the mantilla and the high comb, with the short petticoat, brilliant in color. Nothing could be more becoming, and it makes one doubt whether woman's strongest desire is to please, and whether it is not rather to follow the fashion, when we see a whole nation abandon such a charming attire.

But the white mantilla is *de rigueur* for a bull-fight, and every lady wore one. It was a little odd to see ladies in the open light of a brilliant, cloudless day, and in the gaze of the public, in full (as it is called) costume of the ball-room; but the creamy-white mantillas softened somewhat the too brilliant display, and threw over the whole the harmony of subdued splendor. What superb Spanish lace, blonde, soft, with a silken lustre, falling in lovely folds that show its generous and exquisitely wrought figures, each leaf and stem and flower the creation of dainty fingers! Such work as this, of such a tone and fineness, in such large mantillas, sweeping from the head to the train, is scarcely to be found in the shops nowadays. These were heir-looms,—great-great-grandmother's lace, long yellowing, and growing rich in locked chests, worn only on state occasions, and now brought forth to make a bull's holiday.

We spent a good deal of the waiting time in scrutinizing the packed seats for beautiful women, and, I am sorry to say, with hardly a reward adequate to our anxiety. I am not sure how much the beauty of the women of Seville is traditional. They have good points. Graceful figures are not uncommon, and fine teeth; and dark, liquid, large eyes, which they use perpetually in *œillades* destructive to peace and security. And the fan, the most deadly weapon of coquetry, gives the *coup de grâce* to those whom the eyes have wounded. But the Seville women have usually sallow, pasty, dead complexions. Perhaps the beauty of the skin is destroyed by cosmetics, for there was not a lady at the bull-fight who was not highly rouged and powdered. This gave an artificiality to their appearance *en masse*. Beauty of feature was very rare, and still rarer was that animation, that stamp of individual character, loveliness in the play of expression, and sprightliness, that charm in any assembly of American women. No, the handsome women in the ring were not numerous enough to make any impression on the general mass, and yet the total effect, with the blonde lace, the artificial color, the rich toilet, and the agitation of fans, was charming. The fan is the feature of Spanish life. It is, I believe, a well-known physiological fact that every Spanish girl is born with a fan in her hand. She learns to use it with effect before she can say "mamma." By the time she receives her first communion, it has become a fatal weapon in her hands, capable of expressing every shade of feeling, hope, tantalization. But ordinarily its use is excessively monotonous. It has, in fact, only three motions. It is opened with a languid backward flirt, it is moved twice gently to stir the air, it is closed with a slow, forward action, and then the same process is exactly repeated, — open, two movements of fanning, shut; open, fan, shut, — hour after hour, until the beholder is driven half wild by the monotony of the performance. It is such a relief when there are three fanning movements between the opening and the shutting. In a public drawing-room, in the cars, in the street, in the bull-ring, this is the everlasting iteration of the fan. The effect produced when three thousand women are executing the monotonous manœuvre is exasperating. When the lady is in an attitude of mental and physical repose there is only this mechanical motion. When she is in conversation, and has an object, the fan has a hundred movements and varieties of expression, as the victim learns to his cost.

But let us not forget that this is a bull-fight, and the bull is probably waiting. The attention of the rustling, chattering, fanning audience is suddenly fixed upon the arena gate, which at the sound of a trumpet swings open to admit the procession of performers, — the *picadores* on horseback, the *chulos* or *banderilleros*, and *matador* on foot, and a gayly caparisoned team of mules with a drag of chains for removing the dead animals. We need not detain ourselves here with the details which will be necessary when we come to engage in a serious affair. The performers are all gentlemen, clad in the fantastic dress of the professionals.

The procession makes the round of the arena under a shower of hand-clapping, salutes the president and the bevy of ladies in the central balcony, and withdraws, leaving only the *picadores*, or spearmen, and attendants in possession of the field of honor.

The trumpet sounds a second time, and the door of the *toril*, the dark cage on wheels in which the bull is confined, is opened, and the bull rushes out. He is also an amateur, a two-year-old, of good lineage like his tormentors, but of imperfect development. He has been exasperated by confinement in a dark box, and pricked into a rage by an ornamental rosette of ribbons, which is fastened between his shoulders by spikes that have drawn blood. Astonished at first by the glare of light and the noisy welcome of the assembly, he stands a moment confused, and then runs about the arena looking for some place of escape. He is a compact, clean-built, intrepid little fellow, and probably does not at first comprehend that this is a duel for life, without a single chance for himself. He does not yet know that he is to be stabbed and pricked and baited for an hour for the amusement of these gracious, applauding ladies, and then butchered, to give them a holiday sensation. He does not know how unequal the fight is to be, until he learns by experience that he is deprived of his natural weapon of attack; but we feel a pity for him in advance, as we notice that the points of his horns have been sawn off, so that their thrusts will be harmless. After a circuit or two, he becomes aware that he is among enemies, and see-

THE BULL-FIGHT. 263

ing the *picadores* advancing and menacing him with their spears, he makes a rush at one of them. The clumsy rider attempts a spear-thrust, but the bull disregards that and gets in under the flank of the horse and attempts to gore him. Alas, the blunt horns will not gore; the blinded beast is lifted a little off his hind legs by sheer force of the plucky little fighter, and then the bull turns away in disgust, pursued by the courageous *picadores*. Again and again he is nagged and pricked into a charge, but always with the same result. This sort of thing goes on till both the bull and the spectators are weary of it, and then the trumpet sounds and the merry *chulos* enter to assist the *picadores* in further worrying the bull. These light-clad skirmishers bear darts and long red cloaks. They surround the puzzled bull and torment him, shake their aggravating red cloaks in his face, and when he rushes at one of them, the athlete springs lightly aside and lets him toss the garment; or, if he pursues too closely, the man runs to the barrier and escapes through one of the many narrow openings. When this sport has continued some time, the *banderilleros* come into play. One of them advances with a long barbed arrow in each hand, holding it by the feathered end of the shaft. The little bull looks at him, standing still and wondering what new sort of enemy this is. The man, with watchful eye, comes nearer, in fact, close to him; the bull lowers his head and concludes to try a charge, but he has scarcely taken two steps when the *banderillero* plants the two cruel arrows on the top of his shoulders and springs lightly aside. The bull passes with the weapons sticking into his flesh, loosely swaying, and aggravating him, and the blood flows down his shoulders. The crowd applaud the gallant young gentleman. This operation is repeated by a second *banderillero*, and when this sort of baiting ceases to be any longer amusing, the trumpet sounds again.

This is for the last act in this noble drama. The *picadores* withdraw, the arena is occupied by the skirmishing *chulos*. At a blast of the trumpet the *matador* enters, advances to the central balcony, makes an address, receives permission to dispatch the little beast, throws his cap over the barrier, and advances to his work. He carries in the left hand a small scarlet flag, and in the other, a long, slender Toledo blade. He must kill the bull, but in only one way. The sword must enter in the back part of the neck just between the shoulder-blades, so as to pierce the heart. The blow must consequently be delivered when the bull is charging, head down. It requires a quick eye, a steady hand, and unshaken nerves to plant the sword exactly in this spot. The *matador* advances warily to play with the bull and study his nature; his assistants group themselves about at his command, to goad the bull into action by shaking their cloaks, or to protect the *matador* if the latter is hard pressed. The little bull is tired and bloody and hot, and has had enough of it. But the *matador* is tantalizing, the scarlet banner is irritating, the *chulos* are exasperating. After much irresolution, and turning his eyes to one tormentor and another, he decides to pay his attention to the man with the sword. He makes a rush at the red banner; it flirts in his face; the *matador* steps aside, and as he does so makes a thrust. The sword enters the beast only an inch or two, and in the wrong place. The bull canters away to the other side of the arena to get rid of his tormentors. They follow him and bait him. He turns again upon his cool pursuer. This time the sword is thrust into his neck and sticks there, while the bull runs and bellows at the hurt until he shakes out the weapon. The *matador* recovers it, and the sport continues. There is nothing very exciting about it, but the crowd apparently enjoy the torture of the animal. The *matador* is cool; he is practicing a noble art. After long manœuvring and feinting and false thrusting, he plants his sword in the fatal spot. The bull stops in his career, astonished. An attendant runs up and drives the sword in by a blow on the hilt; the bull falls on his knees, and "the arena swims around him." He tumbles over; the mule team gallops in and drags away his carcass; the hero advances to the central balcony and receives a tempest of applause and a shower of bouquets. He has done what man can do in this land of romance to commend himself to the favors of the gentler sex. Two other bulls are slain with exactly the same prolonged and ceremonious torture, and then the arena is cleared for another sort of performance.

Meantime, the fans flutter with a new meaning, the chatter is continuous, the brilliant behavior of the performers is discussed with earnestness, and boys make their way up and along the tiers of seats with great trays of costly and toothsome bon-bons and sweetmeats, which are gratuitously distributed at the expense of the club.

The next performance is by the gentlemen riders. Sixteen of them, superbly mounted, in morning costume, with tall hats, enter the ring and begin a series of pleasing evolutions. The performance has not the dash and danger of an Arab *jereed* nor the break-neck pace and skill of some of our Western and Indian horsemen, but it is better than most of the riding in our best circuses with trained horses, and is altogether a pleasing sight. The riders sit and manage their spirited horses perfectly, and their complicated evolutions, like the mazes of a dance, in time to the music of the band, are a charming exhibition of grace and skill.

This was followed by riding at the scarf. On a projecting arm in front of the president's stand were rolls of colored scarfs, the end of each roll hanging down with its fringe about six inches. The scarfs of blue, red, white, yellow, and green had been embroidered by the fair hands that were applauding the horsemen, and the capture of these was the prize of the riders. Each horseman carried a long wooden lance with a sharp point. They were drawn up in line on the opposite side of the arena. At a signal one advanced, and put his horse into a gallop around the circle; as he neared the balcony, the pace increased to a dead run. Just before the rider passed under the roll of scarfs he raised his lance and thrust it at the six inches square of hanging silk. He had to estimate the height, to calculate exactly the distance from the balcony, and to hit this small object exactly while guiding his fiery horse at a prodigious pace. If the point of the lance caught the silk, the scarf unrolled and fluttered down, and another one was ready for the next trial. Opposite the balcony, by the side of the track, on a stand about eighteen inches high, lay a bouquet. When the rider had essayed at the scarf, he threw down his lance and, with the horse still at full speed, leaned from his saddle and attempted to snatch the bouquet. I could see how the riders could very well spear the silk and catch the flowers; but how, in all this excitement, with a plunging horse, they could keep on their tall hats, was a mystery to me. There were many rounds made without capturing a scarf. Whenever one was caught down, a footman picked it up and carried it to the winner, who decorated himself with it by passing it over his right shoulder and knotting it on his left hip. In time, the successful competitors presented a gay appearance, with scarfs of many colors. The game went on for nearly two hours, and almost at the last there were some unfortunate riders who had no scarf, while others were ornamented with a dozen of these tokens of affection. I fancied there were some heart-aches in the galleries on seeing so many of the embroidered decorations go to the wrong men. But the supply held out, and when the trial was over every gallant had at least one. No doubt it was a happy night for the heroes who wore a dozen. But what their social rank would be, in comparison with the swordsman who killed the amateur bull, I cannot say.

The high and almost sacred rank the bull-fight holds in Spain may be inferred from the fact that all the important spectacles are on Sunday. As the great *funciones* had already taken place during the Easter holidays in Seville, we were obliged to go to Jerez on the thirtieth of April in order to witness a real engagement. Every town in Spain of any size has a large bull-ring, whatever other public buildings it may lack; and the erection of new ones recently proves that the sport has not declined in popular estimation, although a few fastidious persons are beginning to regard it as a barbarous and unseemly usage. And during some portion of the year, usually during the local fair, or on some high *fête* of the Church, there is in every bull-ring in the kingdom a great *funcion*. There are a few bull-fighters who have a national reputation, whose services are always in demand, and the local fights have to be postponed till one or more of them can be secured. Although it is said that the professional bull-fighter is very low caste in Spain, I think no one, not even the military hero, enjoys so much consideration with the masses as the successful and skillful *matador* of the ring. They are followed by the boys, they are the admiration of the rabble, they are smiled on by the gentle ladies in the boxes, they are dined by the local governors, and they move about in their own social circles with the port of conquerors who subdue hearts as easily as they slay bulls.

There are very few who attain great eminence in their profession, never more than three or four at a time in the whole kingdom; but for them there is profit as well as honor. These great men are the autocrats of the ring when they enter it. Each one has his own train of followers, *chulos* and *banderilleros*, who accompany him in his circuit of engagements, and who are paid as he dictates. A great favorite receives a thousand dollars for a fight, and as he is crowded with engagements during the whole spring, summer, and autumn, he reaps a good harvest. Two fighters whom I saw, one of Seville and one of Granada, had accumulated large fortunes, owned many houses, and lived in considerable, showy ostentation. Bull-fights are very expensive entertainments, costing usually two thousand dollars and more, and the prices of admission are high compared with the wages paid in Spain; the artists must be well paid, and the animals cost much to breed. But there is no difficulty in filling a ring anywhere, for the fight is a passion with the people; children are taken early to the arena, and bred to love it — their common game is a "bull-fight;" and all Spaniards love to see a bull slain, for they seem to have an unconquerable hatred of the animal, and never, I am told, see one in the field without attempting to irritate and insult him. Of the bulls that are bred for this pastime, only the noblest and fiercest are fit for the arena, and the breeders have methods of testing their courage and mettle. The lovers of the sport always post themselves as to the character of the bulls who are to perform, and the reputation of the fighting quality of the forthcoming bulls is an attraction only second to that of the famous artists who are to meet them in the arena; and the latter are esteemed as great actors are with us.

It was fair and horse-race week at Jerez, and the little "sherry" city was crowded with visitors. The culminating interest was in the bull-baiting on Sunday afternoon, and when we found our way to our seats in the vast edifice, at half-past three, it was already packed from the barrier-ring to the top of the walls. And such an assembly! I doubt if a Roman circus could ever have shown a more brutal one. Very few women were present, though there were many children; and there was a sprinkling of ladies in white mantillas in the grand balcony, where the town officials were seated. These functionaries had the air of the judges and important personages on the stand at an American horse-trot *funcion*. The occasion had been anticipated with great eagerness, because the bulls were from a famous Andalusian herd, and two fighters with a national reputation were to officiate: Antonio Carmona, called "El Gordito," of Seville, and Salvador Sanchez, called "Frascuelo," of Granada. These men are both in the first class of the brotherhood, although two of the Madrid fighters are their acknowledged superiors.

I had imagined that a bull-fight, with all its cruelty and much to disgust, must be an exciting and gallant spectacle. I saw, in my mind, the trained spearmen on horseback dashing in full gallop at the bull, dexterously evading his enraged rush, and flying and charging about the arena, alternately pursuing and pursued. I saw the bull, always alert and bellicose, charging the footmen, who pricked and baited and enraged him with their scarlet mantles, who put their lives against his in a closed arena, and only saved themselves by the utmost address and skill. I had imagined, in short, a chivalrous performance.

We had not long to wait. The gate swung open, and the bull-fighting company entered in what was meant to be a gorgeous procession. It had the cheap elements of a spectacular effect in a sawdust arena. The costumes, at least, were showy in spangles and in divers colors, as in the " grande entrée " of a circus, and some of them were rich; and scarlet cloaks and swords and plumes and the courtly, high-stepping march of the fighters imitated, I supposed, the opening of a mediæval tournament. First came four *picadores*. These men wore broad-brimmed Thessalian hats and carried long spears; their bodies were thickly padded, their legs incased in iron and leather, the right one being most protected; they were rusty in appearance, and so incumbered were they with armor and wadding that they sat their horses insecurely.

The poor beasts they rode were worthy of the occasion, thin Rosinantes, old, knock-kneed, stiff-legged, who stumbled along and with difficulty could be urged out of a walk. They were blindfolded. They would be dear purchases at two dollars and a half a head. When you speak to a Spaniard of the cruelty of torturing such poor beasts, he says, "Why, they are worth nothing!" These were followed by a band of foot-fighters, comely fellows in spangled jackets, plumed caps, waist sashes, short breeches, and stockings, bearing on the left arm red mantles. After them walked the two *matadores en grande tenue*, with conscious pride, and the procession closed with a team of six gaudily caparisoned mules. The procession marched up to the judges' stand and saluted; the president threw down the key of the *toril*, or bull-cell, to an attendant policeman, the round of the arena was made amid the roar of nine thousand spectators, and all passed out except the *picadores* and half a dozen of the footmen.

And now came the first moment of intense anxiety, the awaiting of the appearance of the bull. Would he be game or indifferent? would he be boldly savage or slyly murderous, a dangerous customer or a coward? Pending this issue, however, I was aware of a rising tumult on the opposite benches, an angry sort of roar and grumble that spread speedily over the whole house except in our immediate vicinity near the grand balcony; men rose gesticulating and sputtering wildly, and pointing in our direction, until nearly everybody was standing on the benches, half of them not comprehending what the matter was, and eager to see, but all roaring in tones that had no good-nature in them. "They are all looking at you," said my companion; "I think it must be your hat." I was wearing, for protection against the sun, an India pith helmet, common enough all along the Mediterranean, but for some reason apparently offensive to these courteous provincials. The whole arena rose at me. It was some seconds before I could comprehend that I was the centre of such polite attention. The hubbub increased; men shook their fists and howled, and began to move as if they would climb up to our tier. They demanded something most vehemently, but whether it was my head or my hat I could not tell. I did not, however, rise to acknowledge the honor, but sat smiling, much as I suppose the *matador* smiles when the bull is about to charge him; and when the tumult was at its height there was a cry, El toro! El toro!" and the crowd turned to a greater attraction.

The bull was in the ring. He was a noble animal, dun in color, handsomely marked, thin flanks, powerful shoulders, high-bred head with dilating nostrils, large, glaring eyes, and symmetrical polished horns. Affixed to the back of his neck was the variegated rosette, and blood trickled down his shoulders. He stood for a moment facing the nine thousand enemies who roared at him, and then dashed around the ring, head erect and lashing his tail, with blood and defiance in his eye. The *chulos* sought cover, and the *picadores* stood still, awaiting his attention. After his first course, the bull stood for a moment pawing the ground and bellowing, and then, catching sight of one of the weak, blindfolded horses, whose rider was urging him forward, he advanced to the attack, though not with any rush. As he came near, the *picador*, who was swaying clumsily on his horse, made a thrust at the bull with his spear and slightly turned his horse's head to the left. The horse stood still, and the bull inserted his horns under the animal's flank, slightly raising him from the ground. The footmen ran to the rescue with their distracting mantles, and the bull turned in pursuit of them. They nimbly skipped behind the shelters that are erected every few paces in the barrier, and the horse got away with his entrails trailing on the ground, his rider trying to spur him into a gallop. The crowd roared in great delight. The horse was good for sport as long as he could stand. (When the horse is not too weak to keep his feet, the wound is sewed up, that he may be gored again; for seeing the horses tortured is one of the chief delights of the ring.) After a brief interval, the bull was excited to attack another horse. This time the horse was lifted from the ground and thrown on his side, the man under him, and the bull drew back to give him a finishing stroke. The attendants again rushed in, distracted the attention of the bull, pulled the man from under the horse, got the horse up, lifted the *picador* to his feet (for incumbered as he was with armor and wadding he could not rise), and put him on the horse again. The bull, still full of fight, wheeled about in a rage at losing his assailants, who had quickly stepped behind their shelter, and advanced threateningly toward another horse. The *picador* walked his horse to meet him. The same clumsy manœuvres occurred as before. But this time the bull not only overthrew the horse, but gored him severely, and then attacked the prostrate rider. The footmen rushed in just in time to save the man from being tossed. The horse lay dead, and the man was carried out of the ring. It was considered by this time a lively fight, and the *picadores* were reënforced by two more horsemen. The next horse assailed was gored so badly that, although he escaped, he was in a shocking condition; and after his cruel rider had spurred him a couple of times around the ring, he collapsed. The bull continued raging about, stopping occasionally to gore and toss the dead horses or chase the aggravating *chulos* to cover, and then sullenly advancing and ripping open another of the blindfolded steeds. When the trumpet sounded, he had virtually cleared the ring, and roamed around, its master. Six horses lay dead or dying in the sand.

In the second act the *chulos* and *banderilleros* had the field, to torture and bait the noble fighter, who was getting a little weakened by his extraordinary efforts, but still seemed to think he had a chance for his life. These fellows are light and nimble, costumed exactly like *Figaro*, in the "Barber's" opera, and skip about the arena with considerable agility. Their office is to tease the bull, to run toward him and aggravate him by shaking their colored mantles in his face, to distract him to pursue first one and then another, and to elude him, when they are hard pressed, by dodging behind the shelters. The only danger they run is in slipping on the sod when the bull is in pursuit. After this game had gone on for some time, a *banderillero* stepped forward with a barbed arrow in each hand and faced the bull. His object was to plant an arrow in each shoulder. The two looked at each other warily. The bull was studying how he could kill the man. He pawed the ground, he lowered his head, and made a dash; the *banderillero* planted the arrows exactly in the shoulders, and skipped aside, just avoiding the points of the sharp horns. It was very neatly done; and the bull went roaring around the arena, bleeding and trying to shake himself free from the stinging barbs. This operation, after two or three failures, was repeated by another *banderillero*, and the bull was further dispirited by nagging until it was deemed time to kill him. The trumpet sounded for the third and last act.

Frascuelo entered. He was not by any means a bad-looking fellow, and, physically, he deserved a good deal of credit. He advanced straight across the arena with the lordly strut of a great man, conscious of his merit and of deserving the thunderous applause that greeted him, to the president's box. There he made a grandiloquent speech, signifying his willingness to rid the earth of that pestilent bull. Permission was graciously accorded: we are nothing here if not courtly. Frascuelo pledged himself to do his duty, tossed his plumed hat over the barrier, and turned and addressed himself to the work. The bull had been meantime patiently waiting for the oratorical part of the performance to finish, and evidently not caring particularly for any more fighting that day.

Frascuelo carried in his right hand a long Toledo blade; in his left, a scarlet mantle a yard square. He wore a small wig of black hair, with a sort of chignon on the back of the head, and a short cue. His jacket and breeches were of light olive-green velvet. The open jacket and the front of his thighs were thickly crusted with silver spangles. His waist was girt with a red sash; his long stockings were pink, and his shoes were black. He was a cool-eyed, steady-nerved, well-made fellow, and he presented a pretty appearance as he advanced to his duel with the bull. His attendants, with the mantles, were disposed near at hand and under his orders, to excite the bull to the combat and to rescue the *matador* in case of extreme peril.

The two stood face to face; the man fresh and cool, the bull enraged, but weakened by the running and the nagging and loss of blood. The only stroke the *matador* is allowed to deliver is between the shoulders; in order to kill, he must pass the sword down close to the shoulder-blade into the heart. In order to reach this spot, the bull must have his head down, and consequently be charging. The combatants eye each other. Frascuelo shakes the scarlet before the bull's eyes. The bull paws the ground and looks wicked, but distrustful of the blade. Frascuelo comes nearer, never for a second losing the bull's eye. He insults him with the scarlet. The bull dashes at it. Frascuelo delivers a stroke as the bull comes on, flirts the banner in his eyes, and steps aside. The bull is wounded, but not in the vital spot, and speedily turns and faces his foe. Frascuelo coolly wipes the blade on the silk in his hand, and is ready for another turn. The same wary manœuvres follow, with the same result. Then a longer period of skirmishing follows, in which the attendants again nag and torment the now distracted and reluctant animal. In the third round, Frascuelo plants his sword in the right spot, half way to the hilt. The crowd rise and roar with delight. The bull goes bellowing around the arena in pain, blood running from his mouth. As he passes near the barrier, the spectators lean over and, with one blow after another, thrust the sword in to the hilt. The bull falls on his knees and is done for. Frascuelo, still cool, gracious, dignified, advances to the grand balcony. He is greeted with a hurricane of hurrahs, and a shower of hats is thrown at him from the benches. These hats are not, however, gifts. Frascuelo goes around and picks each one up and restores it to its owner. Then the trumpet sounds, the mule team gallops in and drags away the bull and the carcasses of the horses, and the arena is ready for another fight..

THE BULL-FIGHT.

The second fight was essentially a repetition of the first, only this bull was sullen and less enterprising than the first one, though equally strong and dangerous. In the second act an incident occurred that sent a delightful thrill of horror through the spectators for a moment. One of the *chulos*, pursued by the bull, fell, and the brute's horns were just about entering his body, when Frascuelo, who was in the arena, rushed forward with incredible swiftness and address, and, blinding the bull with his cloak, diverted his attention and saved the man's life. It was the cleverest feat of the day.

The *matador* in this fight was El Gordito, a man of fame, but older than Frascuelo, and on this occasion he appeared to be a very clumsy swordsman. Although the bull was much fatigued when he took him, the fight was intolerably long. El Gordito made pass after pass, wounding the bull repeatedly, but never in the right spot. Twice he lost his sword, the bull carrying it away in his neck, and it was recovered and brought to the *matador* by his attendants. Once he thrust it so deeply into the shoulder that it was a long time before it was pulled out, and then by one of the spectators leaning over the barrier when the bull was sulking, and El Gordito had to be furnished with another sword. After twenty minutes of this clumsy work the crowd got very impatient, and did what is very seldom done in a bull-ring — they demanded the life of the bull. The signal of this act of mercy is the waving of a white handkerchief. Soon the whole arena was fluttering with these flags of truce. But the president would not heed them. He probably hesitated to disgrace so notorious a fighter. The farce went on. Again and again the crowd rose, waving handkerchiefs and demanding that the bull should be let go. But the president was inexorable. The fight went on, intolerably weary and monotonous. At the end of nearly three quarters of an hour El Gordito succeeded in planting his weapon in the right spot, though not delivering an immediate death-blow; but the bull, after some hesitation, sank on his knees, and an attendant crept up to his side and dispatched him with a butcher-knife.

We assisted at the killing of one bull more. It was always the same thing. Six bulls were slaughtered that day, but three were quite enough for us. I do not know how many horses bit the dust, but a good many, — I should think twenty-five dollars' worth, in all. Perhaps I should have got used to the cruelty, the disgusting sight of the gored horses, and the cheap barbarity, if I had stayed through the entire performance; but I could not longer endure the weariness and monotony of the show, the tedious skirmishing between bulls that needed to be all the time irritated up to the fighting point, and decrepit, blindfolded horses that could not see their danger, and nimble athletes that could easily skip to a place of safety. It would have been something like fair if the barriers had been closed and the fighters had owed their escape to speed and address. One's sympathy went always with the tormented bull, whose very bravery and courage insured his death, for there was no chance for him from the first moment. There were times when it would have been a relief to see him dispatch one of his tormentors.

The profoundest impressions left with one were of the weary monotony of the show, and the utter tameness and cheapness of the most of it, and the character of the spectators. There were a good many children in the crowd, having their worst passions cultivated by the brutal exhibition. It is an important part of the national education, and the fruits of it are plain to be seen. I am glad to record that a little girl, seated near us, who had enjoyed the grand entry and the excitement of the scene, was quite broken up by the disgusting details, and frequently hid her face on her father's shoulder, crying nervously at the distress of the poor horses. But the great, roaring crowd heartily gloated over all that was most revolting. Long after we left the arena there was ringing in my ears their barbaric clamor.

We went out from the blazing light and tumult of the ring, glad to escape from the demoniac performance, and sought refuge in an old church near by, to bathe our tired eyes and bruised nerves in its coolness and serenity. Here, at least, was some visible evidence that the Christian religion has still a foothold in Spain.

We tried to console ourselves for the part we had taken in the day's sport by the thought that we had once for all discharged the traveler's duty in a study of the great national pastime — the pastime that royalty encourages by its presence, the pastime that reveals and moulds the character of a once powerful people.

CHAPTER XX.

MONSERRAT.

THE queerest freak of nature in Spain, and perhaps in Europe, is Monserrat, the convent mountain on the east coast, about thirty miles from Barcelona. Goethe refers to it in the second part of "Faust," where we read : —

"It is not unamusing to see Nature
From the Devil's point of view."

It is not generally supposed that the devil, whose office it is to destroy, ever created anything, but if he should try his hand at a landscape the result would be something like Monserrat. Whether he would fill its almost inaccessible caves and the holes in the rocks with hermits is a question for the theologians. That he resisted the establishment there of one of the greatest convents of the Middle Ages, I presume there is no doubt, and that he sees with chagrin the one hundred thousand pilgrims annually crowding to its broken shrines is taken for granted. It is not probable, however, with his Mephistophelean sympathy with the "progress of the age," that he is disturbed by the curiosity-hunters, who have, to use his own language, "a devil of a time" in getting there, or by the thrifty spirit which makes a little money out of the desire to see its sacred places and buy pious souvenirs.

We took the rail from Barcelona to Zaragoza, one day early in June, and rode a couple of hours to the little station of Monistrol. The country is broken into low hills and sharp ravines, and although it is absolutely barren of grass and ragged in aspect, it is much better cultivated than most parts of Spain, and presents an appearance of industrious agriculture. By contrast to the thriftlessness elsewhere, it is a paradise of verdure, and when its nakedness is covered by the vines is far from being unpleasing. From the station, where the road runs along an upland slope, we looked down upon the river Llobregat and its valley. There, at the very base of the mountain, lies the straggling village of Monistrol, with its old stone bridge and high, quaint, dilapidated buildings.

Out of this valley rises the scarped, gashed, and flamboyant mountain, as by a *tour de force*, thrust up, with almost perpendicular sides, into the air nearly four thousand feet. It is said to have a circumference at its base of about twenty-four miles. It springs out of the valley an irregular, unique, independent mass of rock, with little verdure apparently, and glowing in the afternoon light with a dull reddish color. I do not know whether it was really thrown up in some prehistoric spasm of nature, or whether its peculiar form is owing to gradual degradation and decay; but it looks like a molten mass spouted from a solid base into fantastic, contorted, and twisted flames, freaky shapes of fire caught and solidified into pointing fingers, towers, pinnacles, beacons, and writhing attitudes of stone. Another mountain so airy, grotesque, and flame-like does not exist. It cannot be anything else than nature from the devil's point of view, and it might well suggest the idea that it is a veritable piece of the infernal landscape flung up here as a curiosity and a warning. This mass of rock is rent by a deep gash on the east side. That this appalling cleft was not there originally, but was formed by a convulsion at the moment of the crucifixion in Palestine, I have only the authority of the monkish writers, who have made this mountain of miracles a subject of deep scientific study. There is this confirmation of the theory: that nobody except the monks can tell when the chasm was made. And there is this, further, to be said: that but for this gash, this ragged ravine, there would have been no place for the convent, and only the poorest sort of shelter for the hermits.

A lumbering omnibus-diligence was waiting at the Monistrol station to take passengers up the mountain. These are sociable conveyances in Spain, having some of the uses and none of the conveniences of railway palace and dining-room cars. Into the interior were jammed nurses, babies, soldiers, priests, and peasants; all talking and chattering, all eating or nursing, all sweltering and half stifled in the clouds of dust that enveloped the coach. It is the fashion in Spain, when one eats his luncheon or dinner in a public conveyance, to offer of his food and drink to his fellow-travelers; it would be very uncivil not to do this. It is the fashion, also, to decline to take it; so that Spain is the land that combines extreme generosity with the least expense. No doubt both the generosity and the economy are genuine. It does one good in his soul to be liberal in the offer of his bread and boiled meat (left from the soup eaten at home) and sour wine to his companions, and they are all put in good humor by declining. We secured places on the driver's seat in front, where we had the full benefit of the dust, and were deprived of the sustenance contained in the garlic-laden air of the interior. We dashed along at a fine rate down into the valley, and clattered into the town with a good deal of importance; but that was the end of our liveliness. Thenceforward, for four mortal hours, we dragged up the side of the mountain at what seemed to be about the rate of movement of a glacier. The town of Monistrol is picturesque at a distance, and unsightly close at hand. Its tall houses, with recessed balconies the width of the front on each story, are piled one above another in shabby disorder, on the steep sides of the river and up the hill. These balconies, which appear to be the living and lounging places of the families, are screened from the sun by curtains of matting, and are gay with garments of all colors and all styles of wear. Before beginning the ascent the diligence halted at a friendly little *posada*, with a flower-garden, where lively and pretty girls served the passengers with such refreshments as they called for. The road climbing the mountain — like nearly all the roads in Spain, where the government has thought it worth while to make any — is splendidly built. It is carried up the mountain side, along ledges and precipices, in a series of gradually ascending loops and curves, constantly doubling on itself, and going a distance of two miles to make a quarter of a mile ascent. Lately, trees — figs, maples, cherries, pines, and aspens — have been planted along this broad highway, so that in a few years its sun-beaten travelers will enjoy a much-needed shade. All the ravines about which the road coils like an interminable serpent are terraced, and carefully cultivated and set with vines.

The slow, creeping movement of the diligence at length became so intolerable that several of the passengers dismounted, and walked on, reaching the monastery before it. As we rose, the capricious character of the mountain became more apparent. Great masses of rock overhung the road; the walls were buttressed like artificial fortifications, and a range of tapering towers, not needles and spires, as in the dolomites and the *pointes d'aiguilles* at Chamouni, but bluntly and clumsily terminated, like fingers and thumbs, stood up in the air. At one point we passed beneath a partially isolated column that is held aloft exactly like a light-house. The mountain is longest from east to west, and the old monks fancied that it had the form of a gigantic ship, with its prow upheaved; a mysterious vessel in which the Virgin Mary conducted her devotees — some of whom, however, suffered shipwreck, according to the legends — to the port of Salvation. It might as well be called a Noah's ark, stranded in a dry time. The mountain in its formation and composition is of the utmost interest to geologists and mineralogists. A near inspection shows that the entire mass, ledges, walls, towers, and pinnacles, is composed of small round stones, of various colors, agglomerated into a sort of pudding-stone, a party-colored mosaic, reddish and greenish and grayish, and very beautiful when the sun strikes it. The mountain is also very rich, for the botanist, in plants and wild flowers.

After miles of weary curving and doubling the road sweeps along the north side of the mountain and enters the eastern cleft, in which the convent buildings and gardens are found. There was no sign of any habitation, or any possible place for one, until we were actually in it. The ravine ends in a horseshoe curve, set about with perpendicular precipices and towers, the latter leaning towards each other in drunken confusion, pointing in various directions into the sky; some the shape of monstrous tenpins, and one, which was my favorite, exactly the shape of a thumb with a distinctly accented nail. In this almost inaccessible spot, nobody except religious fanatics would ever have deemed it possible to obtain standing-room for extensive religious houses. But here, jammed into this crevice, frowned on by precipices all around, with a ragged, yawning gulf in front and below, extending down, down, to the far-off, dreamy valley, are the several houses of a vast monastery, a large church, buildings for laymen, a great restaurant, ruins of fine Gothic edifices destroyed by the ever-barbarous French invaders, some cypresses, and some tiny garden spots. All these structures cluster about the head of the ravine, and rest on ledges over which the rocks hang in threatening attitudes. Standing in the courtyard of the church, about which are the high barracks of the "religious," and looking up to the beetling, impending crags and the blue heavens above the dark mass, one has a conception of the sublime daring of religious faith in the presence of forbidding and implacable nature. Round about, high up among the rocks, are the caves and the ruined stone huts of the old hermits.

It was near sundown when we reached this haven of rest and made a demand on its hospitality for the few days of our pilgrim sojourn. The monastery has a great history, into which it is no part of this paper to enter. It was suppressed over forty years ago, and is no longer of much importance as an active religious community; it has less than a score of monks to occupy its vast barracks. But it is now, as it has been for ages, a thronged place of pilgrimage on account of its famed image of the Black Virgin. Many years ago extensive buildings were erected for the temporary accommodation of pilgrims and lay brothers, and in these strangers are hospitably assigned quarters for three days, or for nine days on special permission, without charge for lodging. But Spain is like other lands, where something is not given for nothing, and the stranger, at the end of his stay, is expected to put into the box of the custodian about as much as he would pay for lodgings at a good hotel, and as much more as his piety dictates.

No enthusiasm was exhibited on our arrival, and there was no one to welcome us or to direct us. We were left on the pavement, where the diligence landed us with our luggage, utterly at a loss how to effect an entrance into any of the stone jails in sight. At length we were directed to the *hospederia*, where a civil brother in a black robe informed us that a lay brother would assign us quarters presently. The lay brother, when he appeared, hardly filled one's idea of a brother, nor had he the neatness that one requires in a chamber-maid, which was his office with regard to our rooms. He showed me into a room in the plain stone building of Santa Theresa of Jesus, as the inscription over the door informed me, built early in the sixteenth century. The room was a dirty, whitewashed cell, with one window and a stone floor, and contained for furniture a narrow bedstead, a rickety, dirty washstand, a shaky chair, and a bit of mirror. To this ascetic den the brother brought sheets, a towel, and a jug of water, gave me the key of it, and set me up in housekeeping. When I had visited the restaurant and bought a fat tallow candle, I wanted nothing more that was to be obtained. The room was comfortable enough, but not calculated to win one to take up a permanent abode in it and abandon the luxury of the world. Yet when I opened the window, in the deepening twilight, and looked out, through the branches of a couple of tall trees that manage somehow to grow in that stony place, down the ravine lying in the shadow of the precipices, on farther into the valley, hazy in a golden mist of early evening, and felt the cool air, not unladen with sweetness, blow up from below, and heard the faint and fainter bird twitterings and the hushed hum of a June night, I think that I experienced, in this high seclusion, something of that calm which hermits term the peace of God. Indeed, one could take his choice of emotions in this solitude, which witnessed strange antediluvian freaks, which was haunted by sylvan shapes in Roman times, where Venus was no doubt a goddess before Mary, which was a hunting-ground of Goths and Saracens, where Charlemagne set up a shrine to Santa Cecilia in the eighth century, where the image of the Virgin wrought miracles in the ninth century, where Philip II. spent vast sums in building to the glory of God and himself, and where, in the chapel hard by, Ignatius Loyola spent a night in meditation before the shrine of the Virgin, on whose altar he laid his sword in the hours when he dedicated himself, her true knight, to the foundation of the Order of Jesus.

The hospitality of the brethren stops with shelter; the pilgrim must go to the restaurant for his food. This is a "Frenchy" sort of establishment, not conducted on an ascetic regimen, and its flaunting presence here, together with the holy booth for the sale of photographs and superstitious trinkets, gives a sort of show appearance to this sacred place. It has become a pleasure resort, — pleasure of a chastened sort. The restaurant has three stories, like a graded school, in which the food served is graded to suit the purses of the pilgrims. The lower floor is rudely furnished, like the peasants' dining-room in a posada; the second is a little better; the third has more pretensions to elegance. The traveler can begin below and eat himself upward into expensive meals, or he can begin at the top and drop down to economy as his purse fails. The natives probably get about as good food in the lowest room as strangers get in the highest. The traveler, however, will fare tolerably well there, and he will be served with that absolute indifference to whether he likes it or not that characterizes the proud caterers of noble Spain.

The glory of Monserrat is the image of the Virgin. It was this that built its monastery and church, drew countless treasure to the coffers of the fraternity for hundreds of years, and that still attracts annually tens of thousands of curious and devout pilgrims. The history of it is interesting, though original only in some points, for there is a monotonous sameness in all these monkish inventions. There was a great strife all through the Middle Ages, among convents and churches, for objects that should attract the pence and excite the piety of the devout, and many a church was built and gorgeously decorated by reason of its possession of some uncommonly attractive relic. Black images of the Virgin are common in Spain. A very popular one is the Virgin of the Pillar, at Zaragoza, over which the Cathedral El Pilar was erected to keep it safe and honor it. In this church is shown the alabaster pillar on which the Virgin stood when she descended to have an interview with Santiago. By reason of this special mark of the favor of the Virgin, Zaragoza claimed the primacy of Aragon. Upon the pillar stands a very ancient image of the Virgin; it is small, and carved out of resinous and very black wood. The Virgin holds the Infant in one hand, and gathers her drapery in the other. The pillar, which is the object of passionate devotion to the people of Zaragoza, can be seen through a small orifice in the marble casing, but the spot in sight is much worn by the kisses of the faithful. Few Catholics visit the church without putting their lips to the sacred stone. In the old Cathedral of San Leo, in the same city, is a spot marked in the pavement where the Virgin stood and spoke to Canon Funes. Toledo, not to be outdone, has also a small image called the Great Queen, carved in black wood. In 711 it was saved from the infidel Saracens by an Englishman, who hid it in a vault. It is one of the treasures of the cathedral, which has also the stone slab on which the Virgin alighted when she conversed with San Ildefonso, who died in 617. To this circumstance Toledo owes its elevation to the primacy of Castile.

The image now at Monserrat has its origin in the love of the Virgin for the Catalanes, who saw with pity their grief at the favoritism shown the Aragonese in the possession of the Virgin of the Pillar. It was probably carved by St. Luke, — the first of the master wood-carvers, — and brought to Barcelona by St. Peter in the year 50. When it was endangered by the Moorish invasion in 717, it was carried to this mountain, hid in a cave, and forgotten for a hundred and sixty-three years. In 880 some shepherds wandering over the mountain were attracted to the place of its concealment by heavenly lights. They informed Gondemar, Bishop of Vique, who repaired to the spot, and, guided by a sweet smell, discovered the image in a cave. This cave, over which is now erected a beautiful and exceedingly damp and bone-chilling chapel, where daily masses are said, is one of the chief places of pilgrimage. It lies on a narrow ledge deep down in the ravine, a mile or more from the monastery. Bishop Gondemar, rejoicing in his discovery, set out with a procession of clergy to bear the image over the mountain to his church in Manresa. When they had toiled up the ragged ravine, and reached a level ledge not far from where the monastery now stands, the Virgin obstinately refused to go any farther. As there was no reasoning with a graven image, it was placed on the spot where it wished to rest, and a rude chapel was built over it, in which it remained for one hundred and sixty years. A cross now marks the spot.

How did the Virgin indicate to the priests her refusal to go any farther? This is one of those skeptical questions which it is easy to ask, and somewhat difficult to answer. It is, however, a scientific fact that if you attempt to carry a wooden image over such a mountain as Monserrat there will come a point in the journey where the image becomes heavy, and apparently refuses to go on without a long rest.

A nunnery was afterwards founded here, which in 976 was converted into a Benedictine convent. In the year 1599 Philip II. dedicated the church which is the present home of the venerated image, where it shines in all the splendor of lace and jewelry high up in a recess above the high altar. Every day after midday mass the pilgrims are permitted to ascend, and adore it. The approach to it is through several apartments by flights of stairs. In the rear of the image is the Virgin's waiting-room, a small chamber, from which the devotees pass round singly to the narrow platform in front of the image. The day of our ascent the chamber was crowded with a devout, or at least devoutly-seeming, throng: worshipers, travelers with note-books and pencils, and artists. Each one in turn passed in front to gaze at or to kiss the object of the pilgrimage. Many a woman returned with moist eyes and deeply moved. The image itself is of black wood; of what sort the custodians are unable to say, but they declare that it is sweetly odorous and incorruptible. It is painted and finely gilded. The figure is seated, with the child in her lap, the latter holding a globe in his right hand. The position of both figures is stiff and archaic, but the face of the Virgin is well carved and pleasing.

In one of the rooms in the rear is the wardrobe of the Virgin, containing many sorts of raiment, rich and ornamented stuffs, the gifts of kings, princes, prelates, and wealthy devotees. Another large chamber contains the votive offerings, the most curious collection in Europe, and not unlike the shop of a thriftless pawnbroker. Those restored to health by touching the sacred image have deposited here whatever was precious to them, and many of the mementos speak the touching thankfulness of poverty. There are wretched pictures of sick-beds, shipwrecks, accidents of all sorts, and rescues; pieces of lace, real and imitation; crutches and canes; an exploded musket; human hair of every color and degree of fineness, — one long and superb braid of glossy black, the wealth and pride of some grateful, and perhaps penitent, Spanish beauty; swords, broken and hacked in service, and parade rapiers; clothing of every description, — gowns of silk and woolen and cotton, underwear of nameless sorts, pantaloons and waistcoats too ragged for a beggar to covet, coats antiquated beyond all fashion plates; hats and caps by the dozen, — hats old and bad, new and shining, hats of silk, of felt, and of straw, sombreros and wide-awakes, belonging to peasants, priests, sailors, and soldiers, all hung up out of gratitude, or weariness of the hat; wax images, without number, of babies, of heads, of arms, hips, bodies, and breasts; bandages and supports; models of ships elaborately carved and rigged; knapsacks; banners of embroidered silk, presented by cities, municipalities, and nobles. An offering that attracted as much attention as any was a lady's necktie, a deft construction of blue ribbon and lace. I saw women looking longingly at it, and wondering, perhaps, how a girl could make up her mind to give up such a fresh and sweet thing.

We made, one day, the ascent of the mountain to the summit, to Monte San Geronimo, where was one of the hermit shrines. The severe climb requires an hour and a half; it repays the trouble, as well for the extensive prospect as for the knowledge it gives of the structure of this fantastic mountain. The way lies up ledges and through ravines and valleys, variegated with sweet shrubs, wild flowers, and verdure, and enlivened with birds, under and around the bases of the detached columns of stone, some of which rise three hundred feet in the air, to the highest point, a bare field of rock. From this windy summit we peeped between the columns, leaning over the dizzy precipice, looking down fully two thousand feet to other ledges below. The prospect is very comprehensive and pleasing to those who enjoy panoramic and map-like views. On a clear day the white snow of the Pyrenees can be seen, the coast and Barcelona, and the Mediterranean and the Balearic Islands. We saw none of these objects in the hazy horizon. Beneath the overhanging rocks is a coffee-house where once the hermit's hut stood, in which travelers shelter themselves from the wind, and partake of a beverage called coffee. It is a very wild and gloomy place, and abounds in curious rocky freaks. We were not alone. A company of chatty, and for Spaniards merry, pilgrims had arrived before us, who were much more impressed with the hardships of the way than with the magnificences and wonders of the mountain. I had the honor — I mention it because it gave a fleeting charm to the barren region — to assist a Spanish beauty, who was painfully picking her way up the rough ascent in satin slippers, and whose husband unsentimentally clung to the shelter of the hut. I carried her formidable fan, a weapon the Spanish woman never parts with, blow it high or low, and when I restored it, on our return from the thrilling expedition of a few rods, I could not have been thanked with more eloquent eyes, sweeter voice, and profounder bow if I had saved her life. How sweet, sometimes, it is to sacrifice one's self for others!

Several hundred feet above the restaurant, in the face of the cliff, and accessible only by a narrow ledge not discernible from the road below, is the cave of Joan Gari. In this hole in the rock that excellent ancient hermit probably passed the last five years of his useful life, never stirring out of it, his few wants being supplied by charitable souls. I found that La Cueva de Gari, when I reached it, was an irregular cavity in the rock, perhaps twelve feet long and not so deep as long, and about four feet high. It is protected in front by a double iron grating four feet square. In it reposes a stone image of the holy man, life-size, with a venerable beard. He lies reclining on one elbow, contemplating a skull, which has lost several of its teeth and is presumably his own, and a representation of the miraculous image of the Virgin and Child. The clasped hands rest upon an open book and beads, and a rude little cross is stuck in the rock before him. Behind him lies his wallet and his staff, a basket that perhaps once held the contributions of the charitable, and a broken water-jug. This primitive furniture is probably all that the apartment ever contained in the days when the entrance to the cave was thronged by devout spectators of a man's ability to lie down on a bed of stone and straw for five years.

The story of Joan Gari is a testimony to the wonder-working power of the Monserrat image. It illustrates also the virtue of penitence, and throws light upon the candid answer of the lovely French catechumen, who, when she was asked, What is it necessary to do in order to repent? replied, It is necessary to sin. I take the story as I find it in the authorized Historia de Monserrat, which I bought at the monastery.

Joan Gari was a hermit of Monserrat in the ninth century, who had a great repute for sanctity and purity and devotion to Santa Cecilia. Naturally, Joan Gari prided himself upon his sanctity, and God determined to put it to proof. There reigned at that time at Barcelona, Count Wilfredo el Velloso, the father of a beautiful and charming daughter, who, for the secret purposes of the divine will, was afflicted with a malign spirit, which, it was declared, would not depart out of her and leave her in health except at the mandate of Joan Gari. And it was necessary that the maiden should seek the holy man alone in the mountain where he abode. Count Wilfredo, moved by his affection, and against all the dictates of prudence, consented to this pilgrimage of his blooming daughter. She departed to the mountain, and never returned. Many years elapsed before her fate was known to the count. The hermit had received her, dishonored her, murdered her to conceal his crime, and buried her body in a crevice in the rocks. Overcome at last by remorse, Joan Gari threw himself at the feet of the image of the Virgin, and begged her pity and help. In order to get an indulgence for his sins he made a journey to Rome, and the Pope absolved him on condition that he should expiate his crime by becoming a beast like Nebuchadnezzar and roaming about on all fours. This Gari did faithfully for six years, crawling about among the rocks on his hands and knees, exposed to the elements, foraging for his food like an animal in the thickets, until he became a hairy, unmentionable monster of the forest. One day in the year 894, Count Wilfredo, with a troop of attendants, went forth to hunt in the wilds of Monserrat. His companions, beating about in the wilderness, routed out a nondescript monster, who permitted himself to be taken alive into the presence of Count Wilfredo. The count was much amused with this capture, and determined to take him as a trophy to Barcelona, whither Gari was nothing loath to go, as he was determined to suffer in silence all the punishment that God and the count might inflict. He was taken to Barcelona, and exhibited as a real monster of the forest, And there God at last saw and accepted the penitence of Gari. One day, when the count had a great feast, he ordered the monster to be brought into the banquet-hall, in order to entertain his guests with the uncouth curiosity. But lo! while they made merry over him at the feast, God spoke out of the heavens, and said, "Arise, Joan Gari! God has pardoned thy sins." All heard the voice, but could hardly believe what they heard. But Gari, emboldened by the heavenly aid, arose and stood upright, and prostrating himself at the feet of the count confessed all. And Count Wilfredo, who declared that it did not become him to withhold a forgiveness that God had granted, pardoned him on condition that he should lead them to the grave of the murdered girl. This Gari did, and when they stood by the grave of his victim, lo! grace succeeded grace. Requilda awoke from her long and tranquil sleep in the arms of Mary the Mother of God, and rose up radiant, and kissed her wondering father. Like a true woman as she was, her first petition to her father was that he should forgive her destroyer, and the next was that she should be permitted to consecrate herself to the service of the Holy Virgin, at this very shrine, in the shadow of which she had been dishonored, murdered, buried, and resurrected after a sleep of seven years. So Requilda became a nun, and Joan Gari crawled, I suppose, into his hole, where he ended a life which diffuses a sanctity over all this region. Whether he is, as I have read, the most beautiful exemplar of *all* the virtues, the reader must judge. It seems to me that he missed some of them. What they were his image is perhaps intended to represent him as inquiring, in his phrenological attitude of studying his own skull.

It is a very soothing and peaceful place to sojourn in, this secluded nook in the mountain. One is lifted up above the world, which is nevertheless in sight, and protected without any sense of being imprisoned. It adds something to the feeling of repose that one can look so far down the ravine, off over the widening valley, and out upon a great expanse of country, which he knows is humming with life, no sound of which reaches him in his secure retreat. If one is in search of a good solid solitude, let him come and dwell here. An air of quiet reigns. All the visitors, pilgrims, and curiosity-hunters do not seem to break it. The ruins, the half-neglected gardens, the gaunt old monastery with its rows of factory-like windows, the antiquated houses of entertainment, the big church hanging over the precipice, the savage rocks, the gashed ravines, the fantastic towers that lean in the background, would subdue the most jaunty spirit; and yet it is not a melancholy place. The birds like it, the flowers bloom there with tender grace, the air is fresh and inspiring. The few friars who glide about the courts and occasionally show themselves at a window, the servants who keep the place in order, the little colony that has gathered there to serve the public, scarcely disturb the ancient quiet. I fancy that the atmosphere of monkish reticence and silence still remains. It is one of the few spots left in the world where a scholar might sit down, undisturbed by any suggestions of an uneasy age, and compose such interminable theological tomes as those that slumber in its libraries, which nobody can read.

CHAPTER XXI.

RANDOM SPANISH NOTES.

SPAIN is for all the world the land of romance. For the artist it is the land of Murillo, Velasquez, Fortuny, and Goya, of sunlight and color. For the student of history it holds the precious archives of the New World adventure and daring, of that subtle and sanguinary policy in religion and war which is typified in the names of Loyola and Philip II. For the lover of architecture it contains some marvels of Gothic boldness and fancy, and Saracenic beauty and grace. For the investigator of race and language it holds the problems of the Basque and the Gypsy. The great races who have had their day there, the Roman, the Goth, the Norman, the Moor, have left visible traces and an historical atmosphere of romance.

And yet the real Spain is the least attractive country in Europe to the tourist. The traveler goes there to see certain unique objects. He sees them, enjoys them, is entranced by them, leaves them with regret and a tender memory, and is glad to get out of Spain. There are six things to see: the Alhambra, the Seville cathedral and Alcazar, the Mosque of Cordova, Toledo and its cathedral, the Gallery at Madrid, and Monserrat. The rest is mainly monotony and weariness.

With the exception of the Alhambra, which has a spell that an idle man finds hard to break, and where perhaps he could be content indefinitely, there is no place in Spain that one can imagine he would like to live in, for the pleasure of living. Taking out certain historical features and monuments, the towns repeat each other in their attractions and their disagreeables. Every town and city in Italy has its individual character and special charm. To go from one to another is always to change the scene and the delight. This is true of the old German towns also. Each has a character. The traveler sees many a place in each country where he thinks he could stay on from month to month, with a growing home-like feeling. I think there is nothing of this attraction in Spain. The want of it may be due to the country itself, or to the people. I fancy that with its vast arid plains, treeless and tiresome, its gullied hills and its bare, escarped mountains, Spain resembles New Mexico. It is an unsoftened, unrelieved landscape, for the most part, sometimes grand in its vastness and sweep, but rugged and unadorned. The want of grass and gentle verdure is a serious drawback to the pleasure of the eye, not compensated by the magic tricks of the sunlight, and the variegated reds, browns, and yellows of the exposed soil and rocks, and the spring-time green of the nascent crops. I speak, of course, of the general aspect, for the mountain regions are rich in wild flowers, and the cultivation in the towns is everywhere a redeeming feature.

The traveler, of course, gets his impressions of a people from the outside. These are correct so far as they go, and it is in a sense safe to generalize on them, though not to particularize. He catches very soon the moral atmosphere of a strange land, and knows whether it is agreeable or otherwise, whether the people seem pleasant or the reverse. He learns to discriminate, for example, between the calculated *gemüthlichkeit* of Switzerland and the more spontaneous friendliness of Bavaria. He can pronounce at once upon the cordial good humor of the Viennese, the obligingness of the people of Edinburgh, the agreeableness of the Swedes, simply on street-knowledge, without ever entering a private house or receiving any personal hospitality. He knows the wily, poetical ways by which he is beguiled in Italy, but grows fond of the sunny race.

In Spain he is pretty certain to be rubbed the wrong way, most of the time. He is conscious of an atmosphere of suspicion, of distrust, of contempt often. He cannot understand, for instance, why attendants in churches and cathedrals are so curt and disobliging, keeping him away, on one pretense and another, from the sights he has come far to see, and for which he is willing to pay. Incidents occurred both at Granada and Toledo that could be accounted for only on the supposition that the custodians liked to discommode strangers. If we had been Frenchmen, whom the Spaniards hate as the despoilers of churches and galleries, we could have understood it.

By reputation the Spaniard is at home hospitable, and on acquaintance gracious, and generally willing to oblige. But the national atmosphere is certainly not what the Germans call *gemüthlich*. In no other European country is the traveler likely to encounter so much incivility and rudeness, so little attempt at pleasing him and making him like the country. At least, the attitude is that of indifference whether the country pleases him or not. Perhaps this springs from a noble pride and superiority. Perhaps it is from a provincial consciousness of being about two hundred years behind the age. But, elsewhere, the pleasantest people to travel among are those whose clocks stopped two centuries ago. Individually, I have no doubt, the Spaniards are charming. Collectively, they do not appear to welcome the stranger, or put themselves out to make his sojourn agreeable.

I should say all this with diffidence, or perhaps should not say it at all, if I had been longer in Spain. But surface impressions have a certain value as well as deep experiences. Some philosophers maintain that the first impression of a face is the true one as to the character of the person.

Spain, then, impresses one with a sense of barrenness, — a barren land with half a dozen rich "pockets." The present race, if we take out a few artists and writers, has produced nothing that the world much cares for. It destroyed and, sheerly from want of appreciation, let go to ruin the most exquisite creations of a people of refinement and genius. The world ought never to forgive the barbarity that constructed the hideous palace of Charles V., in the Alhambra, — tearing down priceless architectural beauty to make room for it, — or that smashed into the forest of twelve hundred columns in the mosque of Cordova, to erect a chapel in the centre. Since the era of the magnificent Gothic cathedrals, Spanish taste and character seem typified in that palace of Charles in the Alhambra, and in the ugly and forbidding pile — as utilitarian as a stone cotton-mill — the Escorial. Modern Spanish architecture is generally uninteresting, and would be wholly so but for the inheritance of the Moorish courts or *patios*, which give a charm to the interiors.

But for these and the few remains of a better age, nothing could be more commonplace than the appearance of the city of Seville, or uglier than its dusty and monotonous plazas. This character is that of the cities of Andalusia. Yet what undying romance there is in the very names of Andalucia and Sevilla! What visions of chivalry and beauty and luxury they evoke! What a stream of the imagination is the turbid Guadalquivir, running through a flat and sandy country! Seville itself is flat, and subject to the overflow of the river. Consequently it is damp and unwholesome a part of the year; in summer it is hot, in winter it has a fitful, chilly climate. In spite of the mantillas and fans and dark eyes, the pretty *patios* with flowers and perhaps a fountain, the iridescent splendors of the Alcazar and the decaying interiors of some old Moorish houses, like the Casa de Pilatos (said to be built in imitation of the House of Pilate in Jerusalem), the magnificent cathedral, which is as capable as anything in this world, built of stone, to lift the soul up into an ecstasy of devotional feeling, the aspect of the town is essentially provincial and common. It is modernized without taste, and yet when the traveler comes away he hates to admit it, remembering the unique attractions of the cathedral and the Alcazar, and a narrow, winding street, still left here and there, with the overhanging balconies high in the air, the quaint portals, the glimpses of flowery courts, the towers white with whitewash, the sharp blue shadows, the rifts of cerulean sky overhead. He tries to forget the staring Plaza Nueva, with its stunted palms, and the Bull-Ring, and the gigantic cigar factory, where are assembled, under one roof, three thousand coarse women, many of whom have learned to roll cigars and rock the cradles at their side at the same time, — three thousand coarse women, with now and then a wild beauty; for it is difficult to keep beauty out of the female sex altogether, anywhere.

The traveler will fare very well in the larger towns of Spain, where the French art of cooking is practiced, with the addition of an abundance in the way of fruit. We were very well off at the Hôtel Madrid in Seville, which has spacious rooms and a charming large interior court, overlooked by verandas, with a fountain and flowers and oleanders and other low-growing trees, and with garlands of vines stretched across it. The company was chiefly Spanish, and the long *table d'hôte* was not seldom amusing, in spite of all the piety of formality which in Europe belongs to the ceremony of dining. Of course none but the best people were there, and after the soup, and at any time during the courses, the gentlemen lit cigarettes, so that we could see the ladies' eyes flashing through a canopy of smoke. It was a noisy table; it was in fact a Babel. The Spaniard, in public, does not appear to converse; he orates, and gesticulates, and argues with the vehemence of a man on the rostrum. He is carried away by his own eloquence; he rises, pounds the table, shakes his fist at his adversary. But it is not a quarrel. His adversary is not excited; he sits perfectly calm, as the listeners do; and then in turn he works himself up into a paroxysm of communication. Occasionally they all talk together, and it looks like a row, and sounds like one. At the first occurrence of this phenomenon I expected trouble, and was surprised to see that nothing came of it, for the talkers subsided, and left the table together in a friendly manner. This exuberance gives a zest to dining.

Cordova is not quite the deadest city in Spain, but it rubs Toledo very hard. If there were to be a fair and a competition for civic deadness, it is difficult to predict which city would win the prize. They would both deserve it, or at least honorable mention. Cordova, however, is not buried, and it is not, like Toledo, a mass of decay. It has simply stopped in a decent commonplaceness; it does not apparently do anything;

it has a vacation. It is whitewashed, and clean enough. But the streets are vacant, and there is a suspicion of grass growing up between the stones. The fifty thousand people here ought to be lively enough to keep it down, but there seems to be nothing to be lively about. And yet if the tourist only had time to take in the fact, this is one of the most interesting cities in Spain. No other, not Seville, preserves so much in its houses the Moorish appearance, which is the charm of Spain wherever it exists. It is a great pleasure to stroll about the echoing streets and note the old-time beauty of the dwellings. Cordova — *Karta-tuba*, an "important city" — had a million of inhabitants from the ninth to the twelfth century, nine hundred baths, six hundred inns, and three hundred mosques. Seneca was born here, and Lucan, and Thomas Sanches, the Jesuit author of "De Matrimonio;" and here Gonzalo de Cordova, the great captain, was baptized. It was once the capital of Moorish Spain, an independent Khalifate; in art and letters an Athens; in wealth, refinement, and luxury the Paris of the time, with an added Oriental splendor; a place of pilgrimage for the occidental world only less sacred than Mecca.

Cordova has now to show the unique mosque, one of the most interesting buildings in the world, the monument of Moorish genius and magnificence, and a monumental statue, *El Triunfo*, — an incongruous pile surmounted by Rafael, the patron saint of the city, easily the worst statue in Europe, and a witness of Spanish taste. This monument stands down by the great stone bridge over the Guadalquivir, from which the lounger has an admirable view of the picturesque old town.

The Great Mosque was begun in 786 by Abdu-r-rahma I., who determined to build the finest mosque in the world; but even his splendid edifice was greatly enlarged in the tenth century. There was an era of good feeling between the Church and Islam in those days. Before this mosque was built, Christians and Moslems amicably occupied different parts of the same basilica, and when the Caliph wanted to enlarge he bought out the Christians. Leo, Emperor of Constantinople, sent one hundred and forty precious antique columns for the new building, and Greek artists to decorate it; and when Cordova was conquered by the Christians, I believe that for some time the two religions held worship in this edifice. It occupies the whole of a vast square. The exterior walls, six feet in thickness, and from thirty to sixty feet high, with buttressed towers and richly carved portals to the different entrances, is the finest specimen of this sort of work existing. Nearly a third of the great square is occupied by the open Court of Oranges, the abode, it will be remembered, of Irving's wise parrot, who knew more than the ordinary doctor of law; still a delightful grove of oranges, with great fountains, where the pious and the idle like to congregate. From this there were nineteen doors, — all now walled up except three, — opening directly into the sacred mosque.

With all these openings, added to the entrances on the other three sides, to admit freely light and air, and to permit the light to play on its polished columns, what a cheerful and beautiful interior it must have been! And what a bewildering sight it is yet! The roof is low, not above thirty-five feet high, and originally it was all flat. The area is about three hundred and ninety-four feet east and west, by five hundred and fifty-six feet north and south, and it is literally a forest of columns. Of the original 1,200, 1,096 still stand; the others were removed to make room for the elaborate choir erected in the centre, which destroys the great sweep of pillars and much of the forest effect. It is fit to make a body weep to see how the Christians have abused this noble interior. It would have been more excusable if it had been done by early Christians, to whom we pardon everything; but it was not: it was done by late and a poor kind of Christians. These columns, all monoliths, and all made to appear of uniform height by sinking the longer ones in the floor, were the spoils of heathen temples in Europe, Asia, and Africa. Many came from Nîmes and Narbonne, some from Seville and Tarragona, numbers from Constantinople, and a great quantity from Carthage and other ancient cities of Africa. They are all of choice and some of them of rare marbles, jasper, porphyry, verd-antique, and all were originally highly polished, and many still retain their lustre. They might, with a little labor, be made again to shine like gems. From the carved capitals of these columns spring round Moorish arches, painted in red and white, which, seen in any diagonal view, interlace like ribbons, and produce a surprising and charming effect.

This mosque was called Zeca, the house of purification; it was equal in rank to Al Aksa in Jerusalem, and its shrine of pilgrimage was second only to the Kaaba at Mecca. If the traveler chooses to walk seven times around the lovely little chapel in the centre, once the holy of holies, he will tread in a well-worn path in the stone made by tens of thousands of Moslem pilgrim feet. This chapel and the Mihrab are brilliant with mosaics, and fine carving in stone, and stucco ornamentation. I have heard some critics contrast the lowness of this edifice with the springing aspiration of the Gothic cathedrals, and say that it oppressed them; but it is one of the wonders of the world.

Toledo, so often figured and described, I am sure needs no description from me. Everybody knows that it stands, with its crumbling walls and towers and decaying palaces, on a high hill of rock perpendicular on three sides, and that the muddy Tagus flows around it in a deep ravine, making it almost an island. I walked and scrambled entirely around it one day, — not on the city side, for that is impossible, but on the high overlooking hills circling it on the opposite side of the river, — and marked well its ramparts and towers. I could n't throw an orange into it from the encircling hills, but from this vantage ground artillery could quickly reduce it to a stone heap. But I do not know as that would much change the exterior appearance of the city. Nothing in the world looks so old, scarred, and battered.

Within it is the city of silence. Not in Karnak is this silence, if one may say so, more audible to the listening ear. There are no carriages, except the omnibus that took us up from the station, over the bridge Alcantara — the high arch beneath which flows the rapid Tagus — and through the Moorish Gate of the Sun, and this can make its way only in a few of the streets; the others are too steep, too narrow, too rough. There is no traffic, and the footfalls have little echo in the deserted streets. But what a museum of the picturesque it is, this stately widow, as somebody calls it, of two dynasties, with the remains of noble façades and the loveliest carved portals and recesses and windows! Everywhere Moorish suggestion and Moorish fancy, a perpetual charm. The tourist goes hunting everywhere for the remains of Saracen genius, and prizes every broken tile, stuccoed room, ornamented wall and ceiling, and quaintly carved door-way.

Ah, well, this is not a guide-book. We stayed, while we were in Toledo, with the sisters Figueroa, descendants, I believe, of a noble house, who dwell in a rambling, high, and gaunt tenement that has seen better days, but not cleaner; for its entrance steps are scrubbed, its bare floors are scrubbed, and I think its hard beds are scrubbed. It is, after all, a comfortable sort of place, though I did not find out exactly in what

the comfort consisted. There is only one other place
of entertainment in the whole city, the inn, and we
were zealously warned against that by all the travelers
we saw who had preceded us. On coming away, we
warned people against the Figueroa. It was the least
we could do. And yet we did it with humorous regret; for the ancient maiden sisters were neat. Ah,
if they had only given us anything we could eat; if
they had not served our morning coffee and bread on
an old salver rusty with age, and not too clean, and
the rusty old coffee-pot had had a handle, and the
bread had been sweet, how different it would have
been! We took a liking to these venerable virgins,
although they were churlish and unaccommodating,
and treated our humble requests for certain conveniences with lofty scorn. But pride and hotel-keeping
must go together in Spain. They must have had good
hearts, these women, although they were not liberal,
for they kept the house full of pets, — quail that were
always whistling, and doves that were always loudly
cooing, especially when we wished to sleep in the morning. We took our frugal repasts in their neat and
stuffy little sitting-room. There was not a book or a
newspaper in the house (in sight), but the walls were
covered with trumpery pictures of saints and madonnas. In the little sitting-room, where the sisters sat
by the deep-cushioned window and sewed, there were
five saints and eleven madonnas. But most pathetic
of all was an *étagère*, on which these dear old ladies
(it was probably our traveled rudeness, and their keen

perception of our ignorance of what was good enough food for anybody, that made them so angular to us) kept the playthings of their far-away youth, — their dolls, their baby-houses, the little trifles dear to girlhood. No, indeed, I would n't have had these excellent women different in any respect, — not in Toledo. For what has Toledo itself except the toys of its youth? It is rather surprising that Toledo is as clean as it is, as it has no water, except what is brought up the steep hill from the river in jars on the patient donkeys. It is in no danger of modern improvements and drainage. I suppose the rains of heaven wash it; and the snow, perhaps, helps, for it is a frightfully cold place in winter. But it makes up for that by a hot summer, when the sun, reflected from the bare rocks about it, blazes away at it without hindrance. Its sole specialty is the beautiful niello work, the inlaying of gold and silver in steel, which is carried on at a couple of shops, and at the ancient factory across the river, ever famous for its high-tempered, inlaid Toledo blades. We made a journey thither, but it was not remunerative, except for its historical associations. A few inferior arms are manufactured there; but as fine blades are probably now made in America and England as Toledo ever tempered; and the inlaying of brooches and fancy scarf pins and other ornamental things is not equal to the ancient work. Still Toledo keeps something of its craft in this exquisite art.

One hesitates to speak of the glory of the place, the cathedral, because no justice can be done it in a paragraph; nor can any justice be done the surly custodians who refused to let us see some of its locked-up treasures, after appointing time after time for us to come. It was a mine of hoarded wealth and art before it was plundered by the French in 1808. The corner-stone was laid by Saint Ferdinand in 1226, and it was completed in the year America was discovered; but its enrichment went on, and the names of one hundred and forty-nine artists are given who for centuries worked at its adornment. I do not know anywhere else a finer example of the pure, vigorous Gothic, scarcely another so nobly and simply impressive, nor any other richer in artistic designs. It satisfies the mind by its noble solidity, purity, and picturesqueness. When you are in it, you are quite inclined to accept its supernatural inception. The virgin is said to have come down from heaven during its erection, and the marble slab is shown on which she stood when she appeared to Saint Ildefonso. But I do not see how that could have been, for the cathedral was not projected till 1226, and Saint Ildefonso died in 617. His body, carried off during the Moorish invasion, was recovered about the year 1270, and is supposed to be buried here. But I believe the legend is that the Virgin made several appearances here, and was present a good deal of the time during the building of the cathedral. At any rate, the stone is here, encased in red marble in the rear of the shrine of the saint, and quite worn with the kisses of the believers, who come still to put their lips on the exact spot touched by the

Virgin's feet. The cathedral has also a famous image of the Virgin in black wood, about which are told the same legends that enhance the other black images in Spain. I confess that I looked with more interest at the banner which hung from the galley of Don John of Austria at the battle of Lepanto. In this cathedral also is the Muzarabic chapel, where the ancient Muzarabic ritual is daily performed. I suppose the litany has some affinity with that of the Eastern Church before the great division. The Muzarabes were Christian worshipers under the Moorish rulers, and were tolerated by them. I saw in the street women wearing yellow flannel petticoats, which are said to be the distinguishing female dress of this sect. I believe there are several Muzarabic parishes in Toledo, but their ritual is performed only in this hospitable cathedral. It is a service of more simplicity than that at the other altars, and probably would be regarded as "low" in ecclesiastical terminology. It is said that the peculiar ritual of this chapel was established here in 1512 by Cardinal Ximenez, as a note of Spanish independence of the Pope.

Madrid, notwithstanding its size and large population — about half a million — and its many stately buildings, a few brilliant streets and beautiful public gardens, is still provincial in aspect. When I saw the ox-carts in the principal streets I was reminded of Washington before the war. It has put on a veneer of French civilization, which contrasts sharply with the lingering Spanish rusticity and provincialism. It has the air of a capital in many ways. Its bull-fights are first-rate; as Paris attracts the best singers, Madrid draws to it the most skillful matadores. The Ring is, I believe, the largest in the kingdom, and capable of seating fourteen thousand spectators. The fight is the great Sunday *fête*, at which the king and the royal family are always present. As the performances are in the afternoon, they do not interfere with the morning church-going. And if they did, an excuse for it might be urged that Madrid has not a single fine church, and, not being a city, it has no cathedral. The town has several fine libraries, besides the Biblioteca Nacional, a splendid collection of armor, and archæological and other museums that properly claim attention. Of course the distinction of the capital is its Royal Picture Gallery, which compels and repays a pilgrimage from any distance. One must go there to see Murillo, Velasquez, and Ribera, and he is almost equally compelled to go there for the study of the great Italian and Flemish masters. The collection is so vast and varied that after days of wandering through its galleries the tourist feels that his acquaintance with it has only just begun.

Almost no one speaks well of the climate and situation of Madrid. Its forced location was the whim of Charles V. The situation offers no advantages for a great city. It is built on a lofty plateau formed by several hills at an elevation of 2,450 feet above the sea; but it is not picturesque, for its environs are sterile plains, swept by the wind. It is the only large capital that does not lie on a respectable river; the Manzanares is commonly a waterless, stony bed. And yet, having heard all this about the detestable climate and the unhealthy location, the traveler, if he happens there at a favorable time of the year, will probably be surprised at the cheerful aspect of the town under the deep blue sky. Within a few years very much has been done to beautify it by planting trees, laying out fine parks, and building handsome villas. It is amazing what money can do in the way of transforming a sterile and intractable place into beauty. Madrid is on the way to be a city of brilliant appearance in the modern fashion, though it is not yet very interesting as a whole. But, for details, in Spain, the traveler is inclined to resent Paris shop windows and Paris costumes. Perhaps the climate is maligned. From what I could hear I should judge it far better than that of Paris, except, perhaps, for a part of the summer. Our minister, Mr. Hamlin, told me that the winter he spent there — which may have been an exception — he found agreeable, with very little frost, almost constant sun, and that it compared favorably with a winter in Washington.

The Spanish people, though reckoned taciturn and reserved with strangers, have a Southern demonstrativeness with each other which does not shrink from public avowal. We had a pleasing illustration of this when we took the afternoon train from Madrid for Zaragoza. A bridal party were on the platform in the act of leave-taking with the happy couple, who entered our car. The tender partings at the house seemed to have been reserved for this public occasion. The couple, as it turned out, were not going very far, but if they had been embarking for China the demonstrations of affection, anxiety, grief, and other excitement could not have been more moving and varied. There were those who wept, and those who put on an air of forced gayety; and there was the usual facetious young man, whose mild buffooneries have their use on such occasions. The babble of talk was so voluminous that we did not hear the signal to start, and as long as we kept the group in sight their raised outstretched hands were clutching the air with that peculiar movement of the fingers which means both greeting and farewell in this land. The pretty bride, it soon appeared, was willing to take all the world into confidence in her happiness and affection. The car was well filled, and, as it happened, it would have been more convenient for her to sit opposite her husband of an hour. But this was not to be endured. She squeezed herself into the narrow place beside him, and began to pet and fondle him in a dozen decent ways, in the most barefaced and unconscious manner. The rest of us were as if we did not exist, and it was in vain that we looked out of the window in token of our wish to efface ourselves in the presence of so much private happiness. She could not keep either hands or eyes off him. And why should she? He was hers, and for life, and we were mere accidents of the hour. The assertion of her possession embarrassed us, but the square-faced and somewhat phlegmatic young gentleman took it as of right and in a serene consciousness of merit. Opposite this delightful couple, who were entering Paradise by such a public door, sat the beau-ideal of a Spanish gentleman and grandee — tall, slender, grave, kindly, high-bred almost to the point of intellectual abdication — and his handsome young son, a most graceful and aristocratically marked lad, with the signs of possibly one step farther in the way of unvigorous refinement; resembling very much in air and feature the young Prince Imperial who was killed in Africa: charming people, with a delicate courtesy and true, unselfish politeness, as we discovered afterwards. I watched to see what effect this demonstration of national manners had upon them; and I am glad to say that their faces were as impassive as if they had been marble images. We all, I trust, looked unconscious, and perhaps we should ultimately have become so if the doting pair — God bless their union, so auspiciously begun! — had not descended from the car in a couple of hours at a little way-station. I hope she did not eat him up.

Somehow this little episode put us all in good humor, and made us think better of the world as we journeyed on in the night through a country for the most part dreary, and came at midnight to Zaragoza, and even brought us into the right sentimental mood to enjoy the moonlight on the twelve tiled domes of the Cathedral El Pilar, as we rattled in an omnibus over the noble stone bridge across the swift, broad, muddy Ebro, — the most considerable and business-like river we had seen in Spain. Zaragoza pleased us in a moment by its quaint picturesqueness and somnolent gravity. My room, in the rear of the hotel, looked upon a narrow street inclosed by high buildings, and was exactly opposite a still narrower street, into which the high moon threw heavy shadows from the tall houses. The situation was full of romantic suggestions, and I was familiar with just such scenes in the opera. As I looked from my window, before going to bed, a brigand in a long cloak and sombrero, carrying a staff in one hand and a lantern in the other, came slowly through this street, set his lantern down at the junction of the two streets, looked carefully up and down, and then in a musical tenor sang the song of the watchman, — " Half-past one o'clock, and fine weather." Then he took up his lantern and glided away to awake other parts of the town with his good news.

We found Zaragoza exceedingly attractive in its picturesque decay. Nowhere else did we see finer mediæval palaces, now turned into rookeries of many tenements and shops. We were always coming upon some unexpected architectural beauty, as we wandered about the narrow streets of high houses. Of the two cathedrals, the old one, La Seo, is the most interesting. It has a curious, lofty octagonal tower, with Corinthian columns, drawn out like a jointed telescope, and on one side some remarkable brick-work of the fourteenth century, inlaid with Moorish tiles, variegated in color. But El Pilar, modern and ugly within, attracts most worshipers, for there is the alabaster pillar upon which the Virgin stood. A costly chapel is erected over it, and upon it stands the blackwood image of the Virgin, blazing with jewels. The pillar cannot be seen from the front, but a little of it is visible in the rear, and this spot is kissed by a constant stream of worshipers all day long. This pillar and figure is the great fact in Zaragoza; it is its most sacred and consoling possession. Many shops are devoted to the manufacture and sale of representations of it, so that this seemed to be the chief industry of the city.

The Maid of Zaragoza is not much attended to, and it was difficult to get any traces of her, or to make her very real. We could not even determine the exact place of her heroic fight during the siege by the French in 1809. It was somewhere near the southwest gate of the city. Here, says the guide-book, which calls this heroine "an Amazon, and a mere itinerant seller of cooling drinks," — "here, Augustina, the Maid of Zaragoza, fought by the side of her lover, — an artilleryman, — and when he fell, mortally wounded, snatched the match from his hand and worked the gun herself." For all that, this plebeian maid, who has an immortal niche in poetry, may outlast Zaragoza itself, or suffice to preserve its memory.

Traveling towards Tarragona, we found dull scenery and a waste country. The land is worn in ragged gullies, and at intervals are mounds of earth, as if left by the action of water, that looked artificial, square-topped, with a button-like knob,—a singular formation. Now and then we had a glimpse of an old castle perched on a hill. At Lareda a genuine surprise awaited us, — the best breakfast we had in Spain. It seems voracious to say it, but it is in human nature to be pleased with something really appetizing after two months of privation. The character of the costume changed here. The peasants wore sandals, often without stockings. The men sported the dull red, or purple, Phrygian cap, hanging well in front. The women wore no distinguishing costume, unless plainness of face is a distinction among the sex, and were more hard-featured than their soft southern sisters. Here is a different and a more virile race, for we are in Catalonia. As we approach Tarragona the country is very much broken into narrow valleys and hills, but all highly cultivated. Everything is dry and dusty. There is no grazing ground or grass, but vineyards, mulberry-trees, and pomegranates.

Tarragona is set on a hill, and from the noble terrace, opening out from the Rambla, one of the chief streets, six hundred feet above the shore, there is a magnificent view of the coast and the sea. The city has a small harbor, protected by a long mole. The commanding position, the dry air, the lovely winter climate, and the historic interest of the place cause Tarragona to be recommended for a winter residence. But I should think it would be dull. There is too much of a decayed and melancholy, deserted air about it. We had another surprise here, not so much in the excellence of the hotel in which we stayed as in the civility of the landlord. But our hopes were dashed of making the *amende* to Spain in this respect, when we found that he was an Italian.

If not for a whole winter, Tarragona might detain the traveler interested for many days, for it is exceedingly picturesque, inside and out. I made the circuit of its high but somewhat dilapidated walls, and marked the enormous stones laid in it. Within, the houses are built close to the wall, and occasionally windows are cut through it, — a very good use for these mediæval defenses. There are ruins of old fortifications on the hill back of the town, and I believe that the town is, in show at least, very well fortified; but we did not inquire into it, having no intention of taking it. The cathedral, high up, and approached by a majestic flight of steps, sustains its reputation, on acquaintance, as one of the noblest Gothic edifices in Spain. We were especially detained by the wonderful archaic carving all over the interior. Attached is a pretty garden with fine cloisters, Moorish windows and arches, and the quaintest, most conceit-full, and amusing carving in the world. We wanted to bring away with us the gigantic iron knocker on the cathedral door, — a hammer striking the back of a nondescript animal. On an unfortunate afternoon, we were roughly jolted in a rattling omnibus — the only vehicle we could procure — three miles along the shore over a wretched road, enveloped in clouds of dust, to a grove of small pines, to see what is called Scipio's Tower. I wished we had never had anything more to do with it than Scipio had. And yet the view from there of the rock-built city, with its walls sloping to the ever-fascinating sea, and the line of purple coast, will long endure in the memory.

To come to Barcelona is to return to Europe. Signs of industry multiply as we approach the town. The land is more highly and carefully cultivated than elsewhere in Spain, but the absence of grass and the exposure of the red earth give the country a scarred, ragged, and raw appearance, which the vines and the few olive-trees do not hide. There is nothing to compensate the Northern-bred eye for the lack of grass and the scarcity of foliage.

Barcelona is the only town in Spain where the inhabitants do not appear self-conscious, the only one that has at all the cosmopolitan air. The stranger is neither stared at nor regarded with suspicion. The people are too busy to mind anything but their own affairs, yet not too busy to be courteous and civil, after the manner of people who know something of the world, and there is a bright vivacity in the place which is very taking. We saw here, however, the first time on this abstemious peninsula, a man drunk on the street. Only once before had we seen any persons intoxicated, and they were a party of young gentlemen accompanying ladies through the Escorial, who had taken so much wine at dinner that even the gloom of that creation of a gloomy mind had no sobering effect on them. The traveler who has been told that Barcelona is too modern and commercial to interest him will be agreeably disappointed. If he likes movement and animation he will find it in the chief street of the place, the Rambla, a broad thoroughfare which runs from the port entirely through the city, planted with trees, and having in the centre a wide *trottoir*, which is thronged day and night with promenaders. On Sunday and Wednesday mornings it offers a floral show which is unequaled. On one side are displayed broad banks of flowers, solid masses of color, extending for something like a quarter of a mile, — roses, carnations, violets, and so on, each massed by its kind in brilliant patches; and the buyers walk along from bank to bank and make up their bouquets with the widest range for selection. If the traveler cares for shopping he will find dazzling shops on the San Fernando, and he may amuse himself a long time in front of the fan and lace windows. As a rule, the windows of Spanish shops do not make a very attractive display, and the hunter after bricabrac and curios seems to be gleaning in a field that has been pretty well ransacked. But everywhere in Seville, Madrid, and Barcelona the most handsome windows are those filled with painted fans. Their prominence is a sign of the universal passion for these implements of coquetry. Barcelona is the centre of the lace manufactory, especially the machine-made. The traveler is also told that he can buy there better than elsewhere the exquisite blonde, which is made by hand. But it is like going to the seaside for fish. The finest blonde, of which very little is produced in comparison with the black, is sent to foreign markets, and in the three largest depots of hand-made blonde lace we found only one sample in each, of the best.

The old part of the town will, however, most attract the Northern wanderer, and if he has heard as little as we had of the cathedral he has a surprise in store for him. Its wide and lofty nave is exceedingly impressive, and the slender columns supporting the roof give it a pleasing air of lightness and grace. There is also much rich ornamentation, and the stained glass is superb. The lover of old iron-work will find it difficult to tear himself away from the cloisters, where he will see an infinite variety of designs and exquisite execution. The cloisters and garden, with flowers and fountain and orange-trees, are altogether delightful. On one side is the court of the tailors, where the knights of the shears lie buried under the pavement, with the crossed shears cut in the stones, as honorable a symbol of industry as crossed swords elsewhere. The shoemakers also come to honor in this democratic resting-place, — God rest their souls! — and the emblem of the boot speaks of a time when honest work was not ashamed to vaunt itself.

It was the eve of Corpus Christi, and the quaint old court was beautifully decorated and garlanded with flowers. An egg was dancing on the fountain jet, and all the children of the town seemed to be there, watching the marvel with sparkling eyes, while a dozen artists were sketching the lively scene. The procession next day, which moved after a solemn service in the cathedral, showed remnants of the mingling of mediæval facetiousness with the religious pageantry. The principal figures were the King and Queen of Aragon, gigantic in size, and gaudy in mock-heroic apparel. The movers of these figures were men who were concealed under the royal skirts and carried the vast frame-work on their shoulders. The tetering motion of the queen, so incongruous with her size and royal state, called forth shouts of laughter. A very pretty sight was the troop of handsome boys on horseback, who followed their majesties, beating drums. Two of them wore white wigs and gowns of scarlet velvet trimmed with gilt, and rode white horses with similar caparison. Four other boys were more elaborately appareled. They were clad in red caps with blue tops and white feathers, a blue satin blouse, a belt of yellow, yellow breeches, scarlet hose, shoes laced with blue, and on the breast a shield of gold with the cross. The admiration of the crowd seemed to nurse the spiritual pride of these boys, who bore themselves with a haughty air. We fancied that the Catalonians, who are politically turbulent and independent, rather delighted in the exhibition of mock royalty made by the King and Queen of Aragon.

We left the cheerful town in the enjoyment of this curious pageant. Almost immediately the railway train took us into a new region. The character of the landscape wholly changed. Grass appeared, the blessed green turf, and trees. The earth was clothed again. And with whatever sentimental regrets we left the land of romance, the verdure so delighted the eye that it was like entering Paradise to get out of Spain.

CHAPTER XXII.

WAGNER'S PARSIFAL.

It is the purpose of this paper to give the impression made by the performance of Parsifal at Baireuth, last summer, in view of certain strictures upon the motive of the drama, and without any attempt at musical criticism. In order to do this, I shall have to run over the leading features of the play, already given in the newspapers. Criticism enough, and of an unfavorable sort, there has been, though I heard none of it in Baireuth, nor ever any from those who had been present at the wonderful festival. Perhaps that was because I happened to meet only disciples of Wagner. I fancy that the professional critics, who did publish depreciating comments upon the new opera, and upon Wagner's methods in general, felt more inclined to that course after they had escaped from the powerful immediate impression of the performance, from the atmosphere of Baireuth, and begun to reflect upon the responsibilities of the special critics to the world at large, and what in particular was their duty towards the whole Wagner movement, assumption, presumption, or whatever it is called, than they did while they were surrounded by the influences that

Wagner had skillfully brought to bear to effect his purpose on them.

I have read two kinds of criticism. One was written by musical adepts, who had not heard the opera, but who condemned it on perusal of the score and the libretto; declaring the latter to be sacrilegious, and the author to be a false prophet among musicians and a charlatan among managers. The other critics, who also set themselves against Wagnerism, described the performance in such terms that all Europe was more and more eager to see it, but compounded for their reluctant enjoyment by finding unworthy methods in a success they could not deny. Whatever the triumph was, they said it was not a pure musical triumph, but one due to the creation of special conditions and favoring circumstances. Fancy Beethoven pushing his music into popular notice by such clap-trap means!

It was a great offense, in the first place, that Wagner should build his theatre in the inaccessible Franconian city, — a city with scant accommodations for visitors, and off the regular lines of travel. It was a still greater offense that, after all, he should be able to attract to this remote and provincial place pilgrims and strangers, not only from every country in Europe, but from America, Australia, and India; and that the theatre should be filled three nights in the week for three months by persons willing to incur the expense of a long, wearisome journey, and to pay thirty marks (seven dollars and a half) for a seat, at the end of it. A success of this sort could scarcely be legitimate. It must be due to some managerial legerdemain and to a misdirected enthusiasm.

Perhaps if we knew all the circumstances, the building of the theatre at Baireuth would not appear to be a whim of arbitrariness. Years ago the King of Bavaria desired to erect a theatre in Munich, on the hill over the Iser. He was so bitterly opposed in the location of the building by the citizens of Munich that he abandoned the purpose, and began the construction of a play-house to suit himself, elsewhere. The new theatre would have been so well adapted to Wagner's purposes that it may be doubted if Wagner would have set up his standard at Baireuth, if the Munich project had been carried out.

Yet it must be owned that the quaint little city, which owes so much of its romantic interest to Frederick's sister, the Margravine, has advantages in its very remotenesses and primitive conditions. The reason why Wagner's operas are enjoyed in Munich, and fail to please in Paris, is not that they are better presented in Munich; nor is the comparative failure in Paris due to the character of the operas, but rather to the atmosphere of Paris and the character of the audiences. Parsifal is scarcely better adapted to the meridian and the operatic traditions of Paris than is the Ober-Ammergau Passion Play.

It is Wagner's well-known theory of the opera that it should be something other than a series of airs, sung by one or two or several persons to the audiences, with spaces or wastes of musical declamation between; with an orchestra merely by way of accompaniment, and a background of scenery that would indifferently fit a dozen plays, and a plot incoherent and without any special purpose. Whether Wagner is successful or not in reducing his theories to practice is still in dispute: but he attempts a production which has purpose and unity, and which excludes everything not consistent with the effects he aims at. A story is to be told, a lesson is to be taught, an impression is to be produced on the hearer and spectator; and to this impression the orchestra, the scenery, and the singing are of almost equal importance. Nothing is admitted that does not forward the general purpose, and the unity of the story is not broken by special appeals to the audience. The effort is made to impress and stimulate the imagination, and to engage the attention in the work as a whole rather than in certain lyrical and melodic details. Wagner desires to move in his audiences sentiments, fervors, aspirations, in particular directions. Why is it charlatanism in him to prepare conditions favorable to his purpose? Why is it not legitimate that he should bring his audiences into such a state of mind, before the performance begins, that they are predisposed to enjoy the entertainment he offers? We know how much the appreciation of a poem depends upon the surroundings in which we read it or hear it. If Wagner has so contrived it that his audiences, arriving at the quiet and primitive city where he is almost worshiped, regard themselves as pilgrims at a special festival, and are in a receptive state of mind before they enter the theatre; if the theatre itself and all the environments heighten this impression; and if, finally, the performance itself seems to them more like a spiritual drama than an opera, where is the charlatanism, even if it can be proved that the impression is largely due to the accessories of the music? If it is said that other great composers would not have resorted to such adventitious aids, I can only think that any composer would have liked to command the best conditions for the production of his compositions. It is of course possible that the crowds at Baireuth were victims of a delusion, and of skillful contrivance. I can answer for many of them that they would like to be deluded again in just that way.

When we arrived at the station in Baireuth, it was at once apparent that the town was *en fête*, and that its sole occupation was the Wagner festival. Our train, which had waited at the last junction to bring hundreds of passengers from the east, was an hour late; it was two o'clock in the afternoon, and the performance was to begin at four. The bustle at the station, the ubiquity of committee-men and town officials, the crowd of vehicles, of all the fashions of the present and the last century, the air of expectation and the excitement were evidence of the entire absorption of the town in the great event. An agricultural fair in a New England village, or a *Fiesta de Toros* in Spain, could not more stir a community into feverish and cheerful activity. If the arriving stranger, carpet-bag in hand, had not the freedom of the city, he had all the city to wait on him, answer his inquiries, and take interest in him as an intelligent and profitable pilgrim. We had secured our tickets by telegraph, and found them ready for us at the banker's. We had also applied to the burgomeister for accommodations for the night, and we found that a committee, in permanent session at the station, had already billeted our party at private houses, to which we were promptly dispatched. Everything was so perfectly systematized that the wayfaring man, though a Wagnerite, need not err therein, and our quarters turned out to be exceedingly comfortable, and given at moderate prices. All the private houses of the place appeared to be at the disposal of the committee, and offered without extortion. If the inhabitants were not all devoted to Wagner, they were devoted to his festival, and the master pervaded the town. The musical works of Richard Wagner were everywhere in sight, and in almost all the shop windows were photographs of Wagner, engravings of Wagner, busts of Wagner, statuettes of Wagner. The other chief objects for sale in the town were photographs of the characters in Parsifal. We liked the old town, at once for its quaintness and single-mindedness, and we admitted that there is only one Baireuth, and Wagner is its prophet.

The pilgrim to the shrine of Wagner is treated like a pilgrim. He is expected to be willing to put his devotion to a further test, after reaching the remote town; for the theatre is set on a hill, half a mile from the city, so that a carriage is needed for the majority of visitors, especially if the weather is rainy, as it was the day of our arrival, and as it was all last summer, four days out of five, in the German land. This hill places the spiritual drama one more remove from the bustle of the sinful world, and helps to isolate the performance from ordinary life. The theatre is an ungainly brick building, erected only with reference to the interior accommodations. The great bulk of the stage rises out of it in defiance of all architectural beauty. The auditorium is surrounded by an open corridor, from which there are entrances for every three rows of seats. Each ticket indicates its entrance, so that the audience assembles and seats itself without confusion, and the house can be perfectly emptied in two minutes, without any danger of a rush or jam. The interior has been so often described that I need not enter into details. There are no proscenium boxes or side seats; the rows of chairs rise from the stage, spread out like a half-open fan, and at the back of the house are a row of private boxes; above them is a shallow gallery. Every part of the stage can be perfectly seen from every seat in the house. A low barrier rises before the front row of seats, separating the auditorium from the stage by a considerable space. In this sunken space, hidden completely from the audience, is the orchestra. The house is almost bare of decoration; only a cool gray color pervades, which is grateful to the senses. All the splendor is reserved for the stage, which is of immense proportions.

At four o'clock the fifteen hundred seats were filled, and a crowd of persons, said to be several hundred, occupied the standing-room in the rear. Most of the audience were standing, and the house was in a buzz of conversation and expectation. Suddenly, at the stroke of a stick behind the scenes, the audience seated itself; the doors were closed, excluding the light; the hall and the people were discernible only in an obscure twilight; a profound silence fell upon the house, indignantly enforced by a hissing "hushzz" directed at a careless whisperer; and at another signal the prelude began. The stillness was phenomenal, and so continued through the entire performance. I had an impression at the time that the audience was in a temper to lay violent hands on any one who should break the silence by any sound.

We sat in the luminous darkness, and the prelude began by the unseen orchestra. From the first note the music was striking; it portended something. It may have been because the players were concealed, but I seemed to hear not instruments, but music. And this music had a supernatural note, an unworldly, not to say a spiritual, suggestion. It rose and fell, more importunate than strident, in pleading, in warning, in entreaty. Whether it was good music or utterly impossible music I cannot say, owing to a constitutional and cultivated ignorance of musical composition; but it affected me now and again like the wind in a vast forest of pines on a summer day. It appealed to the imagination, it excited expectation, it begat an indefinable longing; and now and then a minor strain, full of sadness or of passion, suggested a theme, like the opening of a window into another world, — a theme which was to be renewed again and again in the drama, when it came to us like a reminiscence of some former life. When the prelude had been prolonged until the audience were brought up to the highest pitch of expectation, the great curtains were drawn aside, and the domain of the Knights of the Holy Grail, a peaceful, sunny land of forest, meadow, lake, and mountain, was disclosed.

- The composer has made use of one of the earlier legends of the Grail, at the time when the cup was still in possession of the knights appointed to guard it. The cup which had been drained at the Passover feast and had received the holy blood at the cross was still safe; but the sacred spear, the spear of the cross, which the heavenly messenger had also committed to the knights, had been lost. It was in possession of Klingsor, a recreant knight, who inhabited pagan land, and had by magic transformed a waste desert into wonderful gardens, and created an enchanted castle, inhabited by women of charms infernal, who lured the knights to wicked joys and pains eternal. One of the victims was Amfortas, the king of the knights, who had yielded to the temptations of Kundry, the temptress and the Magdalen of the play, a witch, who was in the power of Klingsor, and forced to do his bidding. When Amfortas fell into the wiles of this bewildering beauty, in one of his expeditions into pagan land, he was overpowered in his weakness, lost the sacred spear, and received a grievous wound in the side. Of this wound of sin he now languished. All the medicines of the world could not heal it; only in one way, by a man without sin, could he be cured. Meantime the spear was lost, and so long as this all-conquering weapon remained in the possession of the enemy, the cup itself was in danger. Klingsor vaunted his purpose to seize it. Kundry, at the opening of the drama, is a sort of impish servant and messenger of the knights, a wild, untrained nature, touched with remorse, but unable to repent or to free herself from the power of Klingsor, and full of unrest and contradictory passions.

The domain of the knights is represented by a charming scene, simulating nature so closely that the leaves are seen to quiver on the forest trees. To the audience, looking at it across an empty space and from a darkened room, it has the delusion of a tableau; but the figures in it seem the real inhabitants of some remote land of myth. Gurnemanz, an aged knight, is attended by two esquires. They are lamenting the sickness and wound of Amfortas, and the danger to the Grail from the loss of the holy spear. To them enters the wild witch Kundry, fantastically clad in a savage garb, with a snake-skin girdle, having a swarthy complexion, piercing black eyes, and black hair flowing in tangled disorder. She comes from the end of the earth, riding on the devil's mare, though, for once, not on the devil's errand. Her self-appointed mission has been to seek some balm for the wounded king, the victim of her wiles. She brings to Gurnemanz a balsam from far Arabia, though well she knows that no balsam can touch his wound. At this moment Amfortas is borne in on a litter, on the way to his bath in the sacred spring, the only alleviation of his suffering. The crystal flask containing the balsam is given to him, and Kundry is bidden to approach. But the wild maid draws away, tortured by a conscience half awakened, and struggling with the wickedness of her unsubdued, animal nature; held by the enchantment of Klingsor, and unable even to repent, but impelled by a blind notion of merit in good deeds to render service to the knights; restless, sleepless, pursued by demons, longing in her fitful despair only to sleep, and to sleep forever, — a lost soul in pitiful helplessness of human succor.

This thrilling scene, interpreted by the wailing and sympathetic orchestra, is at its height, when an interruption occurs that strikes all with new horror. A swan flutters from over a lake, strives to fly further, and sinks to the ground, dying, pierced by an arrow. It is the sacred swan. Who has committed this sacrilege? The murderer appears, a strong, rude hunter, clad in skins, his bow in hand. He is proud of his feat. He is accustomed, in the wilderness, to shoot whatever flies. This is Parsifal, the man of absolute nature, without sin and without virtue, as ignorant as he is innocent. It is with difficulty that he comprehends what he has done, and he slowly understands the woe and horror of the company. As moral sense begins to dawn in his dark mind, he is seized with violent trembling, and falls half fainting. He breaks his bow and casts it from him. Kundry, at sight of him, is as strongly moved as he. On the return of the train of the king from the bath, Gurnemanz asks Parsifal to accompany him to the holy feast. If thou art pure, he says, surely it will feed and refresh thee. What is the Grail? asks Parsifal. The guide cannot say, but knowledge is not hidden to those who are bid to serve it; yet to it no earthly road leads, and no one not elected can see it. Gurnemanz lays Parsifal's arm on his own neck, and, supporting him with one arm, leads him away.

The two appear to be walking slowly through the forest to the left, pausing here and there in weariness. In fact, the scenery itself is moving to the right. The country changes its character. The forest becomes wilder and denser. The travelers make their way painfully, up steeps and amid rocks and fallen trees. The way is still more rocky and wild. Dark caverns yawn, and the trees are more fantastically savage. The music, ever graver, and ever recurring to the minor sadness, expresses toil, and the weariness of the way, and the difficulty of seeking. For moments, behind some giant rock or cluster of trees, the two are lost to view, and appear again, the red cloak of the knight glowing amid the dark green. As the travelers move on, the scene still changes. Touches of the artificial are seen. The caverns and passages in the rock have been enlarged and worked by man's hand. Here is trace of an arch, of cut stone, of a wall buttress. We are passing into the depths of the mountain, by a way in which nature has plainly been assisted. There is a faint sound of chimes; the orchestra itself is on the impatient point of disclosing the secret; there is a second in which all is obscure, and then, in a burst of light, stands revealed a mighty hall, vast as a giant cathedral. The aisles stretch away in dim perspective; the arches are supported on lofty columns of jasper, of verd-antique, of alabaster, of all precious marbles; and above is a noble dome, blue and luminous with golden stars. From the dome streams the light; from it floats down the faint and fainter peal of the chiming bells. Beneath the dome stands a long horseshoe curved table, with the ends towards the audience, leaving the centre of the stage free. In the middle of this open back-ground is a high table, like an altar, with steps leading up to it, and behind it is a raised couch, with a canopy. Upon the communion table are set tall silver cups.

From the far distance in the aisle the knights, clad in robes of scarlet, enter in slow and stately procession, moving with reverence and dignity, and chanting as they approach the table and take their places; from the middle height of the hall come the responsive voices of younger knights; and then down from the very summit of the dome float boys' voices. So angels might hail the Supper of our Lord, leaning over the gold bars of heaven. Immediately, from the other aisle, enters a procession of equal solemnity and splendor: the bearers of Amfortas on his litter, the servitors of the Holy Supper, and the angelic boys who carry and sustain, under its covering, the sacred cup. But for the intense solemnity of the scene, one must note the marvelous skill with which every detail of it, in form and color, has been composed. But it is only afterwards that we vividly recall this. The bearers of the cup are less earthly than Raphael's angels, from whom they may have been copied. And it never occurs to you that they are stage angels. The whole scene, so necessarily theatrical in description, does not impress the spectator so; the art of color and grouping is too perfect, the solemnity is too real. Amfortas is borne to the couch behind the altar. The holy vessel is deposited before him. The servitors attend with baskets of bread and tall silver flagons. At one side, near the entrance of the hall, stands Parsifal, clad in sheep-skin, as rigid as a stone, a mute and awestruck spectator of the scene.

Amfortas, stricken with disease and sin, shrinks from performing the ordinance. At length, urged by the voices from heaven, by the knights, and by the command of his aged father, he feebly rises. The boys uncover the golden shrine, and take out of it the cup of the Grail, an antique crystal cup. As Amfortas bows over it in silent prayer, a gloom spreads through the room; a ray of light shoots from above upon the cup, which begins to glow with a purple lustre. When Amfortas raises it and holds it high, it burns like a ruby, — it is the Holy Grail. In the dusk the knights are kneeling and worshiping it. When he sets it down the glow fades, the boys replace the cup in the shrine, and the natural light returns to the hall. The goblets are then seen to be filled with wine, and by each is a piece of bread. At intervals in the progress of the supper alternative voices of youths and boys from the heights chant in response to the solemn chorus of the knights, and finally down from the dome comes the benediction, " Blessed believing." During the repast, of which Amfortas has not partaken, he sinks from his momentary exaltation, the wound in his side opens afresh, and he cries out in agony. Hearing the cry, Parsifal clutches his heart, and seems to share his agony, but otherwise he stands motionless. The supper over, Amfortas and the sacred shrine are borne away. The knights rise; and as they pass out, and meet, two and two, at the ends of the table, they tenderly embrace, with the kiss of peace and reconciliation, and slowly depart in the order in which they came. To the last Parsifal gazes in wonder; and when his guide comes to speak to him, he is so dazed that Gurnemanz, losing all patience at his unresponsive stupidity, pushes him out of the door, and spurns him for a fool. The curtains sweep together, and shut us out from the world that had come to seem to us more real than our own.

For a moment we sat in absolute silence, a stillness that had been unbroken during the whole performance. There was not a note of applause, not a sound. The impression was too profound for expression. We felt that we had been in the presence of a great spiritual reality. I have spoken of this as the impression of a scene. Of course it is understood that this would have been all an empty theatrical spectacle but for the music, which raised us to such heights of imagination and vision. For a moment or two, as I say, the audience sat in silence; many of them were in tears. Then the doors were opened; the light streamed in. We all arose, with no bustle and hardly a word spoken, and went out into the pleasant sunshine. It was almost a surprise to find that there was a light of common day. We walked upon the esplanade, and looked off upon the lovely view : upon the old town ; upon the Sophienberg and the Volsbach forests in the Franconian Jura ; upon the peaceful meadows and the hills, over which the breaking clouds were preparing a golden sunset. We did not care to talk much. The spell was not broken. How long, I asked a lady, do you think we were in there? An hour, nearly, she thought. We had been in the theatre nearly two hours. It was then six o'clock.

On the esplanade are two large and well-appointed restaurants, adjuncts to the theatre, and in a manner necessary to it. Wagner understands how much the emotional enjoyment and the intellectual appreciation depend upon the physical condition, and he has taken pains to guard his audiences against both hunger and weariness. During the half-hour interval that elapsed between the first and the second act, the guests were perfectly refreshed by a leisurely stroll in the open air, by the charming view, by the relaxation of their intense absorption, by a cup of coffee or a drop of amber and perhaps Wagnerian beer, or by a substantial supper. When the notes of a silver trumpet summoned us back to our seats, we were in a mood to enjoy the play again with all the zest of the first hour.

The second act is of the earth, earthy, and less novel than the first to opera-goers, accustomed to spectacles, ballets, and the stage seductions of the senses. It is the temptation of Parsifal, who has begun his novitiate. The temptation is wholly of the senses and the passions. The scene is the magic castle and the enchanting gardens of the magician Klingsor, — a scene of entrancing but theatrical beauty. The magician is discovered seated in the dungeon keep of his tower, surrounded by the implements of magic. In the background is the mouth of a black pit. Casting something into it, he summons Kundry. A cloud of smoke arises from the pit, growing luminous and warming into rosy color; and suddenly from the chasm rises a most beautiful female form, enveloped in a gauzy tissue, and flushed with rosy light. It is Kundry, no longer in her aspect of witch, but surpassingly lovely; and yet as unhappy as lovely, and responding to the summons of her master with a cry and look of agony. She is bidden to undertake the temptation of Parsifal, who has been seen from the ramparts approaching the castle. She refuses. Her whole nature abhors the office. But yield she must to the power of the charm. Yield she must, and exercise all her power of fascination and seduction, though she knows that it is only by the resistance of her blandishments that salvation can be hers. She knows that only by meeting and being resisted by a sinless one can her own sin be cured, and yet she is forced to put forth all her efforts to secure her own ruin and his.

With a gesture of protest and despair, she vanishes as she came. The tower and the cavern sink away, and in place appear, filling all the vast stage, a tropical garden, and the battlements and terraces of an Arabian castle. Parsifal stands upon the wall, looking down upon the scene in astonishment. From all sides, from the garden and the palace, rush in groups of lovely damsels, arranging themselves in haste, as if waked from sleep. Each one in her dress represents some flower. They are awaiting Parsifal, and as he descends they surround him, and envelop him, and distract him with their voluptuous charms. When their blandishments fail (although the music pleads in all sensuous excitement) to arouse in the pure youth anything more than perplexity and wonder, the maidens leave him in disgust, and with the appearance of the ravishingly beautiful Kundry the dangerous temptation begins.

Gorgeous as is the scene, and opulent as are the female charms of this second act, there is yet something of the cheap and common about it, — tawdry splendors, easily seen to be the stock gorgeousness and the painted temptations of the stage. This seemed to me an ethical mistake in the drama. Such a man as Parsifal should have been approached, to his ruin, with subtler and less gross allurements than these. At least, the guileless nature of Parsifal would have appeared to the audience in more danger of being seduced from his knighthood by the appeals of beauty to his pity, to his sympathy, for an innocent and simple maiden, beset by dangers, and coming to him for aid and comfort; approaching him through his higher qualities, and flattering him into forgetfulness of his mission in the names of virtue and compassionate love. The devil of modern society appears to understand these things better than the traditional devil whom Wagner consulted for this scene. The audience feels from the first that the open solicitations of Kundry must fail, and that Parsifal is in little danger, even when she bends over him and impresses upon his lips a kiss of a duration so long that the spectator is tempted to time it with his watch, like the passage through a railway tunnel. From this embrace, at any rate, Parsifal starts up in intense terror, clasping his hand to his side, as if he felt the spear-wound of Amfortas. I need not detail the struggle and the passion that follow. Failing in this first appeal, the maiden, too late in his aroused suspicion, pleads for his love, in that it alone can save her; his love alone can redeem and pardon her. He resists also this more subtle temptation. "Eternally should I be damned with thee, if for an hour I forgot my holy mission." In rage at her final failure, when Parsifal spurns her as a detestable wretch, Kundry curses him, and calls for help. The damsels rush in. Klingsor appears upon the battlement, with the holy spear in his hand; he hurls it at Parsifal; but the spear remains floating above the latter's head. Parsifal grasps it with tremulous joy, waves it, and makes with it the sign of the cross. Instantly the enchantment is broken: down tumble towers and castle walls; the garden vanishes; the leaves and branches of the trees strew the earth; the damsels lie on the ground like shriveled flowers; and Kundry falls insensible, and lies amid the ruins and the waste of the original desert.

In the background rises a path up a sunny slope to a snow mountain. Purity and nature have taken the place of the baleful enchantment. Parsifal turns from the top of the broken wall, over which he disappears, to look upon the ruin as the curtain closes.

When the act ends, the audience, still under the spell of the music, which had at the end risen out of its soft and siren strains into a burst of triumph and virile exaltation, sat, as before, silent for a moment. Then it rose *en masse*, and turned to the high box in the rear, where, concealed behind his friends, Wagner sat, and hailed him with a long tempest of applause. The act had lasted less than an hour. It was followed by an intermission of three quarters of an hour, which gave the audience time for supper, and for the refreshment of a stroll and the soothing effects of the charming view in the fading sunlight.

In the third and last act we return to the high themes of the first; the touching minor strains of the prelude recur again and again, soothing the spirit agitated by the period of storm and stress. The conflict is over. We have passed through the regions of tumult and passion; we have escaped out of the hothouse air of temptation. Penitence is possible, and through suffering peace is dawning with forgiveness in the torn and troubled heart. The orchestra declares it, and the scene upon which the curtain rises is the sweet and restful domain of the Grail in the springtime of the year. On the edge of the forest, built against a rock, is a hermitage; a spring is near it, and beyond stretch flowery meadows. It is the dawn of day, the sky reddening before the coming of the sun, when Gurnemanz, now extremely aged and feeble, emerges from the hut. Attracted by moaning in the thicket, he moves aside the branches, and discovers Kundry, cold and stiff, lying in the hedge of thorns, which is little better than her grave. He drags forth the nearly lifeless form, bears her to a mound, chafes her hands and temples, calls her back to life with the news that the winter has fled and the spring has come. Slowly the maiden revives, gazes at him in wonder, and then adjusts her dress and hair, and without a word goes like a serving-maid to her work.

To Kundry has come a wonderful transformation. The wildness has gone from her mien and from her eyes; into her face has come the soft, indescribable light of penitence, and a transcendent spiritual beauty. She is no longer the fiery witch, full of disordered passion, contempt, and impish malevolence; she is no longer the houri of the enchanted garden, with the charms of the siren and the bewildering allurements of Venus Aphrodite. Clad in the simple brown garb of the penitent Magdalen, subdued and humble, every movement and gesture and her sad, lovely face proclaim inward purity and longing for forgiveness. When Gurnemanz upbraids her for her silence and thanklessness for her rescue from deathly slumber, she bows her head, as she moves towards the hut, and in a broken voice murmurs, "Service, service!" — her only exclamation in all the act.

Kundry comes from the hut, and goes towards the spring with her water-pot. Looking into the wood, she sees some one approaching, and calls Gurnemanz's attention to the comer. A knight, in complete black armor, weary and worn, bruised with conflict and dusty with travel, slowly and feebly draws near, with closed helmet and lowered spear. It is Parsifal. Gurnemanz, who does not recognize him, hails him with friendly greeting. Parsifal only shakes his head. To all inquiries he is silent, and he is still speechless when Gurnemanz asks him if he does not know what holy day has dawned; that it is the hallowed Good-Friday morn, when he should doff his armor, and trouble no more the Master who has died for us.

After an interval, in which the music of the orchestra pleads as for a lost world, Parsifal rises, thrusts his spear into the ground, places against it his great shield and sword, unbraces and removes his helmet, and then, kneeling, raises his eyes in silent prayer towards the spear's head. Gurnemanz beckons to Kundry, who had gone within the hut. Do you not know him? Kundry assents with a nod. Surely, 'tis he, — the fool whom I drove in anger from the hall of the knights. In great emotion Gurnemanz recognizes the holy spear. Kundry turns away her sad and longing face. After his devotions are ended, Parsifal rises, and, gazing calmly around, recognizes Gurnemanz, and knows where he is. The murmur of this forest, falling on his tired senses, gives him hope that he has come to the end of his journey of error and suffering. He has sought the path that would lead him to the wounded Amfortas, to whose healing he believed himself ordained; but hitherto that path has been denied him, and he has wandered at random, driven by a curse, through countless distresses and battles, — wounded in every fight, since he was not fit to use the holy spear which he bore, undefiled, by his side. The ancient knight assures him that he has come to the Grail's domain, where the knightly band awaits him, with great need of the blessing he brings. Amfortas is still struggling with the tortures of his wound; the shrine of the Holy Grail has long remained shrouded; the Holy Supper is no longer celebrated; the strength of the knights is withered, for want of this holy bread; and summoned no more to holy warfare in far countries, they wander pale, dejected, and lacking a leader; and Titurel, the old commander, to whom was first committed the cup and the spear, the father of Amfortas, hopeless of ever beholding again the refulgence of the Grail, has just expired.

Parsifal hears this with intense anguish, and laments that he has brought all this woe, since some heinous guilt must still cling to him that no atonement or expiation can banish, and that he who was selected to save men must wander undirected, and miss the path of safety. He is about to fall, when Gurnemanz supports him, and seats him on a grassy knoll. Kundry, in anxious haste, brings a basin of water; but Gurnemanz waves her off, saying that only the pilgrim's bath can wash away his stains; and they turn him about to the edge of the spring. While Gurnemanz takes off his corselet and the rest of his heavy armor, Kundry, kneeling, removes the greaves from his legs, and bathes his feet in the healing spring. The armor removed, Parsifal appears clad in a soft white tunic, with a cord about the waist, and his long, light hair, in wavy masses, flows back upon his neck. There is no mistaking the likeness, in this meek and noble face and figure. Shall I straight be guided to Amfortas? asks Parsifal, wearily. Surely, says Gurnemanz, we go at once to the obsequies of the beloved chief. The Grail will be again uncovered, and the long-neglected office be performed. As the knight speaks, Parsifal observes, with wonder, Kundry humbly washing his feet, and gazes on her with a tender compassion. Taking water in the hollow of his hand, Gurnemanz sprinkles his head. Blessed be thou, pure one. Care and sin are driven from thee! Kundry, from a golden flask, pours oil upon Parsifal's feet, and dries them with the long tresses of her black hair, which she has unbound for the purpose. Then Parsifal takes from her the flask, and desires Gurnemanz to anoint his head; for he is that day to be appointed king. Gurnemanz, pouring the oil, declares him their king, and the rescuer from sin. And thus I fulfill my duty, murmurs Parsifal, as he, unperceived, scoops water from the spring, and, stooping to the kneeling and heart-broken Kundry, sprinkles her head. "Be thou baptized, and trust in the Redeemer." Kundry bows her head to the earth, and weeps uncontrollably. As Parsifal raises both hands, the fingers of one extended in blessing, we recognize the figure and very attitude of our Lord in that famous old painting, where he is seated, blessing little children. The Magdalen, shaken with penitence, and yet weeping for joy, is cast at his feet. The aged knight stands in solemn rapture. The scene is inexpressibly touching. The music is full of pathos and solemn sympathy.

How fair the fields and meadows seem to-day! exclaims Parsifal, gazing with gentle enjoyment upon the landscape. This is Good-Friday's spell, my lord! exclaims Gurnemanz. The sad, repentant tears of sinners have besprinkled field and plain with holy dew, and made them glow with beauty. As Gurnemanz discourses of the redemption of man and nature, the transformed Kundry slowly raises her head, and gazes with moist eyes and beseeching look, out of which all earthly passion has completely gone, up to

Parsifal. Thou weepest. See! the landscape gloweth, he gently says, and, stooping, softly kisses her brow. Who would recognize in the pure, sweet, spiritual face of this forgiven sinner the temptress of the gardens? I know not how this whole scene may appear in the coldness of description, but I believe that there was no one who witnessed it, and heard the strains of melting music which interpreted it, who was not moved to the depths of his better nature, or for a moment thought that the drama passed the limits of propriety.

The pealing of distant bells is heard growing louder. Gurnemanz brings a coat of mail and the mantle of the Knights of the Holy Grail, with which Parsifal is invested. The landscape changes. The wood gradually disappears, as the three march on in silence; and when they are hidden behind the rocky entrances of the caverns, processions of mourning knights appear in the arched passages. The bells peal ever louder, and soon the great hall is disclosed. From one side the knights bear in the bier of Titurel, and from the other the litter of Amfortas, preceded by the attendants with the covered shrine of the Grail. The effects of color and grouping are marvelous; and to eyes familiar with the sacred paintings of the masters, almost every figure and dress is a reminiscence of some dear association. The angelic loveliness of the bearers of the shrine, however, surpasses any picture, as much as life transcends any counterfeit of it.

At the sight of the body of Titurel there is a cry of

distress, in which Amfortas joins; and the knights press upon the latter, urging him to uncover the shrine and do his office. With a cry of despair he disengages himself, tears open his mantle and discloses the wound, and invokes the knights to bury their swords in his breast, and kill at one stroke the sinner and his pain. At this moment, Parsifal, who has entered, with his attendants, unperceived, starts forward, and, stretching out his spear point, touches the wounded side. Only the weapon that struck can staunch thy wounded side. Amfortas, who feels himself instantly healed, can scarcely support himself, for joyful rapture. As Parsifal raises high the spear, the shining point is red as blood, and the whole assembly, falling upon their knees, adore it. Parsifal assumes the kingship, takes his place behind the altar, and commands the cup of the Grail to be uncovered. Taking it in his hand, and raising it on high, the crystal burns again like a ruby; from the dome a white dove descends, and hovers over him; Kundry — peace at last, stricken soul! — falls dying; the knights are gazing upward in rapture; and out of the heights come down soft and hardly audible voices in a chant of benediction.

It was nine o'clock when we went out into the still lingering twilight. I, for one, did not feel that I had assisted at an opera, but rather that I had witnessed some sacred drama, perhaps a modern miracle play. There were many things in the performance that separated it by a whole world from the opera, as it is usually understood. The drama had a noble theme; there was unity of purpose throughout, and unity in the orchestra, the singing, and the scenery. There were no digressions, no personal excursions of singers, exhibiting themselves and their voices, to destroy the illusion. The orchestra was a part of the story, and not a mere accompaniment. The players never played, the singers never sang, to the audience. There was not a solo, duet, or any concerted piece " for effect." No performer came down to the foot-lights and appealed to the audience, expecting an encore. No applause was given, no encores were asked, no singer turned to the spectators. There was no connection or communication between the stage and the audience. Yet I doubt if singers in any opera ever made a more profound impression, or received more real applause. They were satisfied that they were producing the effect intended. And the composer must have been content when he saw the audience so take his design as to pay his creation the homage of rapt appreciation due to a great work of art.

A genial exponent of the best American thought. — London Examiner.

WRITINGS OF
CHARLES DUDLEY WARNER

A ROUNDABOUT JOURNEY.
A New Volume. 12mo, $1.50.

Mr. Warner has a genius for traveling. By some mysterious gift he always happens to see the most interesting objects, the most important persons, and the most significant events of the time and country in which he travels. Fortunately for us he has also a peculiar felicity and humor in recording what he sees, so that his volumes of travel are at once among the most informing and the most charming books of modern literature. During the past year Mr. Warner spent many months in Europe, principally in the countries bordering on the Mediterranean, and made an excursion into Africa. The experiences and observations of these months he depicts in the above volume.

MY WINTER ON THE NILE.
New Edition, revised, with an Index. Crown 8vo, $2.00.

This book comprises the first part of the experiences and observations of a journey in the East by Mr. Warner a few years ago. It relates to Egypt, while its continuation, "In the Levant," describes the people and sights of Palestine, Turkey, and other countries bordering on the eastern Mediterranean.

I still feel the fascination of Egypt so strongly that it would have been hard for me to read a book in which it was not apparent. I have read the book from beginning to end without having to stop and shake my head once. If you should think this only negative praise, you must remember that my literary standard is rather high and severe. A book written for the people must be entertaining, first of all; but it may be written so as to carry them a step forward in taste and the appreciation of sound literary work. I think you have done this, and hope you will be rewarded by immense sales. — BAYARD TAYLOR.

Mr. Warner's pictures of Oriental men, manners, and incidents are, to one who has lived so long in the East as I have, positively photographic reproductions. How could a passing traveler so thoroughly appreciate and so sharply outline the peculiarities of all classes of people? — Gen. L. P. DI CESNOLA.

IN THE LEVANT.

With an Index. Crown, 8vo, $2.00.

It is not often that of a volume of recent Eastern travel it can be honestly said that it is more than hard to find a single dull page in the whole four hundred; but even more may be said for Mr. Warner's well-seasoned, graphic record of his adventures. From first to last he has the same unflagging spirit, the same sparkle of humor and power of observation. — *London Standard.*

Being a writer of keen observation, and one accustomed to select what may be called representative features, the result is that his descriptions are remarkably vivid and lively. Besides, there is a vein of refined and delicate humor running through the whole. Part of the time it is latent, but this affords an opportunity for pleasant surprises. In fact the author's chief power lies in the rich humor which pervades both thought and style. In this quality he ranks far above every other American writer. It is seen in its highest perfection in that inimitable creation, "My Summer in a Garden." There the subject was eminently fitted for manifesting that kind of genius; and the work is one which will always be fresh, though it is read for the twentieth time or by the twentieth generation. — *The Churchman.* (New York).

WILLIAM C. PRIME, LL. D., speaking of "My Winter on the Nile" and "In the Levant," says: "Whether one has been in the East, or is going to the East, or does not expect ever to go, these books are of all travel books the best, because most truthful and companionable guides, having in them the very atmosphere and sunlight of the Orient."

MY SUMMER IN A GARDEN.

New Edition, enlarged. 16mo, $1.00. THE SAME. *Illustrated Edition.* With 12 full-page Illustrations, by DARLEY. Square 16mo, $1.50.

You cannot open his book without lighting on something fresh and fragrant. Every page abounds with mellow and juicy fruits, showing that whatever success may attend his use of the hoe and spade, he knows how to handle the pen with admirable effect. — *New York Tribune.*

In the wisdom and wit of the thoughts, and the grace of the style, this book is so good as to bring to the reader's mind, now Holmes, then Curtis, and again Mitchell, and finally to leave the conviction that Mr. Warner is neither the one nor the other, but quite the peer of either. — *Springfield Republican.*

This is a set of humorous papers describing the experiences of an amateur who busies himself for the first time with the cultivation of a garden, humorous with that quiet humor in which, as well as in its very antipodes, the wildly extravagant, the Americans seem to excel. — *The Spectator* (London).

Charles Lamb might have written it if he had had a garden. — *Quarterly Review* (London).

BACKLOG STUDIES.

With 21 Illustrations by Augustus Hoppin. Square 16mo, $1.50.

This book discusses in the most charming way such matters as Criticism, the Great New England Pie-line, the Furnishing of Rooms, the Progress of Civilization, the Worth of Oriental Classics, the Work of Reformers, Women Novelists, the Clothes Question, Gothic Architecture in Modern Churches, Life at Concord, Speech and Custom in Boston, Social Popularity, Misdirected Energy, the Personality of Authors in their Books, the Value of the Stage as a Mirror of Nature.

One might say that the studies are wise and witty, and tender and fanciful, and incisive and shrewd; all that is true, but the whole truth is something more. There is a certain sober dryness and whimsical seriousness about them, which sets Mr. Warner apart from other humorists of our time. — *Boston Advertiser.*

BADDECK AND THAT SORT OF THING.

"Little Classic" style. 18mo, $1.00.

Baddeck is a small town in the island of Cape Breton. However, the interest of the book does not centre there, or anywhere; but it flows all along the very devious route which the author was compelled to take in order to arrive there; and it is an interest which increases with every moment. One of the freshest and most enjoyable books of the kind we have ever read. — *The Churchman* (New York).

For perfect drollery of situation and sentiment, and the daintiest surprises of fun, and for the traveler's good-humored perception of absurdities, told with sprightliness and the most charming abandon, we account Mr. Warner's description of his pilgrimage to Baddeck as one of the most wittily playful things in our literature since the "Sentimental Journey." — *Christian Union* (New York).

BEING A BOY.

Illustrated by Champney. Square 16mo, $1.50.

It is an elderly boy's reminiscences and reflections upon boyhood, the actual boyhood which he lovingly remembers. The book is full of the dry, unexpected humor of which Mr. Warner is a master, and is equally delightful to boys of all ages from six to say sixty or seventy years. It is full of clever pictures, too. — *New York Evening Post.*

It is charming alike in style, treatment, and temper. . . . The chapters on "The Boy as a Farmer," "The Boy's Sunday," "The Grindstone of Life," "The Coming of Thanksgiving," "The Season of Pumpkin-Pie," "John's First Party," "The Sugar Camp," and "John's Revival," are especially readable. — *San Francisco Bulletin.*

IN THE WILDERNESS.

New Edition, enlarged. "Little Classic" style. 18mo, 75 cents.

One great charm of Mr. Dudley Warner's sylvan recreations is that he never repeats himself. His to-days are never yesterdays, but always fresh with the breeze and the fragrance of the passing moment. In this volume he takes us once more to the Adirondacks, trending over the familiar ground of the summer tourist, but always revealing a new beauty in the forest, a new glory in the river, a new joy in the heart of Nature. — *New York Tribune.*

It is as fresh and fragrant of the woods as anything that Thoreau ever wrote, having in it also a spicy flavor of humor that was but slightly possessed by that forest philosopher. — *Philadelphia Bulletin.*

SAUNTERINGS.

"Little Classic" style. 18mo, $1.25.

The book is made up of a series of sketches, written in the most unpretending and familiar manner, concerning peculiarities in the life, customs, and appearance of most of the countries and towns usually included in the "grand tour." It is not only thoroughly entertaining, but exceedingly instructive. — *New York Evening Post.*

His journey was confined to England, France, Belgium, Holland, Switzerland, Bavaria, and Italy, — countries rendered commonplace by the books of innumerable tourists, but which he *Warnerizes*, and makes his own. He not merely addresses his readers; he takes them with him. — E. P. WHIPPLE.

A perfect book of travel. — *New York Evening Mail.*

WASHINGTON IRVING.

In "American Men of Letters" Series. With fine Portrait. 16mo, gilt top, $1.25; half morocco, $3.00.

Mr. Warner has not only written with sympathy, minute knowledge of his subject, fine literary taste, and that easy, fascinating style which always puts him on such good terms with his readers, but he has shown a tact, critical sagacity, and sense of proportion full of promise for the rest of the series which is to pass under his supervision. — *New York Tribune.*

It is a very charming piece of literary work, and presents the reader with an excellent picture of Irving as a man and of his methods as an author, together with an accurate and discriminating characterization of his works. — *Boston Journal.*

A delightfully written book, investing with fresh charm the familiar story of Irving's life and discussing the character of his genius and art with fine appreciation and perception. — *Buffalo Courier.*

HOUGHTON, MIFFLIN & CO., PUBLISHERS, BOSTON.

www.ingramcontent.com/pod-product-compliance
Lightning Source LLC
Chambersburg PA
CBHW020219240426

43672CB00006B/362